# ENDORSEMENTS

I think this is an excellent book. It is well-researched and exceptionally well-written. I particularly like the fact that O'Brien is utterly fearless and critically independent. He writes vigorously and entertainingly and challenges conventional wisdoms at every turn. He knows the literature—literary, historical, empirical and theoretical—thoroughly and brings to it an extraordinarily inquiring and critical mind. There have been a few good books on waste, and this one is certainly among the very best of them. ... Martin O'Brien has established himself as one of the few sociological authorities on this subject and, on this evidence, he is the very best of them.

**Christopher Rootes, Professor of Environmental Politics and Political Sociology, University of Kent**

Overall, this is an excellent, well written, scholarly and exciting book—relevant to policy as well as academia ... It does more than merely 'filling a gap' between historical studies of waste and more 'technocratic' and environmental debates—in effect it sets out a whole new way of conceptualising the constitutive role of rubbish in society and as such its intellectual impact is set to ripple out widely across a range of related debates.

**Elizabeth Shove, Professor of Sociology, University of Lancaster**

# Routledge Advances in Sociology

1. Virtual Globalization
Virtual Spaces / Tourist Spaces
Edited by David Holmes

2. The Criminal Spectre in Law,
Literature and Aesthetics
Peter Hutchings

3. Immigrants and National Identity
in Europe
Anna Triandafyllidou

4. Constructing Risk and Safety in
Technological Practice
Edited by Jane Summerton and Boel
Berner

5. Europeanisation, National
Identities and Migration
Changes in Boundary Constructions
Between Western and Eastern Europe
Willfried Spohn and Anna Triandafyllidou

6. Language, Identity and Conflict
A Comparative Study of Language in
Ethnic Conflict in Europe and Eurasia
Diarmait Mac Giolla Chríost

7. Immigrant Life in the U.S.
Multi-disciplinary Perspectives
Edited by Donna R. Gabaccia and Colin
Wayne Leach

8. Rave Culture and Religion
Edited by Graham St. John

9. Creation and Returns of
Social Capital
A New Research Program
Edited by Henk Flap and Beate Völker

10. Self-Care
Embodiment, Personal Autonomy and the
Shaping of Health Consciousness
Christopher Ziguras

11. Mechanisms of Cooperation
Werner Raub and Jeroen Weesie

12. After the Bell – Educational
Success, Public Policy and Family
Background
Edited by Dalton Conley and Karen
Albright

13. Youth Crime and Youth Culture
in the Inner City
Bill Sanders

14. Emotions and Social Movements
Edited by Helena Flam and Debra King

15. Globalization, Uncertainty and
Youth in Society
Edited by Hans-Peter Blossfeld, Erik
Klijzing, Melinda Mills and Karin Kurz

16. Love, Heterosexuality and Society
Paul Johnson

17. Agricultural Governance
Globalization and the New Politics of
Regulation
Edited by Vaughan Higgins and Geoffrey
Lawrence

18. Challenging Hegemonic
Masculinity
Richard Howson

**19. Social Isolation in Modern Society**
Roelof Hortulanus, Anja Machielse and
Ludwien Meeuwesen

**20. Weber and the Persistence of
Religion**
Social Theory, Capitalism and the Sublime
Joseph W. H. Lough

**21. Globalization, Uncertainty and Late
Careers in Society**
Edited by Hans-Peter Blossfeld, Sandra
Buchholz and Dirk Hofäcker

**22. Bourdieu's Politics**
Problems and Possibilities
Jeremy F. Lane

**23. Media Bias in Reporting Social
Research?**
The Case of Reviewing Ethnic Inequalities in
Education
Martyn Hammersley

**24. A General Theory of Emotions and
Social Life**
Warren D. TenHouten

**25. Sociology, Religion and Grace**
Arpad Szakolczai

**26. Youth Cultures**
Scenes, Subcultures and Tribes
Edited by Paul Hodkinson and Wolfgang
Deicke

**27. The Obituary as Collective Memory**
Bridget Fowler

**28. Tocqueville's Virus**
Utopia and Dystopia in Western Social and
Political Thought
Mark Featherstone

**29. Jewish Eating and Identity
Through the Ages**
David Kraemer

**30. The Institutionalization of Social
Welfare**
A Study of Medicalizing Management
Mikael Holmqvist

**31. The Role of Religion in Modern
Societies**
Edited by Detlef Pollack and Daniel V. A.
Olson

**32. Sex Research and Sex Therapy**
A Sociological Analysis of Masters
and Johnson
Ross Morrow

**33. A Crisis of Waste?**
Understanding the Rubbish Society
Martin O'Brien

# A Crisis of Waste?

## Understanding the Rubbish Society

## Martin O'Brien

Routledge
Taylor & Francis Group
New York   London

Routledge
Taylor & Francis Group
270 Madison Avenue
New York, NY 10016

Routledge
Taylor & Francis Group
2 Park Square
Milton Park, Abingdon
Oxon OX14 4RN

© 2008 by Taylor & Francis Group, LLC
Routledge is an imprint of Taylor & Francis Group, an Informa business

Printed in the United States of America on acid-free paper
10 9 8 7 6 5 4 3 2 1

International Standard Book Number-13: 978-0-415-96098-4 (Hardcover)

**Library of Congress Cataloging-in-Publication Data**

O'Brien, Martin, 1957-
    A crisis of waste? : understanding the rubbish society / Martin O'Brien.
        p. cm. -- (Routledge advances in sociology ; 33)
    Includes bibliographical references and index.
    ISBN 978-0-415-96098-4 (hardback : alk. paper)
    1. Urbanization. 2. Sustainable development. 3. Refuse and refuse disposal. 4. Urban ecology. I. Title.

HT361.O37 2007
363.72'8--dc22
          2007009906

Visit the Taylor & Francis Web site at
http://www.taylorandfrancis.com

and the Routledge Web site at
http://www.routledge.com

'Writers are really people who write books not because they are poor, but because they are dissatisfied with the books which they could buy but do not like' (Walter Benjamin, 'Unpacking My Library')

For Katie and the rubbish of her past
and for William and Isobel and the rubbish of their future

# Contents

*Preface and Acknowledgments*                                   xiii

Introduction: Rubbish Society?                                     1

1   Rubbish Histories                                             11

2   Rubbish Literatures                                           35

3   Rubbish Industries                                            57

4   Rubbish Households                                            83

5   Rubbish Relationships                                        107

6   Rubbish Idealisms                                            125

7   Rubbish Materialisms                                         145

Conclusion: Rubbish Society!                                     169

*Notes*                                                          181
*Bibliography*                                                   183
Index                                                            191

# Preface and Acknowledgments

I have carried this book around with me for more than seven years. I first thought of writing it in the aftermath of a research project on the environmental implications of using waste as a fuel for energy-generation[1] but made no real progress until the summer of 2001. When I conceived of the idea, there were hardly any books on the connections between waste and society; and those that did exist tended to focus on the history of waste in specific places (such as Melosi's, 1983, American-centred *Garbage in the Cities*) or to concentrate on the cultural construction of value (such as Thompson's, 1979, *Rubbish Theory*). The clear exception to this trend was Rathje and Murphy's (1992) *Rubbish!* — a book that applies the methods of archaeology to contemporary America's trash and deduces general 'laws' of garbage as well as acute insights into personal behaviours and social norms. Because of the paucity of available material, I had to do an enormous amount of digging and sifting through libraries, in particular, and through Internet sites (less so) to gather information on the relationships between waste and the societal contexts of its production, consumption and management. This digging and gathering and sifting has left me with such vast heaps of research papers, media stories, social science and engineering books that the small study in my house looks more like a landfill site than a place of scholarly activity. I am surrounded by tottering heaps of paper, stacks of books, scribbled notes, 'post-its' stuck to walls and shelves. Finding anything in the mess involves moving mounds of this stuff from one side of the room to another and then to another spot again when I need something else. In the microcosm that is my study I engage in a ritual that defines waste in modern society more generally – great mounds of stuff are permanently moving from one place to another, and often then moving on yet again. Even the landfill or waste incinerator is often not the final resting place for all this material since landfill mining is becoming an increasingly

1    Funded by the Economic and Social Research Council under the Global Environmental Change Programme, award number L320253136.

used means of extracting useful (or hazardous) materials before moving them on to other sites or back into industrial production and the ash that remains after waste is incinerated is traded in competitive markets. If there is a 'law of garbage' it is that it might look dead but it refuses to lie down: waste flows ceaselessly around society. 'Managing' waste – both in our own private homes and publicly via the 'waste management sector' of the economy – seems to take up more and more time and more and more effort as the years roll by.

If the sheer amount of work involved in gathering together the relevant information is one of the reasons for the book's long gestation period, its production has also been slowed down by another consideration. This consideration has been to find a voice through which to express a series of controversial propositions about contemporary waste. To argue against the easy familiarity of the 'throwaway society' thesis, as I do, has required attention to ensuring some measure of accounting balance. Across the last decade I have become fascinated by the topic of modern waste — by the intricacy of its material forms, by the intimacy of modern society's relationships with its wastes and by the ingenuity with which they are, sometimes, reprocessed into new products. The writerly temptation in this circumstance is to produce a book filled with exclamations and declamations about the wondrous qualities of and crucial roles played by waste in contemporary society. To offset this temptation I have tried to separate description, analysis and theory so that the exclamatory and declamatory tendencies are mostly located in one part of the book's parts.

The first part of the book — Chapters 1 to 3 — is mainly descriptive. The chapters tell stories about the history of waste, the cultural imagination of waste, and the role of waste in industrial development. Although there is some analysis and a small amount of reflection on theoretical questions the purpose of this first part of the book is intended primarily to expose the richness, complexity and crucial societal role of waste today and in the past. The second part of the book — Chapters 4 and 5 — is mainly analytical. These chapters investigate the evidence about what people do with and how they relate to the ordinary waste that we encounter in our lives. The chapters do tell stories, to a certain extent, but their main purpose is to take empirical issue with the idea that contemporary society is uniquely a 'throwaway society' and to explore what the available data can tell us about past and present wastefulness. The final part of the book — Chapters 6 and 7 — is wholly theoretical in that it examines critically the dominant theories of waste in sociology. Of particular importance here are the contributions of Mary Douglas and Karl Marx to sociology's grasp of the nature, origin and consequences of waste.

Although it took several years to accumulate the research materials and begin planning the book's contents, I did publish two short pieces on this topic in 1999 (O'Brien, 1999a; 1999b). One was an account of householders' understandings and relationships with domestic waste and one was an analysis of the commodity value of waste materials. Some sections from these two publications have been reworked for inclusion in the present book, notably in Chapters 5 and 6.

During the years that I have been thinking about, researching and writing this book, very many people have provided suggestions, pointed me in new directions and given me all kinds of help. Particular mention must be made of colleagues and management at the University of Chester who provided enough space in a very busy academic year to enable me to complete the final draft; Elizabeth Shove, Rodanthi Tzanelli and Majid Yar for friendship and for putting up with my obsession with waste; Sue Penna (always) for unflinching support and for letting me turn our shared study into a personal rubbish tip.

Martin O'Brien

# Introduction
## Rubbish Society?

A smooth and well-trodden path may be traversed without danger even by an unsteady wanderer, but where the road must be first marked out and the rough path made smooth, progress is of necessity slow, and each step must be made sure before we extend to the next (Koller, *The Utilization of Waste Products*)

It is entirely uncontroversial to say that waste does not get a good press. Whilst millions of products and services of dubious provenance and utility are treated to extensive marketing campaigns in order to persuade consumers of their merits, there are no equivalents for the contents of your dustbin. At a common sense level, there is no surprise in this. Who, after all, might desire what you have discarded? What possible value could the 'by-products' of your life represent? Since it is you, the citizen, who has to pay to have the detritus carted or flushed away, is it not perverse to imagine that it might, after all, be the object of someone else's desire or, at least, that there are values embedded within it? Put this way waste appears to represent not just the end of a useful life and the absence of value but a transition to *negative* value: the exact opposite of what the term 'value' is normally considered to mean. It is obvious, is it not, that no-one in their right mind would pay money in order to get rid of something that someone else wanted? But, as I will show throughout this book, what is commonsensically labeled as waste has many values and many qualities. It is not necessarily useless or worthless in itself and generating markets for its exchange, institutions for its regulation and industrial processes for its utilisation are, in many ways, hugely impressive social and technological achievements. They are, in short, central elements of how societies are constructed and a plausible definition of 'society' in this characterization would be: organized patterns of collective activity for managing waste.

The centrality of waste to contemporary society is visible everywhere and every day. In my daily life I can walk nowhere, sit nowhere, be nowhere without detritus cluttering up my every horizon. Like the bane of planet earth in Philip K. Dick's novel *Do Androids Dream of Electric Sheep?* (see Chapter 2), I live in a world that appears to conduct a ceaseless war against invading 'kipple' — the slowly accreting effluvia of life that find their way onto my desk, into my car, my home, my coat-pockets, travel- and work-bags; everywhere, in fact. Theoretically, it is possible that I have been somewhere devoid of such detritus but if so I have no recollection of it. The whole of my life has been lived in and through an environment of debris. Let us not forget that it is also visible in the recycled proportions of the newspapers and books I read, the car I drive, the clothes I wear, the glass containers I purchase (and then recycle again); and even the food I eat has, more often than not, been produced by using recycled organic (and inorganic) compounds for fertilizer or feedstock. And where the recycled stuff itself is not the context, means and object of how I live then this very fact, this absence of recycling is visible, tangible, smellable and sometimes tasteable: 'kipple-ization' appears, at first sight, as a law of the failure of recycling.

Nor is it simply the detritus itself that clutters up my landscapes and my living environments. For the war against it generates industrial, politi- cal, economic and social developments and changes the way I live, what I see, what my political and administrative representatives do in central and local government. For example, if, for the moment, I discount the sight and smell of rubbish burning on the domestic fire or in the metal dust- bin outside the kitchen door, my childhood memory of the publicly visible waste business has only two players in it: the Council bin-men on their stop-start weekly rounds and the rag-and-bone man whose horse-drawn cart collected all manner of unwanted textile and metal items and, rarely, glass — in exchange for spare change or cheap children's toys — for return to industrial use. The clip-clop of the horse and cart and the cry of 'RAG- BONE!' — which always sounded like 'RAAHBOAR!' — was one of only two sets of audible signs of the war on waste, the other being the rumble of metal dustbins rolling between the houses on their way to and from the dustbin wagon. Now, a massive commercial sector, more visible in its diver- sity than ever before, stamps its logos on lorries, dustbins, recycling recep- tacles, litter bins and buses. Thousands of lorries and vans daily and hourly whiz around at speed along the highways and byways of town and country alike in their green, red, yellow, white and multicoloured liveries and the rag-and-bone man's cart and cry is hardly anywhere to be seen or heard. Instead, the recycling 'banks' (an interesting choice of word) stand coldly silent and offer nothing in exchange for the rubble of my life except a faint but uneasy sense of self-satisfaction at doing my microscopic bit for the environment. The sounds of waste management have transformed into the clink and crash of bottles being recycled, the squishy rustle of plastic refuse sacks, the metallic grinding of lorry-borne cranes lifting skips from the roadside and the beeping, bleeping and squealing crunch of rubbish com- pactors compressing the stuff *in situ* to the accompaniment, sometimes, of loudly proclaimed profanities as the refuse operatives go about their work. At every turn, I am reminded not only of the massive existence of the kipple but also of the myriad vested interests that thrive on its existence and its continued production, circulation and use. Whether it is PeakWaste or BiffaWaste, EuroWaste or TrentWaste, LakeWaste or BloggsWaste; whether it is the waste-collection authority or the waste-disposal authority or the Waste-Traders and Licensers Club or the Packaging Responsibility Group or any of the other thousands of public and private waste organisations, I have become increasingly conscious of the centrality of the 'war on waste' (see Chapter 3) to the contours of my social environment.

Beyond the confines of my own experiences, the war on waste motivates transnational accords (and disputes) and nurtures the growth of international organisations whose bureaucratic function is to enforce a consensus on how to wage the battle, on what fronts, with what resources and, equally, to carve up the theatre of war into territories upon which different social, political and economic forces will seek to turn back the enemy. A mountain of regulatory guidance and international policy agreements rises up as high as (or possibly higher than) the piles of rubbish that it ostensibly addresses. To switch metaphors, it is sometimes impossible not to see this huge, hydra-headed bureaucratic and regulatory beast as a kind of bloated King Canute, ordering back the oceanic tides of clutter as they wash ever further up the beach. There are times when it is equally impossible not to see this beast as up to its neck in the kipple it seeks to order about or not to notice that one last big wave will finally drown its squawking ineffectuality. In the European Union, for example, a quarter of a century of Council Directives on waste — from Council Directive 75/442/EEC of 15 July 1975 to Council Directive 99/31/EC of 26 April 1999 — failed outright to stop the rising tide. In 1999 Eurostat reported that throughout the mid-1990s, with some variation by country, the quantity of hazardous waste produced across Europe as a whole grew inexorably, reaching 27million tonnes per annum by 1998. This is, as Beck (1992) has already observed in relation to breaches of German environmental regulations, in spite of legions of bureaucrats generating ever-increasing quantities of legislation, guidance and recommendations intended ostensibly to prevent or reduce the production of hazardous wastes.[1]

I remember reading the section of Michel Foucault's *Discipline and Punish* on the 'failure of the prison' where he argued that the 'failure' should be seen not as a negative incapacity of the prison to do its alleged job but as a positive moment in the manufacture of a system of social control — 'discipline' — and in the formation of delinquent targets for its application. In his elegantly polemical way, Foucault portrayed the prison and all of its satellite institutions not as the cure but as the cause of delinquency. If the prison failed to curb criminal impulses and deter criminal acts then, paradoxically, it was working as it should. The laws, institutions and agencies of the criminal justice system existed not to rid society of crime but to produce, regulate and circulate it throughout the social body. Foucault's poststructuralist account of the production of crime and delinquency does not figure in my account of the rubbish society. Yet, his assessment strikes a disturbing chord and urges me to the suspicion that behind or alongside the war on waste another social and political process transpires — virtually without comment — that is aimed at producing, regulating and circulating waste throughout that same social body. The failure of the regulatory complex surrounding waste is not, to quote Mary Douglas out of context, 'a negative movement' but 'a positive effort to organize the environment' (see Chapter 6). In other words, the failure of the regulatory system to achieve its aim of reducing or eliminating useless waste represents the success of a network of institutional, political and economic structures and practices whose cumulative effect is the production and reproduction of a paradox of modern society: useful waste.

In this regard, the present book is partly an exercise in imagination. Specifically, it is an attempt to imagine what a world to which waste is central to people's lives, to economic growth, to political regulation and social engagement, looks like. To put it another way, it is an attempt to imagine the world we live in today. For a long time, a popular imagination devoid of waste has held sway over scholarly debate, political dispute and historical deliberation. From gleaming-white kitchens to gleaming-white teeth, from uncluttered living spaces to uncluttered environments, from shiny new cars to shiny new towns through which to drive them, a rubbish-free sensibility has infested the modern world's outlook on life. This sensibility is a mask or, more appropriately, a cloak that has been worn as ideological protection from what waste really represents and really underpins in contemporary society. The cloak has encouraged a view of waste as ephemeral, as something that can be disposed of and 'disappeared'. Like a kind of socio-economic dandruff it can be brushed from our shoulders and forgotten: it is not something we 'produce' — so it needs no investment; it is not something we 'consume' — so it needs no care. It has been viewed as an accidental afterwards of our normal activities, as if there is no intention propelling its production and no desire feeding its consumption.

In fact, waste is something that is indeed produced, in systems as complex and contrived as those for producing cars or clackerballs. It is also something that is consumed, in public and private networks as sophisticated and organized as a Royal Banquet or a film theatre. The idea that the production and consumption of cars or clackerballs, food or film exists in a reality somehow different to the production and consumption of waste is a classic ideological substitution of fiction for fact. If we did not produce and consume waste, if we did not organize this production and consumption in the most inspired, imaginative and technically sophisticated ways, we would die. Death is when you no longer waste.

In spite of the superclean sensibility that dominates the modern relation to the world, waste is absolutely central to life. It represents its dynamism and its development just as clearly — and just as materially — as the goods and services that comprise the staple diet of modern economic and social thought. And waste is not a 'bad' that can be counterposed to the desired and needed 'goods' of economic theory. What we think of as 'waste' is not something that has *escaped* use or exploitation. It is, much more importantly, what motivates the *search* for use and exploitation. It is involved in some of the most ingenious inventions the world has ever seen. It represents the realisation of an alchemical dream: the conversion of so-called base matter into gold, the valueless into the valuable, the repugnant into the desirable. The alchemical conversion of waste into value is not primarily a technological process even though technology is an important player. It is, instead, a social process of valuation and the industrial, political and economic means of its realisation.

The heart of the book, then, is an attempt to recuperate waste: to retrieve it from the intellectual dustbin to which it is all-too readily consigned in social thought. I attempt this historically, sociologically, politically and anthropologically. In short, I develop a 'rubbish imagination' that is able to begin the process of making links between the practices, institutions, regulations, transactions and transformations that define, organise and govern modern waste. The central proposition that organises the book's contents is that the developed and wealthy societies in the world today should not be construed as 'consumer societies' but as 'rubbish societies'. They have emerged and continue to develop in a quagmire of rubbish relationships, inventions, regulations and institutions: what is commonly understood as waste is a dynamic motor of their growth and transformation that is as important as the motors of production and consumption. I develop this idea by exploring the import of waste for the ways we live today and by exploring aspects of the history of wasting. I suggest that we cannot live without waste and that it is pure fantasy to pretend that the 'problem' of waste can be solved technically. Moreover, there is no possibility of a rational debate about waste unless there is at the same time some appreciation of the complexity and intricacy of its place in society.

Nominally, I use the terms 'waste' and 'rubbish' interchangeably but the discussion running throughout the book rests on the play of a subtle distinction between their everyday transitive meanings. To 'waste' something, in contemporary parlance, means to lose its value, to render the thing unavailable for constructive use. A 'waste of time' is a loss of opportunity or a misapplied effort; to 'get wasted' is to become useless, most often by means of intoxication; to 'waste' a resource is to inefficiently exploit its possibilities or fail to realise its full potential. To 'rubbish' something, on the other hand, is not to lose or inefficiently exploit an opportunity or potential, it is actively to devalue that opportunity or potential; to pluck something from a context of utility or worth and situate it in a diametrically opposed context of worthlessness and futility. This contextual transformation cannot be achieved in private: as any reader who has had their work rubbished by critics will realise, the act of rubbishing is a very public, socially orchestrated process. Rather than the element of worthlessness, it is this element of social orchestration, the degree of co-ordination that dominates the discussion in the following chapters and is signalled by the book's title and thematic organisation. To 'rubbish society' in this context, then, is not to make some rhetorical accusation of futility or worthlessness but to expose some of the ways that waste is central, significant and deeply rooted in personal life, in cultural representation and industrial organisation.

In this sense, the book represents something of a challenge to the popular idea that contemporary society is uniquely a 'throwaway society'. I do not dispute that people today throw things away nor that some of this throwing away is unnecessary, harmful or morally objectionable. Instead, I suggest three things. First, I suggest that industrial societies are and always have been 'throwaway societies' and that this ejecting process has been subject to periodic evaluation and critique on a scale directly comparable with today's common sense complaints. There is nothing peculiarly contemporary about disposing of vast quantities of stuff or lambasting the 'waste' it represents. In fact, whilst beyond the scope of this book, it is plausible to assume that all developed civilisations are 'throwaway societies'. For example, amongst many other instances of ancient disposable cultures, William Rathje and Cullen Murphy refer to the archaeologist David Pendergast who, after studying the Classic Maya site Altun Ha in Belize, concluded that the site's ancient inhabitants 'would have traded in a Cadillac when the ashtray was full' (Rathje and Murphy, 1992: 38). Archaeology, in this argument, is at least partly dependent on the seemingly inevitable practice of discarding rather valuable things. Second, although waste is usually construed as the curse of profit and innovation, the fact is that uncountable wastes have entered, and continue to enter, into industrial production. Some of these wastes have been so central to the social and industrial development of modern societies that it is impossible to imagine what the world today might look like without them. Third, I suggest that the relationships that people and organisations have with waste do not consist in a one-dimensional callous disregard. The idea that people's understandings of and relationships with waste boil down simply to some kind of programmed insatiability and indifference built into consumerism is far too simplistic. Waste is important culturally and personally as well as industrially and socially.

To develop these points the book is divided into seven substantive chapters. The first chapter — 'Rubbish Histories' — tells four stories about the history of waste. They are not four stories about the same history but an attempt to group together some of the dominant historical narratives about the waste, dirt, pollution and litter that characterised the urban landscapes from the medieval period to the dawn of consumerism. The chapter begins with the filth-encrusted world of medieval and Tudor England and moves on to the era of nineteenth century reform before considering the history of early twentieth century consumerism. In its later stages the chapter moves between British and American historical narratives not because the histories themselves run in direct parallel but because the claims made and the stories told become increasingly generalised to the rise of industrial, and consumer, society as such. Of course, the discussion is too short to do proper justice to the historical nuances that have surrounded the emergence of different societal relationships to waste. The point of the chapter is not to depict a total history of waste but to collate key narratives in order to provide readers with some sense of the historical contexts that lie behind contemporary ideas about waste.

Chapter 2 — 'Rubbish Literatures' — presents four stories of a very different kind. Rather than collating historical narratives the chapter examines four fictional constructions and uses them to explore shifting cultural meanings and signals about the personal and social significance of waste. The four fictions — spanning the period from the mid-nineteenth century to the present day — are Charles Dickens's *Our Mutual Friend*, T.S. Eliot's *The Wasteland*, Philip K. Dick's *Do Android's Dream of Electric Sheep?* and Don Delillo's *Underworld*. These fictions narrate four different relationships to waste and, I argue, represent waste's historically unstable meaning and significance. From 'dust' as a foundation of life (Dickens) through 'waste' as the absence or loss of value (Eliot) to the menacing threat of 'kipple' (Dick) and the 'shadow' of garbage (DeLillo) four clearly articulated, and clearly different, aesthetics of waste are recounted. Each of these waste aesthetics reveals something about the cultural contexts in which wider commentary and critique about waste has been embedded as well as the inevitable intersection of moral and sociological assessments in understandings of waste.

This aesthetic contextualisation is partly visible in the stories explored in Chapter 3 — 'Rubbish Industries'. Here, the dependence of industry on waste materials of all kinds and the ingenuity with which these materials have been used in the production of valuable commodities is recounted. Beginning with the importance of paper to the scientific revolution and the ensuing European Enlightenment, the chapter goes on to note the increasing industrial internalisation of waste recycling and reuse. Products as varied as motor transport, modern medicines, dyes and explosives were all dependent on the conversion of what had been understood and treated as the useless, and sometimes dangerous, by-products of industry into useful products. The chapter recounts the shift from the widespread scavenging and collecting practices in the urban centres to the chemical synthesis of new products and notes some of the optimism, and despair, that this synthetic economy seemed to promise to social commentators of the late nineteenth and early twentieth century. It goes on to note the growing disquiet, in the middle of the twentieth century, generated both by the chemical industries themselves and the altered economic and industrial structures in which they came to operate. Finally, the chapter discusses the continued dependence of modern industry on waste products of all kinds and notes the striking inventiveness that accompanies the generation and use of such products.

Chapter 4 — 'Rubbish Households' — is less concerned with stories and more concerned with what the available evidence suggests about the validity of the 'throwaway society' thesis. Here, the available data on household disposal practices in England and Wales from 1919 to 2003 are presented and discussed. The data are placed in the context of a growing population, changing household composition and altered waste management arrangements. What these data appear to demonstrate is that the keyword in household disposal practices is not growth but continuity. As surprising as this finding might appear, when household disposal practices are placed in their appropriate social and industrial contexts, the evidence suggests that contemporary consumers are no more — or not grossly more — profligate than their forebears. In fact, there are many reasons why patterns of household disposal today are different than those of our parents and grandparents but the evidence does not point towards a society increasingly characterised by callous disregard for post-consumption waste — at least this is true at the level of the household. In short, it appears that our parents and grandparents were as likely to discard reusable items as we are — even if the character of the items themselves has changed.

Where Chapter 4 looks at the available evidence on callous disposal, the following chapter — 'Rubbish Relationships' — teases out some of the rich complexity that characterises contemporary relationships with wastes. If the callous, profligate, and insatiable epithets are too simplistic then what kinds of relationships to waste to people have? The chapter opens by considering Jeff Ferrell's immersion in the 'scrounge' economy of urban American trash-pickers and dumpster divers. In Ferrell's hands, the intimate details of this 'outsider' economy are described in almost loving detail in order to portray a landscape where discarded materials are revalued, reworked, reused or returned to the industrial economy either as a means of marginal survival or as a positive statement against consumerism. Where Ferrell finds material recuperation in the marginal economy of scrounging, Nicky Gregson, Louise Crewe and colleagues find it in the mundane worlds both of second hand exchange and the careful dispersal of used goods to places where their inherent values can be redeemed in second, third and further uses. The chapter goes on to discuss the meaningful personal relationships that people invest in the 'junk' of their lives and notes how the social contexts in which these junk objects are situated are crucial in grasping the significance they hold for individuals and families. The significance of these 'useless' items — comprising everything from plastic bottles to old video tapes — derives from their ability to signal memories and attachments in personal histories and relationships. By contrast, the chapter concludes by investigating a very different set of contexts in which junk and waste are valued by exploring the conversion of waste into commodities rather than personal objects of desire and memory. Here, the institutions and organisations responsible for this conversion situate these same objects in very different valuation frameworks that enable waste to release its commodity values for exploitation.

Chapters 6 and 7 turn to debates in social theory. Chapter 6 — 'Rubbish Idealisms' — begins with the work of Mary Douglas and her famous dictum that dirt is 'matter out of place'. Whilst this dictum is repeated *ad nauseam* in books and essays on waste, its underlying theoretical and analytical context is invariably ignored. Instead of treating the dictum as a fact, I take a close look at why Douglas used it in her investigation of primitive cultures but not in her work on modern cultures. Anyone who reads Douglas's *Purity and Danger* is presented with an array of interconnected arguments and analyses that provide the dictum with some force in understanding *non-modern* cultures. Yet, in spite of its regular repetition in the literature of waste, Douglas's general thesis does not translate easily from its primitive context and its applicability to the modern world is questionable. Following a detailed exploration of Douglas the chapter goes on to examine what latter day idealists have done with her central proposition and shows how it has been necessary to fill in her original thesis with a variety of supplementary arguments and theoretical injunctions in an attempt to secure its relevance to a world beyond the 'tea cups' of small scale cultures.

Chapter 7 — 'Rubbish Materialisms' — begins with the work of Karl Marx. Here I unpack three different theses on 'waste'. These are Marx's analysis of the 'passively rotting mass', or 'social scum' that is the lumpen proletariat; the 'overproduction' of capital; and the 'reconversion' of the 'excretions of production'. The chapter shows that, for Marx, the production of social refuse is inevitable, the over-production of commodities is inescapable but, except in some special circumstances, the production of waste materials is not. Thus, although Marx observed and condemned the squalor and filth in which the proletariat was forced to subsist and acknowledged the rubbish-filled environment that was nineteenth century capitalism, he could not explain the generation of the substance of that filth — in what it materially consisted — as an inbuilt logic of capitalist production. In order to answer the question 'why is there waste and what role does it play in capitalism' later social theorists took Marx's original work in a variety of different directions. Veblen emphasised the role of 'conspicuous waste' in distorting industrial production; Baran and Sweezy recounted the rise of 'monopoly capitalism' and its dependence on wasteful expenditures; and Bauman returned sympathetically to the lumpen proletariat, characterising their outcast status as 'wasted lives' built into 'liquid modernity'.

Aside from some short comments at the end of the chapters I have saved a summary and conclusion for the last chapter of the book — 'Rubbish Society!' Here I return to the book's key themes and propose that waste should take its rightful place in our understanding of the world in which we live. That is, it should be understood and treated as a *central* rather than *superficial* dimension of personal, social and industrial organisation. Instead of understanding 'waste' as that which is left-over *after* production or consumption I propose that it should be grasped as *what* modern society produces and consumes. Waste is not one thing and one thing only. It is a rich, abundant and significant dimension of how we live. Whilst my aim is not to celebrate the waste of modern society, it is certainly to show that it is now, and long has been, a crucial component of social organisation and cultural understanding.

# 1    Rubbish Histories

[Behind] every embassy, court, palace or Grand hotel where history, as men record it, is made, in every city in the world, there is a row of battered dustbins. We have come a long way from the ape and the man who only threw away fruit peel that rotted where it fell, and we can measure our progress through the centuries by how fast our dustbins are filled. (Wylie, *The Wastes of Civilization*)

Writing histories of waste is not a typical undertaking. Library shelf upon library shelf is filled with histories of how societies have produced and consumed things; whole academic departments of scholars and researchers are devoted to teasing out the historical minutiae of making things and using them. Yet there are hardly any detailed, historically sensitive studies of how societies have dealt with their wastes and, conversely, the role that those wastes have played in historical development and social change. The histories that have been written tend, with few exceptions and where they delve sufficiently far back, to recount a linear legislative track from the mediaeval rakers of the mid-fourteenth century to the current 'crisis of waste' and the 'throwaway society'. By and large, where the nettle of historical rubbish has been grasped firmly, it has generated fascinating insights into how people relate to the world around them and to each other. Melosi's (1983) *Garbage in the Cities*, Strasser's (1999) *Waste and Want*, Miller's (2000) *Fat of the Land* — all, incidentally, American — demonstrate that waste is a key to understanding social, economic and political organisation.

In the British context the historical focus has tended to emphasise public health and hygiene, rather than waste as such. Wright's (1960) *Clean and Decent*, McLaughlin's (1971) *Coprophilia*, Wohl's (1983) *Endangered Lives* are classic examples of the British coprologist's art. Somewhat more concerned with the cultural mores surrounding the creation, rather than the disposal, of sewage, Inglis's fascinating (2001) *A Sociological History of Excretory Experience*, attempts to trace the historical intersection between toilet technologies and 'defacatory manners' but is still well within the British canon. True, many books on recycling and 'green' thought seek to evaluate contemporary waste management practice against historical data but these do not dig into history's rubbish piles in order to relate their contents to the societies that generated them (see, for example, Gandy, 1993; 1994; Tammemagi, 1999. See Chapter 4). This latter task has been left to archaeology but even here it is uncommon to find significant work on the importance of the waste itself, rather than on the social contexts of production and consumption illuminated by it. The tendency has been to view history's waste through the lens of current understandings and treat it simply as an afterwards of production and consumption — as a leftover or excess that somehow escaped its social system.

Yet societies, contemporarily and historically, are built upon and, in important senses, fabricated out of waste. Waste is, quite literally, the ground upon which they stand, a crucial resource that has driven their development, and a key substance out of which they are, at least partly, historically composed. My main concern in this book is to investigate modern waste; that is, the roles that waste has played in social and industrial change in the period following the industrial revolution — from the middle of the nineteenth century to the present day. In this first chapter, however, I want to try and set the scene for the investigation by looking briefly at how the period immediately following the industrial revolution compares with earlier ways of dealing with waste. I begin with the swamp of filth that was mediaeval England and progress to the beginnings of the consumer society in the early twentieth century. If there is a moral to the drawn from the story it is that if you think contemporary industrial societies are facing a crisis of waste, you should spare a sympathetic thought for the living conditions of your (not-so-distant) ancestors.

## FILTHY HISTORY

Following his murder in December 1170, a select band of disciples gathered to undress Thomas à Becket — Henry II's 'meddlesome priest' — in preparation for burial. Terence McLaughlin (1971: 19–20) describes the body's many layers of clothing:

> Outermost there was a large brown mantle; next a white surplice; underneath this a fur coat of lambs' wool; then a woollen pelisse; then another woollen pelisse; below this the black cowled robe of the Benedictine order; then a shirt; and finally, next to the body, a tight fitting suit of coarse hair-cloth covered on the outside with linen, the first of its kind seen in England. The innumerable vermin which had infested the dead prelate were stimulated to such activity by the cold that his hair cloth ... "boiled over with them like water in a simmering cauldron."

December can be a very cold month in England so, in the absence of central heating, it is little surprise that Becket's frame was layered against the elements. His 'innumerable' passengers, although seemingly there only for a free lunch, must have made an extra layer, helping to keep the drafts out and thereby contributing to much appreciated bodily warmth. Being ignorant of the potential dangers that fleas might herald — the plague had not struck England seriously for a very long time and even when it did return the potential role of the flea in its transmission was unknown — mediaeval folk of all social stations often put up with them for the whole of their lives. Anyway, given that Becket had a coarse hair-cloth next to his flesh, there may have been some difficulty distinguishing between the flea- and louse-feast and the general skin irritation deriving from the garment itself. Of course, the level of infestation also suggests that, if he had ever experienced a bath at all, it had been some considerable time before his death. More likely, Thomas à Becket and, equally significant, his clothing, had passed large phases of his adult life un-immersed in any cleansing water.

Even if Becket's coarse hair shirt was worn as a religious penance, the condition of his body was no different from the population at large. The idea that energy might be expended in regular bathing — or even washing, either of the body or its apparel — was an alien concept to the majority of our mediaeval ancestors, including much of the monarchy and nobility. It is not that no one *ever* washed or bathed in these times. Lawrence Wright's *Clean and Decent*, for example, presents several instances of medieval tubs and lavers, and communal bath houses which, in relatively short time, descended into houses for gossip and loose living. King John (1199–1216), for example, was said to have taken a bath 'about once every three weeks' (Wright, 1960: 39) — although no mention is made of his laundry arrangements. The point is that, in general, people passed their lives in a state of accumulated filth, and the places where they lived were no different. Houses were begrimed in dust, mud and all manner of dirt both outside and in. The streets of towns and villages were awash with refuse and excrement. In spite of the efforts of the rakers, who were instructed to remove deposits of filth, the tide of rubbish was simply too large to control. In London, the Fleet and Thames rivers were choked with refuse and sewage, and the town ditch, a defensive moat completed in 1213, regularly overflowed with accumulated detritus. 'Human and animal dung and household rubbish,' observes McLaughlin (1971: 28) 'all discharged into the streets and left to find their own way into the river or the town ditch, were supplemented by the by-products of slaughtering and butchering.' The remaining entrails of the slaughter trade, mixed up with excrement, blood and bits of carcass, gathered along the banks of the Thames to be washed over the side at the next moderate rain. The combined piles of household, industrial and excremental matter often blocked the gutters that ran down the streets, causing many houses to flood with the liquid run-off and encouraging some to put boards at the front of their doors to keep out some of the disgusting deluge.

The stench of medieval urban England, as can be imagined, was foul in the extreme. So pervasive was the stink of excrement, rotting carcasses and offal that few ever noticed anything amiss. McLaughlin recounts the case of two men who were prosecuted for piping 'ordure' into a neighbour's cellar and who were caught not because anyone in the house noticed the smell but because the cellar overflowed. Given the tendency of street ordure to wash into houses, this circumstance is not as extraordinary as it may at first appear. When the plague did strike England in 1348, it added a new pungency to the normal stink of life. Bubonic plague carries its own peculiar, and fearful, odour. Combined with the smell of the rotting corpses that gathered in quantities too numerous to dispose of, the inhabitants of England's towns and villages locked their doors, sometimes being forced to do so by panic-stricken authorities, and burned ineffective fumigants — such as incense — to ward off the invading stench. In a strange kind of association, to contemporary sensibilities, at least, many also believed that one foul stink could defeat the menacing consequences of another so it was not uncommon for householders to squat over their earth closets, breathing in the fumes to offset the threat of the black death.

If medieval England comprised a swamp of filth and rubbish, the Tudor period fared better only superficially. Houses, furnishings and clothes became more decorative but behind the grandiose décor and style lurked the same accumulations of refuse and dirt. Elaborate hooped skirts, extensive padding at shoulder and waste, ruffs and frills of huge variety, tapestries, textile hangings and covered furniture, for those who could afford them, still hid infestations of fleas and lice and provided an outward show of ornamentation overlaying an inner reality of grunge and grime. The Tudor era may have provided close stools and prototype water closets (the latter were considered an eccentricity) for the wealthy, but it did little to improve on the means of disposing of the accumulated cloacae. Nor did it do much for the state of the larger towns and villages. Street gutters were still filled with all manner of refuse, and rubbish was piled in such abundance on the highways that wagons often became completely stuck in it (see Mitchell & Leys, 1964: 161). As if the ground-level catastrophe were not enough, from the late sixteenth century onwards, houses and manufactures became increasingly dependent on coal, instead of wood, for heating. Supplies of wood for urban domestic fires and industrial production had all but dried up in many larger towns so, although the better off could still afford to buy some wood, the mass of the urban population and many urban industries had to exercise frugality by purchasing cheap coal — 'sea cole' — shipped from Newcastle. By the time of the Restoration in 1660, a million tons of coal was being mined in England every year, around half of it being consumed in London alone. Indeed, 'Seacoal Lane', near Ludgate Circus in London, is almost certainly so named in recognition of the coal-laden barges that landed there after sailing up the Fleet river. As a consequence of the substitution of coal for wood, the inside, as well as the outside, of houses was often choked by a fug of acrid smoke. Now, added to the excrement and refuse piled in the thoroughfares, overflowing cesspools and rank waterways, came ever-growing quantities of thick, black soot deposited from the belching chimneys of the breweries, dye-works and soap-makers as well as from the houses themselves. So dense and obnoxious was the foul miasma that in 1661 Sir John Evelyn was moved to present to King and Parliament a tract entitled *Fumifugium: or the Inconveniencies of the Aer and Smoak of London Dissipated together with some Remedies Humbly Proposed* which he opens with an illustrative anecdote:

> It was one day, as I was Walking in Your MAJESTIES Palace, at WHITE-HALL (where I have sometimes the honour to refresh my self with the Sight of Your Illustrious Presence, which is the Joy of Your Peoples hearts) that a presumptuous Smoake issuing from one or two Tunnels neer Northumberland-House, and not far from Scotland-yard, did so invade the Court; that all the Rooms, Galleries, and Places about it were fill'd and infested with it; and that to such a degree, as Men could hardly discern one another for the Clowd, and none could support, without manifest Inconveniency.[1]

The change from wood to coal as fuel for domestic heating and industrial production had other effects, apart from blackening the air of major towns and depositing concentrated Tudor acid rain on town and country alike. The ash from burned coal is a more effective binding agent than wood ash. In consequence, when piled on the streets with all the other effluvia of industrial and domestic life, it was progressively fused into a relatively durable mass by successive waves of traffic, causing the level of the roads to rise. By the early nineteenth century, using coal ash for making garden paths was recommended to American householders precisely because it can be trodden to a consistency more durable than brick (see Strasser, 1999: 23). In some cities today the roads stretch atop multiple layers of mixed refuse and coal ash going down as far as fifteen feet. In Edinburgh and other ancient cities the rising road level, rather than the builder's shovel, explains the existence of some of the cellars (see Wylie, 1959: 32–3).

If the urban stench became particularly ripe, persons with spare cash were able to purchase perfumes with which to soak their gloves or handkerchiefs and thus mask the worst of the odour. However, 'perfume' is a rather fanciful term for the substances most commonly in use. Whereas today's perfumeries may use, for example, tiny fractions of *essence* of musk — well disguised in compound fluids — the Tudor practice often was to apply the much less adulterated secretions of musk deer, civet cat, Russian beaver, or ambergris — this last being a putrefying emanation of dead whales. Civet is particularly interesting, in that it is produced by a gland near the penis of the civet cat and, in order to extract it, the collector frequently would first 'tease' the cat. It was a valuable substance, worth several pounds sterling per ounce at today's prices — but how many people today would deign to arouse a very annoyed and potentially ferocious wild cat in order to earn a meagre living? Still, the notion that it is preferable to walk around smelling of slightly sweetened tom-cat spray than to inhale the raw air of urban England surely confirms that the smell at times was intolerable even to those for whom it was a fact of daily existence.

Still unaware of the role of the flea in spreading the plague, and oblivious to the place of *Mus rattus*, the native black rat, in the transmission cycle, post-Tudor England's filthy towns and dwellings stored up the conditions for the return of the plague. Although the town and village authorities made some rudimentary connections between the dirt and disease, the measures enacted to sanitise the streets were both ineffective and often not implemented. Given also that designated places for excreting were few and far between, and given that the labour power expended on ridding the streets of the mixed human and animal droppings, rotting carcasses and refuse remained woefully inadequate, enacting provisions for cleaning up the towns was a deed with more than a little of the King Canute about it. Numerous, and vehement, public laws had been issued since the mediaeval period (see Salusbury, 1948) but no abatement in the tide of deposited filth could be discerned. The last true epidemic of Bubonic Plague struck England in 1665–66 and, in London, at least, inhabited by something of the order of a fifth of England's population, the 'cure' was drastic indeed and had nothing to do with public sanitation measures. On Sunday September 2, 1666, a small fire started in Thomas Farynor's bakery in Pudding Lane. Five days later, one and a half square miles of London and its environs lay in ashes and the new 'Great Fire' of London (exceeding that of 1212) entered the historical record. Over 13,000 of London's close-packed wooden houses were destroyed along with every scrap of refuse upon which the black rats had been feeding, thus encouraging *Mus norvegicus*, the more aggressive and more prolific imported brown rat, finally to supplant its plague-carrying cousin in England's capital city. London was about to be reborn and whilst there were some improvements — notably in the construction of many more buildings from brick and stone instead of wood, and a better system of barging refuse to the food-growing suburbs — the rivers and streets very soon overflowed with filth once more.

Obviously, it did not help that the common practice, ingrained over centuries of habituation, was for householders, and manufacturers, whenever it suited them (and whenever they could get away with it), simply to disgorge any and all detritus straight into the street or, for those 'lucky' enough to live near running water, into the nearest stream or river. Excrement, bones, fish waste, feathers, metal and fibrous industrial discards, and effluents, worn out items of every kind, household dust and debris, dead dogs: you name it and out of the door or window it went. Walking beneath the windows of Edinburgh lodgings required that you be alert to the characteristic cry of *Gardy-Loo* ('Gardez L'eau!') and shouted, as quick and as loud as you could, the appropriate response *Haud yer han* in order to avoid being showered by the contents of chamber pots. In fact, since beer, rather than water, was the usual beverage of the common urbanite, the condition of the slops thrown from the windows can hardly be imagined. If you happened to be out when nature's call was felt (and even, sometimes, if you happened to be in), little embarrassment attached to an abrupt dash and squat in the nearest doorway or street corner. Even during the eighteenth century, that period of Enlightenment and progress when the minds of men and women turned to the rational exploration of the natural and social universes, it was still necessary to wade through the slime and grime of urban life. In these circumstances, if you could afford it, a thick-soled wooden 'patten' or galosh came in handy. Designed to maintain several inches between foot and smut, it just goes to show that the platform shoe was an in-demand item centuries before the 1970s and that there is indeed nothing under the sun (or very little, at least) that is new.[2] The faecal morass was not a peculiarly British phenomenon: the whole of urban Europe was caked in the stuff. In Paris, according to Corbin (1986: 27), 'excrement was everywhere: in alleys, at the foot of milestones, in cabs,' and the stink of that city was matched, if not surpassed, by the choking odours of Bordeaux, Rouen and Clermont.

Although the streets of England and Scotland slowly and spasmodically became cleaner as the century progressed, and although increased access to water meant that, for some people, greater cleanliness was theoretically possible, urban waterways deteriorated even more. A major reason for this was the growing popularity of Alexander Cummings's water closet, patented in 1775 and subsequently improved by Joseph Bramah. In spite of a tendency to find its own natural course to the waterways, at least a portion of the 'nightsoil' customarily had gathered in earth closets or on the streets, or was collected by nightmen either for fertiliser or to be dumped in laystalls, but now increasing quantities were flushed through crude sewers or into open street channels straight into the rivers and streams that supplied the water drunk by the urban population. The seventeenth century had been struck by a plague it did not understand and whose origins were not of its people's own making. The eighteenth century, in contrast, began to ferment a perfect organic culture in which to nurture its own epidemic: typhoid (or 'enteric fever'), which, by the end of the century, was already signalling the tragedy that was to follow in several large-scale epidemics after 1836.

## REFORM HISTORY

The turn of a century means nothing in itself, yet the arrival of the nineteenth century was marked by a fitting event since 1800 was the year of Edwin Chadwick's birth. Chadwick bestrode the Victorian public health movement like a sanitary behemoth, producing schemes for social reform in every sphere from accident insurance to 'preventive policing' and sewage management. Chadwick, in fact, epitomises the soul of Victorian urban reformism. He was not a philanthropist, he was a social engineer seeking to mould the physical character of urban England in the service of a higher plan — and a quick profit in the process. A utilitarian through and through he became secretary to Jeremy Bentham but soon exceeded the latter's capacity to devise practical schemes for social development. The prime mover behind the 1834 Poor Law Ammendment Act and the 1848 Public Health Act, Chadwick's influence extended across the Atlantic to encourage successive waves of American urban reform.

Looking back at nineteenth-century Britain, it certainly appears that reform was necessary. The filth and squalor that had characterised the medieval and Tudor towns was simply intensified in rapidly growing urban areas like Leeds, Manchester, Birmingham, Glasgow and London. The rivers were still filled with all manner of discards, the streets ran with sewage and were covered in refuse, the air was a dense, nauseating fug. The rising population and expanding industries generated greater and greater quantities of rubbish and filth, overwhelming the expurgatory capacities of even the most industrious dustmen and scavengers. In order that thoroughfares remained passable, and in order that crossing from one side of a road to the other did not result in the pedestrian becoming bogged down in the grime, major urban areas fair teemed with crossing sweepers who, like Moses repeatedly parting the Red Sea, made paths through the grunge so that the thoroughfares of larger towns and cities came to resemble three-dimensional geometric figures. So many of these operatives were there in London, and so significant was their work, that Henry Mayhew devoted more than two dozen sections of his book to the various different pliers of the trade (Mayhew, n.d: 381–410). From the juvenile gangs sharing three or four crossings together, to the elderly and infirm individuals who swept the same crossing every day, they were too numerous for Mayhew to count. 'We can scarcely walk along a street of any extent,' notes Mayhew, 'or pass through a square of the least pretensions to "gentility," without meeting one or more of these private scavengers' (ibid.: 381). Some were paid regularly by householders, shopkeepers or banks in order to maintain navigable pathways to their doors. Others relied on gratuities from pedestrians who used their crossings. The very existence of these sweepers, and their uncountable number, indicates something of the condition of the roads in mid-century London and, by extension, the accumulated urban detritus which was the Victorian norm.

Hector Gavin, writing in 1847, attributed London's high mortality rates to defective paving and drainage, population density, and impure air as well as to the 'filthy state of the dwellings of the poor and of their immediate neighbourhoods; to the *concentration* of unhealthy and putrescent emanations from narrow streets, courts and alleys' (cited in Wohl, 1983: 5). He might have taken the passage from Engels, whose *The Condition of the Working Class in England* had been published in 1845, were it not for the fact that it was published only in Germany. It did not become available in English for another forty-two years. In the report, Engels describes the labourers' housing in England's great cities (he also describes Edinburgh and Dublin), including London, Leeds, and Bradford. Looking down from a bridge over the river Irk — a 'narrow, coal-black, foul-smelling stream, full of debris and refuse' — Engels portrays the condition of mid-century Manchester:

> Below the bridge you look upon the piles of debris, the refuse, filth, and offal from the courts on the steep left bank; here each house is packed close behind its neighbour and a piece of each is visible, all black, smoky, crumbling, ancient, with broken panes and window frames...

> Everywhere heaps of debris, refuse, and offal; standing pools for gutters, and a stench which alone would make it impossible for a human being in any degree civilised to live in such a district. (Engels, 1974: 83)

No surprise, then, that the Victorian mortality rate from preventable diseases — among the poor, in particular — was appallingly high, nor that the infant mortality rate was nothing less than a long-running tragedy. In England, during Victoria's reign, the infant mortality rate (that is, deaths per thousand of children under one year old) stood at a staggering 153, according to official, and probably conservative, estimates. 'Every year', writes Wohl (1983: 11), 'well over 100,000 infants died before their first birthday in England.' It was a feat, he goes on to imply, that would have impressed Herod himself. This figure, of course, represents only the average over a number of years and is drawn from the later decades of the century. It does not take into consideration the huge increases in death rates that occurred during the severe epidemics of the 1830s and 1840s when cholera, typhoid, smallpox, scarlet fever and influenza combined to wipe out tens of thousands more — adults and children alike. 'Scarlet fever,' notes Haley (1978: 7), 'was responsible for nearly twenty thousand deaths in 1840 alone' and typhoid took over thirty thousand souls in a single year in 1847.

The conditions inside the houses of the urban poor were hardly better than outside. With intermittent access to (invariably contaminated) water, overcrowded, damp and unsanitary rooms heated by open grated stoves in the 'kitchens' (where such designated spaces existed), infested with parasites and other insect life, often unventilated — although, given the stench of the streets, this might have been considered a mixed blessing — urban populations were squeezed together more tightly than tinned sardines and in far less hygienic conditions. Henry Mayhew describes the state of several London lodging house districts, including the rookery of St. Giles and, in volume two of the *Morning Chronicle Survey* (1981: 140), recounts the plight of two women, seven men, and four children living and working in two rooms, the largest of which was no more than eight feet by ten.

In these circumstances it may seem somewhat paradoxical that the Victorian social reform movements did not begin with the living conditions of the poor. They began, instead, by penalising the unemployed through the Draconian 1834 reform of the Poor Law, then moved on to combining the supply of water with the removal of filth from public places following Chadwick's 1842 *Report on the Sanitary Condition of the Labouring Population of Gt. Britain* before eventually attempting to systematise the provision of charitable relief through the Charity Organisation Society from 1869 onwards. Yet, there is no paradox when you realise that early Victorian social reform was fundamentally a utilitarian endeavour. The abstract goal may have been, ultimately, to improve the lot of the population as a whole but the method was not to reach out to the poor and needy themselves, nor to address the gross inequalities of wealth and status that kept them poor and needy. The method, instead, was to rationalise all of the institutional structures by which society was organised and controlled and thereby establish the conditions for progressive efficiency and rationality in the political economy. This latter 'progress' would ensure the social improvements necessary to combat epidemics, unemployment, crime, fecklessness and immorality. To suggest that the system itself generated poverty, disease or death was tantamount to an admission of national (and intellectual) failure. What the poor needed, according to Chadwick and his supporters, was not better wages, more food or greater equality but water, sewage- and refuse-management. Fashioning a sanitary urban environment, properly organised and well-administered, would create the conditions for the (deserving) labouring classes to thrive.

For centuries the practice had been for dustmen and scavengers of various kinds to collect what rubbish they could (although vast quantities remained rotting and festering in the streets) and either reuse it or trade it — notably by selling materials to dealers and manufacturers and either carting or barging portions of it up- or down-river to the food-growing suburbs of the major urban areas. Of the large number of scavengers and rubbish-removers who inhabited London's nineteenth-century streets, the dustmen had it, comparatively, pretty good and the lower orders of bone-grubbers, rag-gatherers, toshers, cigar-end finders and the rest could only dream of rising to the rank of dust contractor. Originally, the latter were required to pay for the privilege of removing the mixed rubbish and nightsoil left by householders and industry. However, London's dustmen, at least, realised that they had the upper hand and were able to extract payment from the authorities for their services. Mayhew (n.d: 346–7) recounts the dustmen's struggle against the London authorities and the striking success of their tactics:

> The Court of Sewers of the City of London, in 1846, [..] were able to obtain from the contractors the sum of 5,000*l.* for liberty to clear

away the dirt from the streets and the dust from the bins and houses in
that district. . . . [By 1851] the amount paid by the City is as much as
4,900*l*.! This is divided among the four great contractors, and would,
if equally apportioned, give them 1,250*l*. each.

Thus, the dust contractors became the only operatives to be paid twice
for the same material: first by the City for removing the dust and second by
the agricultural and industrial businesses who bought the products of their
labours. This double payment was won because the contractors formed a
cartel and forced payment for their services. All parties to the exchange
— the contractors and the City authorities — knew that London's dust was
a valuable commodity and that the contractors were able to get good prices
for its sale. However, whilst the contractors could afford to let the dust
accumulate as a weapon of industrial dispute, the City authorities were
aware that the streets would too quickly become impassable unless some
means of removing it were arrived at.

This practice — of removal for resale by contractors — continued
to be of central importance in managing urban waste for decades after
Chadwick's intervention. However, Chadwick's main concern was to rid
the streets and public places of the foul miasmas arising from the rotting
rubbish rather than to think through a workable and practical method of
disposing of what was collected. In consequence, his first schemes simply
involved flushing the filth into the nearest waterway (usually the Thames)
and hoping that the water would get rid of it somehow. But, at the same
time, Chadwick was also planning to construct several miles of sewage
pipeline in order to transport London's filth to the outlying districts where
it could be used to fertilise the soil, for a fee. Combining the flush system
with the pipe system meant that the cost of supplying the water, and a
not inconsiderable profit for his 'Towns Improvement Company,' could be
recouped from the sale of street dirt (see Miller, 2000: 30–1).

Chadwick was disappointed that his scheme initially foundered through
lack of scientific and political support. But the idea did not go away. Instead,
it transformed into a plan not only for the fertilisation of food-growing
soil, but also for reclaiming land. The Sewerage Utilization Act (1865),
extending and consolidating provisions of the 1848 Public Health Act, created sewer authorities and made provisions for health authorities and town
councils to take responsibility for sewage. This responsibility required that
councils and allied authorities had to find ways of disposing of that sewage.
So, in the same year in London, there appeared a Special Report from the
*Select Committee on the Metropolis Sewage and Essex Reclamation Bill*
which had been charged with inquiring into 'the most useful and profitable means of disposing of the Metropolitan Sewage on the North side of
the Thames.' The Committee recommended the Chadwickian scheme, put
forward by Messrs. Hope and Napier, of irrigating 'by sewage in whatever quantities may be found useful of a considerable area [i.e., Essex!]

particularly well adapted for such a purpose'[3] and allowing for all unused material to be shipped for coastal land reclamation. In fact, the scheme was not implemented but only because its two proponents could not raise the necessary financial backing. It indicates clearly, however, that Londoners have never had many qualms about defecating on Essex — even though the inhabitants of that County have for long been less sanguine about the arrangement (see Luckin, 2000: 212).

Part of the problem faced by Chadwick in his efforts to achieve the same support as Messrs. Hope and Napier later did, was that there was insufficient separation between sewage and all the other rubbish. Chadwick's scheme involved flushing just about anything and everything down the pipes with the consequence that its nutritional value to agriculture was suspect. Given that quantities of industrial effluent and discards would also be mixed in, as well as general refuse from domestic life, the practicality of fertilising or reclaiming land with the piped ordure was far from apparent. In 1865 this problem remained — although there was a slowly growing distinction between general rubbish and sewage proper, street refuse, offal, excrement and industrial discards were still mixed together in urban areas. Various Acts of Parliament after 1848 had made inroads into this state of affairs, constituting and reconstituting Boards of Health, making provisions for the removal of nuisances, and regulating some industrial emissions via the Alkali Act of 1863 and subsequent measures. But it was not really until the Public Health Act of 1875 that conditions in most urban areas began to improve noticeably and local authorities started to take over the systematic collection of household rubbish — slowly but surely putting to an end the practice of indiscriminate scavenging and (eventually, via a series of measures to improve the dwellings of the labouring classes and the erection of 'destructors' — i.e., waste incinerators — in many urban settings) the general mixing of 'sewage' and refuse. Support for the scheme of Messrs. Hope and Napier was helped, of course, by the fact that more and more households began to install water closets as the century progressed until, by the early part of the twentieth century, they were increasingly to be found in working class, as well as bourgeois, homes.[4]

In important respects, what was happening in the later part of the nineteenth century was a more systematic separation of wastes — house refuse, industrial discards and sewage came to comprise different categories of 'waste' and began to flow through different physical and administrative channels. The moderate success of the Alkali Act of 1863 (and the more forceful provisions of ensuing Acts), for example, was in part consequential upon the activities of the chemist Robert Smith, who was appointed as Chief Inspector under the Act's provisions. His capacity to persuade the chemical industries to re-route their wastes into alternative productive processes — notably the transformation of waste hydrochloric acid into commercial products such as bleach for the textile and paper-making industries (Wohl, 1983: 228–30) — encouraged industrialists to comply with wider controls over the emission of gasses and effluents. Similarly, as the century progressed, particularly following the Public Health Act of 1875, there was a tendency, increasingly regulated under Byelaws, for household wastes to be collected more systematically by different operatives — nightsoil, where it was not flushed immediately into drains or sewers, being collected separately from the mixed refuse that was to be found on the streets and in communal ash pits.

## POLITICAL HISTORY

The history of sanitary reform is not a simple or straightforward narrative of enlightened progress from dirt to hygiene. It is a complex interweaving of political, economic and social agenda in which some kinds of reform progress apace, whilst others move much more hesitantly and encounter many more barriers. Thus, Bill Luckin's (2000) tale of reform in English cities is careful to acknowledge the 'inhibiting' role of local politics and technological incompetence on urban environmental intervention. In particular, he notes that different elements of the problems of urban contamination were addressed in different ways, at different times and in different places. The provision of sewage systems across Britain's towns and cities was a largely uncoordinated process and produced rather different outcomes for different communities. As we have seen above, some nineteenth-century communities had their sewage pumped away but only to be deposited on the doorsteps of other communities. The 1865 plan, for example, to pump sewage from London and deposit it on Essex, in reality ratified a practice that had been going on for a long time but was intended to change the financial and bureaucratic locus of control over the conveyed filth. Glasgow acquired safe drinking water as early as 1859 but prevaricated over financing a properly constructed sewage system until 1888, when the company that was to build the underground railway agreed to remodel the system for free as a fillip to winning the contract. The tales of trade-offs and deals were not confined to the early history of sanitary reform but continued into the twentieth century. So, whilst safe drinking water was (generally, but not everywhere) available following the programme of chlorination during the Great War, effective smoke abatement had to wait a further forty years — or, depending on your historical perspective, four centuries after Evelyn's *Fumifugium* — and, even then, different cities implemented policies differently as a consequence of the various combinations of more or less powerful industrial, political and citizens' lobbies. This story of British rubbish, as we will see in later chapters, has parallels today. The most detailed and insightful studies of the political character of waste's history, however, are American and they are mightily instructive about the role of rubbish in urban planning and development.

For obvious reasons, there is much less to relate about the urban American experience in the mediaeval and Tudor periods but by the late eighteenth and early nineteenth century American dirt and waste were generating problems of their own. There were some similarities in the accumulation of urban filth and in the reforming zeal applied to it but there were also significant differences in the ways that these problems arose and were tackled. Some of the differences can be accounted for by the different paths of industrialisation and urbanisation followed by American cities, others by the different political cultures organising America's urban power bases.

By the late eighteenth century, the eastern cities — of New York and Washington, D.C., for example — were already caked in filth. But it was only as the nineteenth century progressed that, with large-scale immigration and urban growth, the familiar grubby scenes of densely populated European cities were reassembled in America. As Engels, Gavin, and Mayhew had commented on the condition of towns and cities in mid-century England, so later American commentators, notably Jacob Riis (1890), reflected on the noisome and unsanitary tenements into which communities had been squeezed following successive waves of immigration after the 1840s and on the filthy tracks and alleyways that passed for thoroughfares in the rapidly expanding cities. By the mid nineteenth century, writes Martin Melosi (1983: 21):

> Heaps of garbage, rubbish, and manure cluttered alleys and streets, putrefied in open dumps, and tainted the watercourses into which refuse was thrown.

As in England, responsibility for the sanitary condition of cities was passed, initially, to health departments. But the spur to action was less a utilitarian dream of rational institutional organisation and more a 'budding environmental consciousness' (ibid.) that persuaded municipalities to address both the unsightly and unhygienic state of the urban milieu. Anyway, it was difficult for American urbanites to square an ambition to utilise their waste rationally with the fact that they produced so much of it that, left untreated, the market for it too often tended to zero. Even by the time of the Great War — two decades after organised street cleaning had been first implemented — the flood of litter and refuse still confounded the efforts of the street cleaners. Added to the problem of sheer magnitude were transport difficulties in getting the organic fractions out of cities to farms where they might be used, and finding suitable sites to erect facilities for converting the rubbish into saleable goods.

What was missing from the waste-to-wealth equation was a political machine that would enable profits to be channelled from the streets to the elites. Certainly, in line with changing ideas in Europe about the values of waste, American commentators later began to argue that city refuse represented a significant loss of wealth from the American economy and that applying more scientific methods to its recovery and treatment would more than offset the costs of collecting it. Amongst other examples, Melosi (*op cit*: 182) cites a pamphlet circulated to promote the activities of the United States Reduction Company in 1902, which claimed that 'The fortunes of the future will be made from the crumbs that fall from the world's table,' implying that waste would be the source of future prosperity. Like their English counterparts, however, American commentators initially failed to realise that the greatest strides in waste recovery and re-utilisation would derive (and were already deriving) not from municipal wastes, but from industrial wastes (see Chapter 3).

Also like their English counterparts, American reformers tackled the problems of removing the filth and disposing of it as two separate processes; it was not uncommon for street and house refuse to be collected from one district and simply dumped on the doorstep of another or tipped into the nearest available stretch of water. Thus, an important spur to the budding consciousness of urban environmental contamination was the very visibility of the waste problem, which itself was partly attendant on developments in transport and other municipal amenities. As well as the widely dispersed piles of rubbish despoiling American cities, by the mid 1880s, there were in the region of 100,000 horse- and mule-drawn vehicles criss-crossing America. The inevitable solid and liquid emissions of these animals created immediate nuisances and hazards for urban dwellers. However, with so many animals circulating the tracks of America, the disposal of their carcasses also generated significant problems. In 1880, New York scavengers had to remove 15,000 horse carcasses from the streets and even in 1912, when motorised transport had become dominant in many urban areas, 10,000 such carcasses still had to be cleared (Melosi, 1983: 25). Combined with human and other animal befoulings, ash, cinders and litter of all descriptions, the horse problem was simply the tip of a rubbish heap of urban blight. The visibility of the late nineteenth century solid waste crisis encouraged American municipal authorities (as in Europe) to devote energy initially to street cleansing rather than to organised and systematic management of municipal solid waste. Thus, as in England, the American 'garbage problem' was tantamount to the 'filthy streets' problem, indicating the extent to which dirt, rather than waste as such, underpinned the urban sanitary reform movements.

This last observation is of some significance because it emphasises a crucial difference between contemporary ideas about waste and those of our late nineteenth-century forebears. Dirt, in the nineteenth century, was simply 'matter in the wrong place', as Lord Palmerston had observed. What needed to be tackled, in the urban sanitary reform movements, both in England and America, was the *accumulation* of refuse and other nuisances, first on the streets and later in the waterways, of urban areas. The *production* of these nuisances, except in some very specific cases, was not seen as a major problem. In fact, given the concentration of polluting and dirty industries in the cities, potentially the main contributors to urban blight were not individual households but the manufacturers themselves. Accumulating industrial scrap and discards, poisonous emissions, liquid disposal directly into waterways and the leakage of industrial effluents down streets and into ground water all compounded the hazards of city life then, as they do today. Sewers would occasionally vent poisonous industrial gases and some refuse piles contained corrosive and otherwise injurious chemicals. Whilst the miasma theory of disease (where illness stems from exposure to an unwholesome atmosphere and noxious smells) was giving way to the germ theory (where illness stems from personal infection by pathogenic agents) by the late nineteenth century, the latter had little to say about the toxic and otherwise health-threatening substances that debilitated urban populations in the absence of germ-transmission.

Important reasons for the focus on dirt, as opposed to waste, in nineteenth-century industrial societies were the inability, and unwillingness, to police the behaviour of extractive and manufacturing businesses combined with a wide variety of political cultures at the local level. Much has been written about the altered scientific and public health outlook that followed the discovery of 'germs' and their role in disease transmission. Very much less has been written about the political scaffolding that upheld the urban spotlight on the accumulation of filth, rather than the production of waste. An outstanding, and rare, contribution to this task is Benjamin Miller's (2000) *Fat of the Land*. Tightly focused on the complexities of New York's history, the book contextualises America's historical rubbish not in terms of domestically-generated refuse piles but in terms of the Machiavellian politics of (often corrupt) urban elites.

Miller recounts several instances of the politically charged historical contexts of New York's sanitation services, beginning as early as the 1840s with the rise to prominence of Alfred White as New York City inspector. White had no interest in making New York's businesses more efficient in order to reduce the quantities of waste they produced, and little interest in controlling the kinds of waste that were disgorged into the city. Instead, he viewed the accumulations of detritus as an urban gold mine, declaring, in 1849, that the filth of New York's streets represented 'the greatest chance for a fortune I ever saw' (Miller, 2000: 38). Following Chadwick's lead in England, the street-cleansing project began to grip America's major cities with a similar fervour and, like Chadwick, White and others were not slow to grasp that power over dirt could be translated into substantial personal profits. If a company could be formed with a monopoly on collecting organic street refuse, well-remunerated by the City authorities for the service, and then convert the piles of muck into saleable products — by recovering reusable materials, dealing in bones and blood, rendering the leftovers into a serviceable fertiliser (whilst discharging the remaining effluent, free of charge and regulation, straight into New York's waterways) — then, he surmised, like London's mid-century dust contractors, such a company would be paid twice for the same business venture. White and his colleagues (in spite of the fact that White was legally debarred from doing so) duly established a reduction plant first on South Brother Island in the East River and, when this was forced to close, on Barren Island in Jamaica Bay and commenced to turn the 'greatest chance' into financial reality. The conditions on the Island were atrocious: a wooden factory, rudimentary housing for the labourers, thousands of hogs to eat what was not boiled in the reduction plant, festering piles and pools of offal, rotting food and other organic matter and a stench to rival mediaeval England, the Barren Island scheme nonetheless held many portents for America's garbage future.

By manipulating City Hall, falsifying bids for rubbish contracts, leaning on friendly legislators, White and partners planted filth firmly in New York's entangled political and business machine. Unlike the common practice of indiscriminate dumping and scavenging, which, comparatively speaking, provided an elementary democratic division of the spoils, White's plan added impetus to the long trend towards monopolisation of the rubbish industry: channelling city (and later federal) funding, together with market-derived profits, into the hands of business and political elites. It was a move that set many precedents for municipal waste management in New York and across America more generally. It made waste a key factor in the civic empires that later came to control the building of roads, subways and airports (through real estate trading and access to preferential funding streams) and perhaps the greatest monument to human productivity ever conceived: the Fresh Kills landfill site on New York's Staten Island. In an ironic circularity, Robert Moses, the civic architect of this massive rubbish monument, had borrowed many of the dodgy bureaucratic and financial means to push through his city engineering projects from Baron Haussman — who had converted the muck pile of Montfaucon into the Parc des Buttes Chaumont and found the means to pay for the boulevards of Paris in the process — but Moses did not live to see plans to transform Fresh Kills into precisely the same kind of amenity (he died in 1981). Faced with the site's imminent closure as a landfill, the New York City Department of City Planning invited submissions to re-engineer the festering pile and, in 2001, announced that they had been pleased to receive common visions 'of a park that includes the active recreational needs of Staten Islanders and that also values and restores the delicate ecology of the site'.[5] It is a vision that Moses would have gleefully shared, and almost certainly would have wheeled and dealt and traded and persuaded in order to gain control.

From Montfaucon to Fresh Kills the rubbish monuments of industrial societies make up the physical, financial and political subsoil of contemporary boulevards, expressways, parks and airports. Thus, the history of rubbish is as much a history of political horse-trading and civic empire-building as it is a history of hygiene and sanitation. The intermeshed business and political cultures that emerged around the control of street dirt in the nineteenth century have determined the shape of waste management in Britain and America ever since.

## CONSUMING HISTORY

Consumerism has been blamed for just about every ill in the modern world — from high crime rates to deforestation, from depression to obesity. It is no surprise, therefore, that it is blamed also for the contemporary waste crisis. Whilst it is a commonplace to hear that the consumer society and the throwaway society are inextricably bound together, hardly anyone has undertaken any detailed historical exploration to substantiate the claim. Indeed, it can be suggested that waste in historical study is in the same circumstances today as was consumerism two decades ago, when consumption and the world of goods, as Agnew (1983: 68–9) remarked, were treated by historians 'as the outcome of other historical developments — industrial capitalism, for example — that are felt to be more compelling.' At the present time, waste is similarly seen as the outcome of other 'more compelling' processes, none more so than rapacious mass consumption.

So, for example, Young (1991: 20–1), expressing this widely held view in a report for the Worldwatch Institute, claims that the 'profligacy' of the developed economies can be measured through the quantities of domestic waste they generate and that these quantities, in turn, arise from the 'voracious demand' generated by a consumerist lifestyle. Quoting Vance Packard (1967) with approval, Young suggests that consumerism is the foundation of the throwaway society (ibid.: 12) and, like many commentators, situates this 'historical aberration' in the period following World War II. Young was simply picking up on a long-held assumption that contemporary industrial societies are more wasteful than their pre-industrial predecessors and that they signify, in the words of the Nobel Prize winner Dennis Gabor and colleagues (1978), a peculiarly modern 'age of waste.' Yet, the origins of mass consumerism are to found not in the late twentieth century, but in the late nineteenth, and are part and parcel of wider social, economic and political changes that were affecting all developing industrial economies. These changes taken together, and not merely the development of individual consumerist lifestyles, were responsible for encouraging new kinds of relationships with industrial goods and services. In addition, whilst there is a tendency in these literatures to treat the history of the consumer society entirely negatively, it needs to be remembered that many of the changes signalled vast improvements in the life-chances of industrial society's poorest constituencies.

For example, rising incomes in late nineteenth-century Europe and America certainly meant that people could afford to widen the range of materials they brought into their homes. But of particular importance to those on lower incomes was the opportunity to diversify a traditionally dull diet. It is not necessarily that people purchased food in greater quantities as a consequence of rising incomes. The tendency was to spend the extra money on more expensive items, especially meat. In England, during the early part of the industrial revolution, three quarters of the income of the poor was spent on bread alone, with a fraction of the remainder being spent on potatoes. By the end of the nineteenth-century dietary diversification had become a widespread priority, which is no surprise in such stodgy circumstances. Greater prosperity also meant the ability to buy more clothes and furnishings as well as increase fuel consumption. Now, not only could poorer people afford to keep warmer and better nourished inside their homes, they could also afford to stay warmer and better nourished outside them. Although fuel consumption went up, it actually became somewhat more efficient because the domestic gas cooker came into extensive use, stimulated by the development of the slot meter. Coal was certainly cheap in comparison, and was still used for household heating, but it was exceptionally wasteful whereas, with piped gas, cooking fuel, at least, could now be used only when it was required (see More, 1997: 161–3).

Whilst not equally distributed, rising incomes applied to both men and women and increasing numbers of the latter found themselves in relatively stable employment before (and often during) marriage with the consequence that more money was available for purchasing what had once been seen as 'luxury' items — such as carpets and china-ware, curtains, books and stationary. In response to expanding purchasing power, major cities became home to giant department stores — Lewis's opened stores in Manchester, Birmingham and Sheffield in the 1880s, and Jaeger Company opened in London in the same decade. Other stores, including Burberry, Debenham, and Gorringe rebuilt, refurbished and expanded to attract more custom until, in the early part of the twentieth century, the giant Selfridge emporium opened in Oxford Street and Harrods expanded to fill four and one-half acres of prime London real estate (see Adburgham, 1989: 271–82).

The expansion of the great stores was part of an emerging supply chain for mass produced goods. The techniques for turning these out had been in place for some considerable time but the means to distribute them, and the funds to purchase them, lagged behind by several decades. In consequence, Richard Robbins (1999) suggests that the second half of the nineteenth century faced a crisis of overproduction (see Chapter 7) the solution to which required major changes in a variety of social institutions and not merely in individual lifestyles. These included educational and cultural institutions, industries, government agencies and the family itself. According to Peter Stearns (2002), during this period intensified consumerism was certainly in evidence everywhere. Not only were there greater quantities of consumer goods, but the idea of consumption also made in-roads into child-rearing practices and leisure pursuits — including holidays, spectator sports and, later, movies. Obviously, throughout the nineteenth century, city dwellers in particular had been buying, using and disposing of goods in unprecedented quantities. But the platform for modern 'mass consumption' — including wider political and social rights, better diets, increased longevity, improved housing and educational provision, greater employment stability, higher wages and an extensive range of parallel social improvements for which our great grandparents had fought long and bitter struggles — began to solidify as that century was drawing to a close.

The historical intersections between waste and consumerism, however, are far from clear and, with very rare exceptions, not explored either by historians or social scientists studying the consumer society. One such exception is the social historian Susan Strasser who, in a series of intensely detailed books, has charted the emergence of mass consumption, and its impacts on women in the household, in late nineteenth and early twentieth-century America. Strasser's guiding thesis — what unites her books on housework (*Never Done*, 1982), the growth of the American mass market (*Satisfaction Guaranteed*, 1989), and garbage (*Waste and Want*, 1999) — is succinctly stated in *Never Done*. The thesis is that, in America at least, the decades between 1880 and 1930 saw a transformation of American production and consumption methods, and a consequent realignment of the relationships between households and industry. Referring specifically to the textile industry, Strasser sums up the case by suggesting that the production, first of the cloths and eventually of clothes themselves, 'progressed through the stages of economic development, from home production for home use, through the independent crafts stage to industrial manufactures, affecting all classes of people long before the century's close.' (1982: 126).

She observes the growth of consumerism through the kitchen window, so to speak, looking at the economic and social changes it effected from the point of view of women's work in the home and the ways and means by which marketing firms recruited housework to the cause of mass consumption. Interweaving personal tales of housework, strategies for manipulating the purchasing practices of consumers, and the emergence of giant distribution chains for mass produced goods, Strasser investigates the changing relationships between people and everyday household objects that ensued from the growth of the new system. Thus, she writes (1999: 12) 'Most Americans produced little trash before the twentieth century.' Up until that time, households and cities, but not industry, resembled 'closed systems' where 'waste to one part of the system acts as resources to another' (ibid.: 14). From the late nineteenth century onwards, the urban and household 'systems' progressively opened up with the consequence that:

> The late-twentieth-century city takes in most of what it uses by truck and train and aeroplane, and flushes its waste into landfills, sewage treatment plants, and toxic dumps (ibid.: 15).

In the past, in the absence of consumerism, people made do and mended and, therefore, generated much less waste than today. Cast-offs, cut-offs, leavings of all descriptions were reused, recycled and revitalised. Part of this history of 'trash-making' is a story of the death of the bricoleur — the person who, inventively and creatively, works what is at hand into useable and desirable goods — and the birth of the consumer-disposer — the person who, destructively and belligerently, eradicates potentially reusable materials and discards what are potentially valuable resources. Today's consumers, in this tale, are such a wasteful lot! Gone are the skills, the know-how and the social contexts supporting the repair and restoration of the lost objects of desire that now comprise the contents of the throwaway society's massively monumental landfills. But it needs to be recognised that the transformation from bricoleur to consumer-disposer was not a straightforward identity-swap, nor was it a simple progression from recycling to dumping. On the one hand, industrial societies did not simply stop recycling. Rather, they changed the means by which household and industrial discards were recovered and re-used. On the other, some activities became more wasteful with the advent of consumerism and some became less so.

For example, instead of the widespread practices of doorstep donation to itinerant collectors and disorganized scavenging by gangs of poor citizens, salvage and recycling became progressively more disciplined and industrialised. A major player in America's trash-trade was the Salvation Army, which, from the 1890s onwards, following William Booth's (1890) vision of a social reformist charitable agenda, began to run rubbish operations in major cities, including New York. The premises in which these operations were carried out were given the apt name of 'industrial homes' and they combined waste storage facilities, repair workshops, lodgings for the poor labourers who conducted the salvage work, and canteens. According to Strasser (1999: 143), these homes multiplied until, by 1904, 'forty-nine institutions accommodated about eleven hundred men and employed about seventy officers. ... [The] homes contributed substantially to the Army's nearly £2 million annual income in the United States, and their buildings were a large part of its £1.5 million real estate holdings.' The homes salvaged and reused clothes and rags, shoes, bottles, paper, and old furniture amongst many other 'waste' commodities. The Army's strategy was mirrored by other large charities — including the Society of St. Vincent de Paul and, later, Goodwill Industries. If each of these charities operated at similar levels of turnover and ran premises equivalent to the Army's, then, by the early twentieth century, when consumerism was already well-entrenched in American society, the three of them alone would generate an annual income of $6 million and own $4.5 million dollars of real estate. This, of course, is merely the tip of a huge financial mountain and takes no account of the wealth generated by the legitimate (and illegitimate) trash businesses that also collected, salvaged and sold America's refuse.

In these profitable circumstances, there was widespread suspicion of municipal collection systems — with good reason, given the corrupt and self-serving practices of city administrations (see above) — and, in some urban areas, such as Cleveland, Ohio, the early municipal systems failed because residents simply would not give their trash to the city collectors. Suspicion, and refusal to hand over household waste, was displayed not only by residents of American cities. George Soper (1909: 66) had observed the same problem in London, where 'the number of these refusals in Hackney alone [amounted] in 1905 to some five or six thousand per week.' Where municipal collection systems did function, they comprised bewilderingly complex mixtures of mechanical and human labour power to extract useable items from the mixed rubbish. By the early twentieth century many American cities had opted for the 'English method' of waste disposal — burning it in dedicated incinerators — although there were also numerous reduction plants, and open dumping still remained common. In both English and American systems, however, much energy was expended on recovering valuable items from the mixed rubbish before disposing of the remainder. Soper (op. cit.) undertook a European tour in order to investigate different street-cleaning and waste management systems. He comments on the work of the Paris rag-pickers, the use of Hamburg's incinerator wastes to supply building materials, and Manchester's municipal 'country estates' at Carrington and Chat Moss where rubbish-manure was used to fertilise root and grain crops. John Kershaw (1928) describes several different operations in English cities — including incinerators, reduction plants, municipal tips, and a gasification plant in Halifax — and details how, in each of these works, tin, iron, glass, paper, clinker, and manure were all recovered or, in the last case, prepared for sale. Strasser, similarly, notes that at America's early twentieth-century incinerator plants, before burning, the rubbish passed along conveyor belts at either side of which stood pickers: one was employed to rescue tin and glass, one to rescue shoes, one paper, and so on until all recoverable items had been separated out. As elsewhere, some of the remaining treated ash was used as a fertiliser when the market for it was not depressed and, in general, the rest was dumped.

At the same time that municipal waste management and treatment became more disciplined and more industrialised, a vast range of manufacturing and agricultural operations began to cash in on the value of the over-produced materials that had traditionally been discarded. With increased demand for a wider range of products, there emerged a greater research and development effort to transform wastes into commodities as well as greater linkages between waste-commodity producers. So, for example, whereas the fisheries of Europe and America had traditionally wasted upwards of half of every catch, because there was no market for what could be made from the offal and bones and there was no taste for some of the fish species netted, rising demand made it feasible to manufacture products from the previously discarded half. Of particular note are the products Isinglass — used in glues and cements, court plaster (a medical dressing combining Isinglass and silk), stiffening for jellies, and in the clarification of wine and beer, — oils for cooking and lubrication, and fish manure (see Simmonds,

1876: 138–46; Spooner, 1918: 278–81). This last became a more lucrative commodity as rising demand for foodstuffs stimulated extra demand for fertiliser. Now, instead of leaving millions of tons of fish offal to rot in the sea or on the beach, industrial and agricultural businesses found markets rapidly opening up. The fruit-growing districts of California, for example, had greater need for fertilisers as demand for fresh produce grew. Like the fisheries, however, they also found ways of using what had previously been unwanted or for which, previously, there were only very small markets. Citric acid and lemon oil, charcoal briquettes, concentrated fruit juice and pectins, all made from the 'culls' — unmarketable fruit — or by-products of California's fruit-harvest began to appear on the shelves of shops and in the catalogues of wholesalers for their remains to become post-consumer waste instead of the producer waste from which they were made.

The point I want to draw from this brief historical survey is that the platform upon which mass consumption was built was not an inherently wasteful structure. There was nothing in the changeover from bricoleur to consumer that necessarily delivered a throwaway society that was essentially different to what preceded it. Or, more modestly, the evidence for a direct association between them is weak. Certainly, there were changes in the quantities of materials flowing through households, and changes in people's relationships to those materials. But the demise of one pattern of resource recovery and reuse — the demise of the bricoleur, make-do-and-mender — was paralleled by the emergence of other patterns of recovery and reuse — industrial and technical innovation in resource retrieval. Some patterns of activity became more wasteful as consumerism took off, others became less so.

# 2    Rubbish Literatures

Here is your monument and it stands high!
The cars which you wore out, the clothes you tore,
The cans you emptied, furniture you broke,
And all the shit with which you clogged the drains.

('Citizen Bacillus' in John Brunner, *Stand on Zanzibar*)

In Chapter 1, waste, pollution, dirt and detritus were shown to be germane
to and embedded in the very fabric of historical societies. The so-called
'crisis' of waste has been central to the lived realities of our ancestors for
centuries: it has, in short, a very long pedigree and has taken many different
forms — from filth-encrusted clothing and households through industri-
ally-polluted living conditions to discarded consumer remnants. The brief
historical survey in Chapter 1 was not intended as a definitive statement
of the reality of historical waste. Rather, its aim was to suggest that waste
has been represented as a problem, in various different guises, for a very
long time. Always, in these representations, some things are emphasised
and some things are all but ignored — whether it be the 'smoake' of London or Paris's excrement-spoiled cabs, the miasmatic ordure that inspired
Chadwick's urban reforms, the filthy streets of urban Britain and America
or the massification of consumption and the demise of the eco-friendly bricoleur — the representation of waste always exceeds a critique of the waste
that is its ostensible target. Any assessment or critique of waste, I suggest, is
always a form of social criticism that espouses an evaluation of the society
in which the alleged waste is situated. Indeed, to invoke a 'crisis of waste'
in any systematic sense is effectively to invoke a moral and sociological
appraisal of how things are in society in general — and how they might
otherwise be.

With this in mind, when contemporary academics, government spokes-
persons or media pundits talk about waste it is tempting to aver that they
are invoking 'what everyone knows', the common-sense of the modern citizen. Surely, it cannot strain the imagination to grasp what 'waste' means

to the modern way of life and to each modern individual in the present industrial-commercial order of things. It seems transparently obvious that 'waste' means the unwanted, discarded, useless and valueless by-product of what is produced and what is consumed individually, collectively and industrially. In such a common-sense imagination this is what 'waste' *essentially and elementally is.* But the question that immediately rears its head when such a construction is addressed analytically is: where has this imagination come from? Does it signify something timeless about waste — i.e., waste has always been grasped as this excessively unwanted leftover — or does it signal something about the peculiar understandings of how the world works today and the dominant sociological and moral judgments about the contemporary scene?

This question arises because waste, dirt, filth or dust represent not only material objects. They also represent social sensibilities. They encapsulate personal, social and aesthetic relations to the world at large and how they are signified and symbolized indicates as much about moral and cultural norms and mores, hopes and dreams, fears and aversions as about the disposability of objects. When waste is the central topic rather than simply the critical context of analysis what emerges is a richness, complexity and abundance of representations and relationships that render waste meaningful and pliable to social action. It is this richness and abundance that is at the heart the present chapter in which I investigate four important dimensions of the cultural imagination of waste. I suggest that this imagination has undergone important historical changes and that these are visible in major works of literature and poetry in which waste is the central topic or crucial context of the work.

In particular, I want to explore some of the ways that the cultural imagination of waste has changed between the publication of Charles Dickens's *Our Mutual Friend* (first published in 1865) and Don DeLillo's *Underworld* (first published in 1998). In between Dickens's tale of dusty London and DeLillo's garbage-filled America are two important transformations in that imagination. The first of these, already underway before the Great War, is exemplified in T.S. Eliot's *The Waste Land* (published in 1922). The second, pricking social consciences from the late 1950s onwards, is captured exactly in Philip K. Dick's *Do Androids Dream of Electric Sheep?* (published in 1968). Through a detailed critical survey of these four fictions, I will show not only that the imagination of waste has changed but also that it is embedded in a wider network of moral and sociological judgments about personal action and about the character of the surrounding societal context. To imagine waste is to imagine much more than the by-products, the discards and the valueless things that occupy centre stage in so much contemporary scholarship and policy: it is fundamentally to imagine the intersections between morality and society.

## FROM VICTORIANA TO MODERNISM:
## DICKENS AND ELIOT

### *Our Mutual Friend*

Published in 1865, *Our Mutual Friend* is Charles Dickens's last completed novel. It is a book of very many parts. There are four volumes and, including the 'Postscript', fifty-four chapters detailing the exploits of at least (depending upon how you count them) twelve central *dramatis personae* and a host of secondary actors. It concerns, amongst other things, the deception of appearances: things are not usually what they seem. In particular, beneath the dust of London life is character in abundance. Some of this is villainous, some of it virtuous but it is impossible to know which is which without digging into the dust to discover what treasures lie hidden therein. The world in which the tale transpires is made of dust. But 'dust' here refers not to a thin film of powder that can be wiped away without thought. Instead, in Dickens's tale, it is the material substance that holds together the solid universe in which all of London life meaningfully exists. According to Adrian Poole, 'the word "dust" was as capacious then [i.e., in nineteenth-century London] as the word "waste" is now' (see Dickens, 1997: 805). It certainly covered the religious connotations of Genesis 3:19, but dust also referred to money and wealth as well as to the detritus of London life. Digging through the dust is a guiding principle of the narrative — things of value are hidden inside it and morally bankrupt characters find themselves consigned to it. In a twist to this narrative principle, immersion in the dust-clogged River Thames provides personal redemption or ruin and the story both begins and ends with characters emerging from or descending into the filth of London's waterways.

The book opens with Gaffer Hexam and his daughter Lizzie sculling a small boat, covered with slime and ooze, through the filth and debris that passed for the Thames River. Lifeless and rank, the river is, nonetheless, 'meat and drink' to the father and daughter, their best friend and their living. 'The very fire that warmed you when you were a babby, was picked out of the river alongside the coal barges,' Gaffer tells his daughter. 'The very basket that you slept in, the tide washed ashore. The very rockers that I put it upon to make a cradle of it, I cut out of a piece of wood that drifted from some ship or another' (p. 15).[1] In spite of the fact that the river is devoid of aquatic life, poisonous, detrimental to human life, and filled with all manner of human, commercial and industrial waste, it nonetheless supports legions of the London poor. It provides firewood, clothing, utensils — and cash. The boat is towing a corpse that has been in the river for some time. Corpses are, in the main, how Gaffer and Lizzie earn a living. Collecting corpses for the inquest fee — and acquiring any valuables the corpses happen to have about them — provides the two with money to survive. Gaffer and Lizzie live in a world of old, discarded, grimy and decayed objects that yield to them sufficient values to sustain life. They inhabit a part of London where river and land are metaphorically united in the image of London's dust. They live 'down by where accumulated scum of humanity seemed to be washed from higher grounds, like so much moral sewage, and to be pausing until its own weight forced it over the bank and sunk it in the river' (p. 30).

In utter contrast, between the finding and the (mis)identification of the retrieved body, Dickens introduces Mr and Mrs Veneering, who were:

> ... bran-new people in a bran-new house in a bran-new quarter of London. Everything about the Veneerings was spick and span and bran-new. All their furniture was new, all their friends were new, all their servants were new, their plate was new, their carriage was new, their harness was new, their horses were new, their pictures were new, they themselves were new, they were as newly married as was lawfully compatible with their having a bran-new baby, and if they had set a great-grandfather, he would have come home in matting from the pan-technicon, without a scratch upon him, French-polished to the crown of his head (p. 17).

Of course, as their name implies, this is really the veneer of newness, not newness in itself: 'And what was observable in the furniture,' continues Dickens 'was observable in the Veneerings — the surface smelt a little too much of the workshop and was a trifle stickey'. Here, Dickens alludes that the Hexams and the Veneerings differ only in the superficial gloss that envelops the latters' life: beneath the polish, the Veneerings inhabit the same degraded, filth-encrusted world as Gaffer and Lizzie. The distance between the 'accumulated scum of humanity' and the 'stickey' newness of London's well-to-do is infinitesimally small and fundamentally unstable: the meaning and the truth of London life lies *beneath* the stickey veneer and the encrusted dust. This is why the story opens with the apparent contrast between what is old, degraded, discarded and dead and what is new, gleaming, 'French polished' and alive. Dickens uses the theme to set the intellectual scene for the remainder of the story. The reader is induced to remember the contrast when following the tale of the main character's ascent from apparent penury to wealth and status.

The corpse that Gaffer and Lizzie have gathered from the oozing Thames is thought to be a certain John Harmon, the only son of 'a tremendous old rascal who made his money by dust' and who:

> grew rich as a Dust Contractor, and lived in a hollow in a hilly country entirely composed of Dust. On his own small estate the growling old vagabond threw up his own mountain range, like an old volcano, and its geological formation was Dust. Coal-dust, vegetable dust, bone

dust, crockery dust, rough-dust and sifted-dust, — all manner of Dust. (p. 24)

The social standing of John Harmon — as heir to a fortune founded on dust — renders his death a matter of keen topical interest. The death of his father — 'Old Harmon', who built the fortune in the first place — occupies no place at all in the story. John Harmon's death, on the other hand, 'like the tides on which it had been borne to the knowledge of men . . went up and down, ebbed and flowed, now in the town, now in the country, now among palaces, now among hovels, now among lords and ladies and gentle-folks, now among labourers and hammerers and ballast-heavers, until, at last, after a long interval of slack water it got out to sea and drifted away' (p. 40): only to return again later, in a different guise — like much else in Dickens's story. John Harmon had in fact been attacked and did nearly drown but the corpse was that of another whose identity was mistaken because the two had swapped clothes.

The opening structure of Dickens's dusty tale, then, completes a cycle: from the discarded, the degraded and dead, through the recently acquired, newly-burnished veneer of respectability to the degraded, the discarded and the dead, again. The whole point of this narrative cycle, of course, is to expose the façade of Victorian veneer. It is an exposé to which Dickens returns again and again in the novel, sometimes as part of its plot, sometimes in the form of rhetorical asides for his readers' edification. The cyclical structure is used to render all of the main characters as betwixt and between, their status is ambiguous and their identities uncertain, as if in a 'state of suspended animation', says Adrian Poole, in his introduction to the book. The principal female character, Bella Wilfer, arrives in the story in mourning for a man (i.e., John Harmon) whom she has never met: 'a kind of widow who never was married' (p. 44), who loves the veneer of money and wealth but who fears its consequences for her identity and morals, who falls in love with a man who is not whom he appears, and who oscillates throughout the novel between foppish sentimentality and steely determination. The principal male character, John Rokesmith (i.e., John Harmon's assumed identity), has a name that implies a maker of fog or mist ('Roke'), and thus insubstantial, yet anchors the moral sentiment of the tale by his flexibility and sensitivity. He takes things as they are, not as they should be and works unstintingly for the best of each of his friends and acquaintances.

The young Harmon's fortune is worth in excess of £100,000, but rather than claim the inheritance immediately, he has cooked up a scheme to pretend to be someone else in order to check up on his prospective wife, Bella Wilfer. The discovery of the body in the river, and the mistaken presumption that it is the young Harmon, extends the period of this deception much longer than he had initially anticipated. His presumed death results in the fortune passing into the hands of his late father's servant, Boffin, whose conscience is uneasy at inheriting such a large sum. So large is this fortune that Boffin is given the sobriquet 'the Golden Dustman' and the connections between dust, gold and wealth are regularly exposed in the story. The inheritance encourages Mr and Mrs Boffin to move from their lowly cottage where they had lived in old Harmon's dustyard to a 'fashionable' London residence. On their departure, a large crowd gathers and some of the more boisterous elements shout 'down with the dust' — a slang expression for 'show us your money'. At their new house, the Boffins are introduced to John Rokesmith (John Harmon's assumed name) by the Wilfer family and he is here referred to as the 'mutual friend' of the book's title. Sensing a way of putting his deception to good use, Rokesmith takes on the role of secretary to the Boffins.

As readers are introduced to the virtuous natures of one set of its leading characters, another set of much less virtuous characters also emerges. These are, principally, Silas Wegg, Roger 'Rogue' Riderhood and, later, Bradley Headstone. Wegg is installed at the Boffin's old cottage and given the task of reading to Mr Boffin for a fee. Whilst there, he is forever rooting and sifting through the dust piles in search of valuable objects but, in particular, in search of a will that he believes lies buried therein and which he hopes might secure him an opportunity to blackmail Boffin. He fancies that his scheme is coming to fruition and is unaware that he has been rumbled by Rokesmith, who hatches a secret plan with Mr Boffin to teach him a lesson. Rokesmith and Boffin decide to sell the dust piles. For the whole period of their removal — day and night for 'a stretch of months together' (p. 761), giving indication of their size — Silas Wegg has watched over the process 'with rapacious eyes' in case any valuables were buried therein. But there were none. 'How could there be any, seeing that [old Harmon] had coined every waif and stray into money, long before?' (p. 759). Whether old Harmon had 'coined' every penny or not, it is instructive that the mounds are still valuable enough for sale.

However, the value of the remaining mounds is not of interest to Dickens. The point about this part of the story is to portray Wegg's villainy and its consequences. Wegg looks greedily at the piles of dust because he believes they contain treasure within them, treasure which he can acquire and use for his own nefarious ends. He does not see the dust piles as anything other than an encasement, a wrapping that might contain something valuable rather than a source of value in themselves. This failure of character determines Wegg's ultimate fate, which is to be consigned to the dust by being thrown into a large dustcart:

> A somewhat difficult feat, achieved with great dexterity, and with a prodigious splash. (p. 770)

The 'splash', here, might be attributed to the possibility that there was some overlap between the dust collectors and the collectors of night-soil or it may be that Dickens is using the catch-all term 'dustcart' to refer to the slop wagons that collected kitchen waste. It is nonetheless instructive that Dickens should use the word 'splash' because it associates Wegg's fate with that of John Harmon as well as a series of other characters whose destiny is determined in watery encounters.

The first of these, Riderhood, is a 'rogue' of the first order and seeks to claim a £10,000 reward for information leading to the capture of John Harmon's murderer by falsely alleging that the deed was committed by Gaffer Hexam. He is never able to claim the reward because Hexam drowns. Riderhood himself nearly drowns following an accident with a steamer. He is fished out of the river and looks dead. Nonetheless, on examination, the Doctor suggests that 'it is worthwhile trying to reanimate' him (p. 439). After much exertion on the part of the Doctor and various volunteers they perceive an 'indubitable token of life' and though 'Niether Riderhood in this world, nor Riderhood in the other, could draw tears from them; but a striving human soul between the two can do it easily.' As Riderhood struggles back to consciousness, the volunteers and spectators sink into a melancholy mood as his 'low, bad unimpressable face is coming up from the depths of the river, or what other depths, to the surface again. As he grows warm, the Doctor and the four men cool' (p. 440). Like John Harmon, Roger Riderhood had almost drowned in the filth of the Thames. In contrast to Harmon, Riderhood did not use the opportunity to emerge from the filth and change himself into a new character, a new self. This omission later proves to be his fatal undoing.

Bradley Headstone is Schoolmaster to Lizzie Hexam's brother, Charley. He falls in love with Lizzie but she refuses his advances. Thereafter Headstone nourishes a raging jealousy of a lawyer, Eugene Wrayburn, who, at the end of the novel will become engaged to Lizzie. Headstone is obsessed with Lizzie and develops an uncontrollable hatred of the lawyer. His jealousy is not entirely unfounded but his hatred is misplaced: Lizzie refuses the lawyer's advances, too, because the difference in their social stations is too great. In spite of her refusal, Headstone determines to murder Wrayburn, which he attempts in book four by viciously beating the latter and leaving him in the river to drown. Wrayburn recovers in Lizzie's care and the near-drowning leaves him dependent on this care, thus reducing his social standing and enabling Lizzie finally to accept his marriage proposal. Like Harmon, and unlike Riderhood, Wrayburn's near-drowning results in him becoming a new character and it is his 'rebirth' as a different social self that enables Lizzie to accept his advances. Meanwhile Riderhood has witnessed enough of Headstone's deeds to know what has transpired, and Headstone murders the former, simultaneously committing suicide, by pitching them both, gripped tightly together, into the oozing Thames.

There is a common theme running through these deaths, near-deaths and rebirths: immersion in the filth teaches moral lessons. As Dickens himself plunged into the dust and dirt of London's soiled landscape, so too do the characters in the story — in the dust piles and dustcarts and the debris-strewn Thames. Dickens uses his own immersion to reflect on the morality and character of London life, he uses the lessons of dusty London to narrate a tale of virtue and villainy: the dustiness itself is the foundation of this moral division. In the story some characters find themselves unwittingly submerged in the same dust and filth — either metaphorically, in the case of Silas Wegg's obsession with the dust piles, or literally, as in the case of John Harmon, Eugene Wrayburn, and Roger Riderhood. Whilst Harmon and Wrayburn used their unwilling encounter with the filth to reconstruct their characters and learn the lessons that their immersion taught, Wegg and Riderhood fail the test. Thus, instead of being reborn into a new social status they find themselves cast back into the mire either to subsist there for the remainder of their days or to perish in the cloying ooze of the lifeless river.

The storyline of *Our Mutual Friend*, including the near-drowning of John Harmon and Eugene Wrayburn, parallels a short tale that appeared in *Household Words* in July 1850, attributed to R.H. Horne, entitled 'Dust: or ugliness redeemed'. In this story, a small group of virtuous but poverty-stricken scavengers are sifting through a large dust pile to recover items they might sell (or eat) and discover a title deed that had been lost by a man who had thrown himself into the river in self-mortification. Not only do the group retrieve the title deed, they also use the dust to revive the man — by immersing him inside it to warm his freezing body. The man, in gratitude, arranges the purchase of a cottage for the scavengers in the vicinity of the dust heap so that, initially, they may continue their virtuous life of scavenging from the comfort of their own home. The tale ends with the revived stranger marrying the daughter of the dust heap's owner and the heap being exported to Russia for forty thousand pounds 'to rebuild Moscow'. The heap to which Horne, and Dickens, are referring is almost certainly the enormous dust heap that began to accumulate in the wake of the Great Fire of 1666 and that, by 1780, had grown to some eight and a half acres in size. The heap was in fact sold to rebuild Moscow, following the destruction of 1812 and is still commemorated in London's Laystall Street (see McLaughlin, 1971: 98). The tale, and the context from which it derives, is a useful reminder that, in nineteenth century London, and not just in Dickens's personal imagination, 'dust' was considered to be valuable not only for what it would fetch at sale in its own right but also for what may be enveloped within it. Dust could revive the dead, return what is rightfully due, provide an income, sustain life. In contrast to our own commonsense notions of the negative and dangerous character of waste, there are important senses in which nineteenth-century dust was construed as valuable in financial, social and moral senses. Dust itself can be redemptive, as Horne and Dickens acutely observed. It is this sense of dustiness that Dickens seeks to convey in the ambiguous characterisations, near-deaths and rebirths, and in the emergence of virtue and villainy: dust is both life's material foundation and the fate towards which it inexorably travels. Dustiness — that is, value and futility, birth and decay, origin and terminus — represents the elemental cycle of human and material existence.

## The Waste Land

*Our Mutual Friend* narrates a very particular set of personal relationship to waste and dirt of all descriptions. It is not merely a tale about the possibility of retrieving value *from* waste; it is a tale about the value *of* waste: a moral fable about the essential 'dustiness' of life and the thin veneer that separates virtue from villainy, respectability from notoriety. Between this mid-nineteenth century myth of dust and redemption and our own stories of surplus, detachment and crisis are two significant challenges to and reorientations in this Victorian aesthetic of waste and dirt. The first of these, the transformation in world-view between the Victorians and the moderns, is captured perfectly by T.S. Eliot.

Like the work of Dickens, the poetry of Thomas Stearns Eliot has generated a massive academic industry devoted to interpreting and criticising his intellectual and artistic output. Nowhere is this industrial architecture more visible than in relation to Eliot's most complex and allegorical work *The Waste Land*. My intention, in keeping with the theme of the book as a whole, is to explore the poem through the lens of its 'waste' theme. Much of what the full poem addresses, therefore, is by necessity absent from the following remarks and observations. It is much easier to explore the poem through its 'land' theme — partly because 'Eliot's London' has been written about extensively. On other hand, Eliot's 'waste' has generated far fewer books and essays and the character or status of the 'waste' of the land about which he writes is more difficult to articulate. Of particular interest in the following commentary are the connections and contrasts between Eliot's poem and Dickens's book. My argument is that Eliot presents a very different notion of what 'waste' comprises compared to Dickens. Between the publication of *Our Mutual Friend* and *The Waste Land* there is an intellectual ocean so that whilst it is possible to note some common motifs between the two works they might better be seen to represent different mental eras — different 'sensibilities' as Marshall Berman (1983) would have it. Compared with Eliot, Dickens's work looks like a collection of Victoriana. Compared with Dickens, Eliot's work looks like a modernist temple whose form is pressed into the service of its functional goal, partly because of Ezra Pound's vigorous editing. Of course, these caricatures only appear when the works are set against each other in isolated contrast and their connections and distinctions are in fact much more subtle. Nonetheless, Eliot encapsulates a modernist outlook on waste that is the negation of Dickens's Victorian outlook. This change in outlook is the guiding principle of my interpretation of *The Waste Land*.

There is no doubt that Eliot was familiar with Dickens's work and held him in some admiration. Almost certainly he had read *Our Mutual Friend* since the working title of *The Waste Land* — 'He do the Police in different voices' — was a quotation taken directly from Dickens' book. The quotation appears on page 168 of the 1997 Penguin edition. Betty Higden, upon introducing Sloppy to the Boffins, bristles with some pride as she announces: 'You mightn't think it, but Sloppy is a beautiful reader of a newspaper. He do the Police in different voices.' Indeed, the multiple voices of the poem are the first, and perhaps clearest, indication of what it is: a lyrical snapshot of a moment frozen in time and filled with as-yet unknown futures. Inside the poem, according to Murphy (1991: 255), is a 'cacophony and almost choking abundance.' So abundant are its voices and themes that contemporaneous reviewers were confused as to the poem's structural integrity, wondering whether it comprised a 'kaleidoscopic confusion' or an '"emotional ensemble" with "a kind of forced unity"' (Mayer, 1991: 265).

The poem opens, in 'The Burial of the Dead', with a reversal of the normal outlook on spring. Whilst April is usually greeted with celebratory anticipation — it brings the rain that nourishes the soil and presages the seasonal turn to more pleasant temperatures — Eliot describes it as the 'cruellest month':

> April is the cruellest month, breeding
> Lilacs out of the dead land, mixing
> Memory and desire, stirring
> Dull roots with spring rain. (p. 63)[2]

It is the cruellest month because it forces life and wakefulness upon the sleeping consciousness of nature. It heralds the obligation to begin again, to grow again, to remember again. Whilst winter, according to the poem, keeps the dull roots warm under a blanket of 'forgetful snow', April rekindles dreams of ambition, love, and desire and thereby once more opens the path of life and forces movement, requires decisions, and threatens hardships and ordeals. Waking up in April implies that withdrawal from the world is no longer an option: the future beckons and must be faced.

The poem, in fact, takes place in that tick of time that separates winter from spring, in the instant of wakefulness between the sleepy past and the demanding future. It suggests that mortal life, everyday existence, is passing in that tick: neither in the long sleep of winter, nor yet in the full bloom of spring, but at the exact point of their intersection. Ezra Pound described it as the longest poem in the English language, running from April to Shantih (i.e., eternity) and yet none of its characters move through time (Woodward, 1991: 46). Instead, Eliot leaps between confusing voices: each voice is simultaneous, no time elapses in the waste land except in memory and projection. The poem is 'suspended in a continuous present' (Wright, 1984: 198). Voices remember what once was and imagine what is yet to come but they do not become their future selves. The tick is an instant of anticipation and also of trepidation.

This tick of suspension clearly references the uncertainty and social ambiguity that followed the Great War. The old European order has been smashed to pieces, ground into the mud of Belgium and France but what will emerge from the waste land of this conflict is unknown (and unknowable). There are the victims and the vanquished, the survivors and the casualties but what the new Europe holds for any of these identities cannot be predicted. For, the return of life after the long death-sleep of winter of the Great War will be different, filled with potential dangers. It heralds the possibility of unwelcome and uncertain change — like the pub scene (in 'A Game of Chess') where the character Lil is harangued by an interlocutor and urged to smarten herself up, get a new set of teeth and prepare for the return of her husband (Albert) from the war. At the same time, Albert himself will be different. After the long winter of the Great War he will be a changed man: his return will signal the restart of their family life but neither of them will be the same people they were the last time it was spring in Europe. They are in the waste land — between winter's snowy blanket and spring's verdant reincarnation.

Eliot ponders what the future holds for this generation in the immediate aftermath of the Great War. The new spring cannot return in its old guise: the world has shuddered violently into a new era, so he asks:

> What are the roots that clutch, what branches grow
> Out of this stony rubbish? Son of man,
> You cannot say, or guess, for you know only
> A heap of broken images. (p. 63)

'You know only a heap of broken images' because in the waste land that is all that people are: reflected fragments of former and potential selves. Like Dickens's characters in *Our Mutual Friend*, everyone is in-between: neither quite dead nor yet quite alive, neither consumed with passion for their fellow questers in the waste land nor unsympathetic to their needs and desires, neither fully masculine nor fully feminine. The blind Tiresius embodies (literally) this last condition — 'Old man with wrinkled female breasts', s/he labours under the belief that s/he can see what others cannot. 'What Tiresius *sees*' says Eliot in a footnote to line 218, 'is the substance of the poem' yet really s/he sees, as Pinkney (1998) suggests, precisely nothing. For, in itself, the waste land is nothingness, it is in essence the fearful anticipation of an emergent new world and the existential angst that such anticipation engenders.

This is one of the main reasons why Eliot's *Waste Land* can be depicted as a modernist poem. Notwithstanding its technical and structural innovations — 'fragment and juxtaposition, counterpoint and irony' (Murphy

1991: 253) — at its heart is the ambivalent indecision and uncertainty over the *next* instant of time. The innovative character of *The Waste Land* was recognised immediately on its publication. Blackmur (1928/1991: 80) suggested that Eliot's poetry had created 'the new way of feeling, the new forms for the combination of feelings' and that this 'change in sensibility is equivalent to a change in identity, a change in soul' (ibid: 73). Although Blackmur believed that Eliot was a 'classical' poet, Ezra Pound asserted unequivocally that *The Waste Land* on its own had provided a 'justification of the "movement" of our modern experiment since 1900' (cited in Woodward, 1991: 49). This 'movement' of 'feeling' is precisely the coming of the modernist sensibility and the movement is captured perfectly by Eliot.

April, to return to the opening of the poem, is so cruel because it threatens the arrival of a certain kind of consciousness of the future. The dread of this consciousness persuades Eliot, finally, in a reference to Kyd's *The Spanish Tragedy*, to buttress the ruins of his past with fragments of memory, lest the coming world tear down everything he has known, experienced and loved — much as the winter of the Great War has torn down the social fabric of Old Europe. This is not at all to say that the poem as a whole is bereft of hope: it is not a nihilistic excoriation of post-war Europe. But it seeks hope outside of the waste land: in classical literature and mythology, primarily, but also in the remembered minutiae of everyday life. It places post-war Europe firmly in the waste land (Wright, op. cit.: 168) whilst simultaneously hoping there is an escape or a salvation in the memory of beauty, in the memory of other springs and summers of European civilization.

However, the poem offers no specific hope. Neither its allegorical nor mythological references signal any definitive way out of the waste land. Smith (1991: 129) observes that Eliot's characters seem to 'belong to a drama they do not understand, where they move like chessmen toward destinations they cannot foresee.' Although the message of the poem is that 'life may be changed, transcended' (Mayer, op. cit.: 265), and although it may contain an injunction to turn away from the emptiness and desuetude of the Great War's aftermath (Smith, op. cit.), Eliot provides no directions or guidance as to which way to turn, except, perhaps, along an ill-defined path of Christian virtue.

Take the section on 'Death by Water', for example. Here, 'Phlebas the Phoenician, a fortnight dead/Forgot the cry of gulls' and his bones have been picked 'in whispers' by a 'current under the sea'. In spite of his death he is still, it seems, capable of forgetting the 'cry of gulls', thus suggesting there remains some kind of consciousness to which the verb 'forget' can be applied. It is said that the reference here may be to the myths in Frazer's *The Golden Bough* where Phlebas is linked to the God Osiris, as Spears Brooker and Bentley (1991: 244) explain:

> whose body was placed in a current that carried it from the place of his death to the place from which it could be taken from the water as a symbol of rebirth.

A different way of locating the watery fate of Phlebas in Eliot's poem is to note that it lies somewhere between the redemption of John Harmon — who almost drowns but does not, who changes his identity and is thus 'reborn' as someone else before finally returning to his own more mature (and thus different) self — and that of Roger Riderhood — who almost drowns, fails to change his identity (and thus remains the same self), and then finally does drown. Whatever the mythological allusions *The Waste Land* draws upon it remains the case that Eliot ensnares and forestalls, in one allegorical passage, the two possibilities that Dickens had used to contrast how life may come from death and vice-versa. Perhaps Phlebas's death consists in his forgetting that he is alive or forgetting that from death life can spring. Perhaps, in keeping with Eliot's own fragments shoring up the ruins, Phlebas needs to *remember* — rather than merely passing 'the stages of his age and youth' — in order to be reborn and live again. Failure to use memory positively to change, in the 'waste land' context of post-war Europe, may well imply that the latter will share the fate of Riderhood rather than that of Harmon.

Thus, Eliot's poem, like Dickens's story, takes death — or near-death — by water as a crucial metaphor for personal change but Eliot reconfigures the theme to present post-War Europe with a warning not to forget its roots, a warning that Dickens did not need to declare because those roots clung to his characters in the form of dust. For Dickens, life's foundations are not in the memory or recuperation of things past but in the decay and rebirth of the present. At the same time, whilst Dickens is intent on distinguishing virtue and villainy through the dust of London — and uses death by filthy water as the decisive act of redemption or demise — Eliot refuses the either/or logic of this textual device and portrays the wasteland as suspension and deferral. For Dickens, life in the dust is rich, varied and valuable; for Eliot, life in the waste land is dissolute, horrifying and not a little tawdry. Dustiness is significance, solidity, connection; the waste land is emptiness, ephemerality, dissonance. In Eliot, in spite of the complexity and abstruseness of the poem, we see an important transformation of the aesthetic of waste laid out in its clearest form: the 'waste' of *The Waste Land* is loss or absence of value, the personal and moral paralysis into which society has slipped under the trauma of the Great War's aftermath.

Now it is much easier to see the contrast between Dickens and Eliot and, by extension, the intellectual and aesthetic movement that separates their respective takes on waste. For Dickens, all life is essentially dusty, out of dust value emerges — in monetary and moral form — just as unto dust value descends. Dust — the inevitable product and firm foundation of solid life — is a real and substantial component of psychological, social and economic existence. Unlike Dickens, Eliot understands the 'waste' in *The Waste Land* not as substance but as nothingness, as empty of value and merit, as the other side of certainty and solidity. It is a void into which Europe has unwittingly slithered and out of which he hopes it can again arise. The tick of time that is Europe's waste land is not the substantial reality of dust but the fearful angst attendant on the loss, and the pressing demand to reinvigorate, the value of life.


## FROM MENACING KIPPLE TO THE SHADOW OF GARBAGE: DICK AND DELILLO

### Do Androids Dream of Electric Sheep?

Philip K. Dick's novel of a post-apocalyptic world, set in San Francisco in the year 2021, appeared in print in novel form in 1968. It was the epitome of a series of science-fiction explorations of human-android relationships, including *We Can Build You* (1972). The book was made into a film in 1982 (directed by Ridley Scott) and the film's reconfigured plot of the struggle between a policeman/bounty hunter (played by Harrison Ford) and a group of android 'replicants' made the story globally famous. Unlike the film, the book's characters inhabit a half-deserted waste land where nuclear fall-out continues to rain down following 'World War Terminus', an event that has sparked the Earth's abandonment in favour of space colonies. Those left behind are either unable to depart — because of the jobs they have or because they are unsuitable for migration — or have vested (economic and/or political) interests in remaining on the hell that is planet Earth. All the Earth's inhabitants fear for their future and receive regular medical inspections to ensure they are fit to breed. There are so few Earth-dwellers left that there is insufficient labour power to do all the jobs that need to be undertaken. In consequence, each citizen is encouraged to conduct their own private war on the 'kipple' — litter and waste — that threatens to occupy their living space. The kipple, and the war on it, is in no way central to the story. Its place in the unfolding existential drama of the book is, however, highly instructive in terms of the shift in the rubbish aesthetic from the nothingness or negativity of Eliot's *Waste Land* to a consciousness of threat and invasion. The book's publication date, at the end of the 1960s, sounded the death knell for the ultra-clean consciousness that had been developing since the end of the Second World War. The dream that waste would simply go away and leave the home and the environment spick-and-span had been breaking apart since before the publication of Rachel Carson's *Silent Spring* in 1962. In Philip K. Dick's novel, a new sensibility of ceaseless and, ultimately, fruitless endeavour against the invasion of dust and decay is played out on the margins of a fable of what it is, morally, to be alive. Coupled with a Carson-inspired theme of species extinction, *Do Androids Dream of Electric Sheep?* is an unremitting bleak reflection on social and industrial change.

In the book, conditions on Earth are so bad that its inhabitants depend on a 'mood organ' to determine their emotional states in order to cope. Dialling 'a 481' on the organ induces 'awareness of the manifold possibilities open to me in the future' and 'new hope', whilst dialling 888 induces 'the desire to watch TV no matter what's on it' (pp. 6–7).[3] The buildings are half or completely empty; radioactive dust falls regularly on Earth-dwellers, persuading the men, at least, to wear 'Mountibank Lead Codpieces' to avoid contamination of their sexual organs. Contaminated individuals are labelled 'specials' and, if the contamination has affected their intelligence, 'Chickenheads'. What disturbs the characters as much as the physical threats to their lives is the aching silence of apartment buildings: the absence of people outside of the central metropolitan areas, the experience of the void (p. 18). An empty world breeds loneliness and the fear of loneliness. Real animals (as opposed to manufactured counterparts) are so rare that each citizen has a moral duty to possess and care for one, resulting in fierce trading and exorbitant prices. All of Earth's emigrants are provided with an android for company and service in the space colonies and, on the occasions that the latter return, illegally, to Earth, they are hunted down and 'retired' with extreme prejudice.

The abandoned buildings, and much of the rest of Earth's living space has been 'kipple-ized', as the character J.R. Isidore explains:

> Kipple is useless objects, like junk mail or match folders after you use the last match or gum wrappers or yesterday's homeopape. When nobody's around, kipple reproduces itself. (p.56)

It is impossible to win against kipple, 'except temporarily and maybe in one spot' because the First Law of Kipple is that 'kipple drives out non-kipple'. In consequence, eventually, everything will be filled with and covered in 'pudding-like kipple' so that the entire Earthscape will merge and become faceless and identical (p. 18). This fate is unavoidable because it is an incontrovertible law that 'the entire universe is moving toward a final state of total, absolute kipple-ization' (p. 57). The process is particularly agonizing for J.R Isodore because, as a 'Chickenhead', contaminated and socially excluded, he, too, is 'moving toward the ash heap. Turning into living kipple', a useless human object (p. 63). Here, Dick expresses the radical conception of entropy and decay that blossomed in the later 1950s and 1960s and was taken up most famously, and abstrusely, by Bataille (1991). Late nineteenth century fascination with entropic decline viewed this as an inevitable fate, about which humans could do nothing — as depicted, for example, in Elihu Vedder's 'The Last Man' (1891). In Dick's book, in contrast, 'kipple-ization' is both naturally inevitable and, at the same time, human-induced.

The omnipresence of kipple, its inevitable march upon the lives of Earth's remaining inhabitants, has resulted in the rise to prominence of the garbage collection and disposal industries. 'The entire planet had begun to disintegrate into junk, and to keep the planet habitable for the remaining population the junk had to be hauled away occasionally' (p. 74). Eventually, however, there will be nothing left to haul — even Mozart's music and the very name of Mozart is fated to disintegrate and 'the dust will have won' (p. 84). Thus, the war against kipple is futile also because kipple has a strong ally in the struggle: 'dust', both the radioactive dust that falls from the sky and the disintegrating kipple-dust that blurs every solid surface under an ever-thickening film. Kipple and dust comprise an immediate and terrifying threat to all living creatures, they have become 'pollution'. The rubbish-littered rooftops of the apartment buildings are so depressing because they underscore an inescapable consequence of unregulated industrial progress: environmental and, ultimately, self-destruction.

Philip K. Dick's book belongs to the 'Science Fiction' genre, yet its contextualisation of human industrial progress might have been taken from Rachel Carson's (1962) text. She, too, prognosticates on polluting futures in terms that Dick might well have borrowed directly. *Silent Spring* opens with a 'fable for tomorrow' in which Carson postulates the fate of a 'town in the heart of America where all life seemed to live in harmony with its surroundings.' But, she continues:

> a strange blight crept over the area and everything began to change. Some evil spell had settled on the community: mysterious maladies swept the flocks of chickens; the cattle and sheep sickened and died. Everywhere was a shadow of death ... There was a strange stillness. The birds, for example — where had they gone? (Carson, 1994: 2)

She depicts a scene of lifeless roadsides and streams, 'withered vegetation, as though swept by fire'. Then, presaging Dick's own vision of a future post-apocalyptic world, she writes:

> In the gutters under the eaves and between the shingles of the roofs, a white granular powder [i.e., 'dust'] still showed a few patches; some weeks before it had fallen like snow upon the roofs and the lawns, the fields and the streams.

> No witchcraft, no enemy action had silenced the rebirth of new life in this stricken world. The people had done it themselves.' (ibid.: 3)

As Carson asks about the whereabouts of birds, so, too, does Dick's book comment upon them being the first casualties of the dust. As Carson depicts the bleakness of a lifeless landscape, so, too does Dick:

> In the early morning light, the land below him extended seemingly forever, gray and refuse littered ... Once, he thought, crops grew here and animals grazed. What a remarkable thought, that anything could have cropped grass here.' (Dick, 1999: 196)

The point is not to claim that Carson was Dick's inspiration — even if there is some truth in the proposition. The point is to note the change in the rubbish imagination that is represented in Philip K. Dick's novel. Antithetical to Dickens's dusty London, a filling in of the emptiness of Eliot's ephemeral waste land with threatening, invasive kipple, *Do Androids Dream of Electric Sheep?* exemplifies the reimagining of waste as a dangerous pollutant arising from industrial development. Dust, in Dick's book, is not, as it was for Dickens, the source of value, progenitor of life, that which underpins and revitalises moral worth: no-one and no thing, ugly or otherwise, is redeemed through the post-apocalyptic dust of Dick's vision. Instead, it is the enemy: a constant, threatening, invasive presence that wipes out entire species, interferes with human reproduction, disintegrates everything of value into a 'faceless and identical' undulating landscape. It provokes profound depression and renders the urban and rural environment lifeless and sterile. Thus, kipple and dust are not Eliot's 'waste' either: they are far too potent and invasive to be nothingness. In the world of 2021 the waste land's tick of time has moved on, the decisions have been made, the degraded and ever-degrading future is a certainty, not an ambiguity: the next tick of time will be just like the last — only worse. The death of the world is produced by industrial society, from the 'by-products' of its feats and wonders. In the San Francisco of 2021 there are mood organs, hover cars, twenty-four hour television, advanced laser technology and much, much more. But there are also invading androids, deadly dust and disintegrating kipple. The two poles of 'progress' march hand-in-hand towards an empty, despoiled future.

Of course, Philip K. Dick's prophecy of an emptied world, traversed by lonely, disconnected isolates represents only one version of the polluting vision of industrial society's future. Harry Harrison's *Make Room! Make Room!* (1966), like John Brunner's *Stand on Zanzibar* (1968), reverses the proposition and portends an overpopulated world that has used up virtually all of its natural resources. Set in 1999, Harrison's book, too, presages a rubbish-filled, ruined environment where food and water are so scarce they are the major stimulus for riots and public disorder. Buildings are piled high with debris and rivers are open sewers whilst two billion rusting cars provide shelter for the homeless. The only things left to eat for most people in this world are 'weedcrackers', processed plankton bricks and, rarely, steaks made of soya beans and lentils, i.e., 'soylent' (not made, as in the film *Soylent Green,* from 'recycled' people). It differs from Dick's book in its contextualisation of industrialism's future but its core message — that humans are responsible, by their rapacious consumption and wanton pollution, for the environmental destruction that foreshadows their own ruin — is precisely the same. 'One time we had the whole world in our hands,' says the character Sol, 'but we ate it and burned it and it's gone now' (Harrison, 1986: 189). Harrison's book serves to reinforce the suggestion that the aesthetic appreciation of waste had developed another important dimension in the period following World War II. A blighted futurology was not simply the wild outpouring of Philip K. Dick's dystopian subconcious. Instead, an altered sensibility was visibly and clearly fuelling the rubbish imagination: waste is destruction and pollution.

## Underworld

If Dick (and Harrison) represent a degraded vision of the world's refuse-filled industrial futures, Don DeLillo's *Underworld* paints a far more subtle, poignant and human-centred picture of America's garbage at the end of the twentieth century. First published in 1998, it is described as 'magnificent' by Salman Rushdie, as an 'epic' by the *Observer* and as 'some kind of implacable monument at the end of the [20th] century' by the *Daily Telegraph*. Its 827 pages of multi-character narrative, travelling backwards and forwards between the 1950s and 1990s certainly marks a book of epic proportions and ambition. But to what is Delillo's novel a monument? What epic legend does DeLillo recount? In the simplest terms, woven between the multiple story-lines, plots and characters is an allegory of America's cultural coming of age. It is a story of America's historical relation to its present, a story about what American history is and how Americans exist historically. It is a story about being 'ninety-nine and nine-tenths percent' certain of the historical authenticity of contemporary American culture whilst at the same time accepting that the authentication can never truly be completed (p. 96).[4]

Elaborating upon a series of themes introduced in DeLillo's earlier *White Noise* (1985), it is an enormous literary undertaking, comparable in scope and depth to Dickens's *Our Mutual Friend*. It might best be described as a symphony to a century's end, so rhythmically does its reflection on American identity beat out its complex narrative. The book opens and closes with a movement of apparently discarded junk. At the epic Dodgers versus Giants baseball game of October 1951, the fans, arranged in tiers above the field of play, toss paper — ticket stubs, old shopping lists and newsprint, crushed traffic tickets and 'work from the office' (p. 37) — which cascades like snow onto the ground below. It is 'happy garbage now, the fans' intimate wish to be connected to the event, unendably, in the form of pocket litter, personal waste, a thing that carries a shadow identity' (p. 45). At the end of the book, the principal narrator, Nick Shay and his granddaughter visit a giant recycling centre and watch in awe as discarded junk once more rushes past. This time the paper, tin, plastics and Styrofoam 'flies down the conveyor belt, four hundred tons a day', in a place that is 'loved' by visiting kids and teachers alike (p. 809).

Each of these flying junk episodes is celebratory, in its own way, which is why they mark the opening and closing spectacles of the book. They represent the cultural flows of everyday life: flows that are entirely material yet bursting with meaning and import. Between the opening excessive rain of personal effluvia and the closing industrialised channelling of commodified detritus lies the meaning of American life, a meaning that is captured in the one item at the baseball game that is given back to the litter-bugging crowd by the objects of their devotion — the baseball itself: a 'five-ounce sphere of cork, rubber, yarn, horsehide and spiral stitching', a 'priceless thing somehow' that manages to connect each game to every game that has gone before (p. 26). In that small object subsists a historical connection that helps to situate 'the dusty hum of who you are'; a 'solemn scrap of history' that connects each person to 'what they did before you' (pp. 16, 22, 31), as the character Bill Waterson says to Cotter Martin. The baseball, and more importantly, the game itself, represents the 'flesh and breath' of the people's history but, like the streaming paper, it is destined to fall 'indelibly into the past' (p. 60).

What DeLillo is attempting is to recover the lives behind apparently useless things, to excavate the cultural effluvia of everyday life and re-site the personal and social histories that created and sustained them. What is discarded — in celebratory or industrial flows — retains meaning, induces memory and possesses significance. In the thematic organisation of *Underworld* the baseball carries most, but not all, of the narrative weight of this proposition. It is an object of personal reverence for Nick Shay. At times, he cannot avoid handling it, or simply staring at it in wonderment. Yet, it is just a ball, 'deep sepia, veneered with dirt and turf and generational sweat — it was old, bunged up, it was bashed and tobacco-juiced and stained by natural processes and the lives behind it, weather-spattered and charactered as a sea-front house' (p. 131). Nick asks himself a thousand times why he wants the baseball, why has he searched and searched to acquire it. His answer is that he is consumed by the passion of lived, real history, of the deep desire to connect with those who went before. In Nick Shay's world, the stuff of real history is passionate, and he wants to get inside the 'thingness' of history: to dig into it and recover its meanings. He wants to 'reassemble a crucial moment in time out of patches and adumbrations' even though he knows he can never find the final link that defines *this* baseball as *that* baseball: *the* baseball, the Thompson homer from *the* game (see p. 181).

It is entirely apt that Nick Shay should be so consumed. He works in a 'shimmering bronze tower' for a company called Waste Containment: he is a waste handler, a waste trader and broker, a 'Church [Father] of waste in all its transmutations', a 'cosmologist of waste.' He has 'travelled to the coastal lowlands of Texas and watched men in moon suits bury drums of dangerous waste in subterranean salt beds many millions of years old, dried-out remnants of a Mesozoic ocean. It was a religious conviction in our business that these deposits of rock salt would not leak radiation. Waste is a religious thing. We entomb contaminated waste with a sense of reverence and dread. It is necessary to respect what we discard' (p. 88).

Nick's employers design and manage landfills: 'We built pyramids of waste above and below the Earth. The more hazardous the waste, the deeper we tried to sink it. The word plutonium, comes from Pluto, god of the dead and ruler of the underworld' (p. 106). Thus, the title of the book connects with Nick Shay's job and with the religious reverence with which he and his colleagues inter America's culture in landfills and caverns.

The religious and reverential references to American garbage underscore the story's running subtext: the discarded and degraded items of American culture comprise the stuff of human behaviour, the material substance of people's desires, impulses and needs. It is handled systematically, 'esoterically', venerably because it represents the meaning of each individual's life. Even if, in the normal course of events, it is overlooked and forgotten, garbage is, nonetheless, vital to progress on both an individual and social scale. This message is reinforced when the characters Nick Shay, Brian Glassic and 'Big Sims' go to visit the Landfill being constructed by their company. There they meet with Jesse Detwiler, a 'garbage guerrilla' of the 1960s. He explains to them that garbage is the key to civilisation:

> Civilization did not rise and flourish as men hammered out hunting scenes on bronze gates and whispered philosophy under the stars, with garbage as a noisome offshoot, swept away and forgotten. No, garbage rose first, inciting people to build a civilization in response, in self-defense. We had to find ways to discard our waste, to use what we couldn't discard, to reprocess what we couldn't use. Garbage pushed back. It mounted and spread. And it forced us to develop the logic and the rigor that would lead to systematic investigations of reality, to science, art, music, mathematics. (p. 287)

In homage to the socially and emotionally crucial role of garbage, the landfill has to be regular, organised, clearly defined, constructed like the Great Pyramid of Giza, monumental in its design: a fitting burial ground for the lost objects of desire that will fill it. In complete contrast to Old Harmon's dust-piles, which were thrown up like an old volcano, *Underworld's* 'dust-piles' are engineered with a precision to match the space programme. Similarly, they do not represent the *beginning* of a useful life — either through recycling, reuse, reprocessing or resale ('to rebuild Moscow' — see above). They represent the *end* of a useful life. By the time the garbage has arrived at the landfill, the work of sorting, sifting, classification and recovery has been completed. *Underworld's* 'dust piles' contain the husk, the 'shadow' of American identity rather than, as *Our Mutual Friend's* dust piles, the essence of identity. The modern landfill is the graveyard of 'quotidian' culture and, as such, its contents must be solemnly and respectfully handled:

> At home we wanted clean safe healthy garbage. We rinsed out old bottles and put them in their proper bins. We faithfully removed the crin-

kly paper from our cereal boxes. It was like preparing a Pharaoh for his death and burial. We wanted to do the small things right. (p. 119)

If Dickens's Harmon encrusts dust upon dust, heaps 'all manner of Dust' together in a dusty landscape, DeLillo's Nick Shay represents an entirely different relationship to his waste. At home, Nick Shay:

> ... removed the wax paper from cereal boxes. We had a recycling closet with separate bins for newspapers, cans and jars. We rinsed out the used cans and empty bottles and put them in their proper bins. We did tin versus aluminium. On pickup days we placed each form of trash in its separate receptacle ... We used a paper bag for the paper bags ... There is no language I might formulate that could overstate the diligence we brought to these tasks. We did the yard waste. We bundled the newspapers but did not tie them in twine. (pp. 102–3. See also p. 89: 'we were careful not to tie the bundles in twine, which is always the temptation' and pp. 803–4, 807).

Nick Shay obsessively sorts, cleans, bundles, *separates* waste from value. He alludes to and, indeed, performs, an altogether different relation to waste than does Harmon. Harmon suffers no obsessive temptations, he does not wish to distinguish between entwinement and non-entwinement nor, in contrast to Nick Shay, diligently to reserve Tuesdays only to do plastic, 'minus caps and lids' (p. 120).

Here is a clue to the division that separates Dickens's world of 1865 and DeLillo's world of 1998. Dust is dust, waste-inchoate, inhabiting a world of only roughly divided objects and materials, where life and death, being and non-being *cannot* be certainly sorted:

> The idea of a completely finished product is a fiction, and so is the idea of a purely raw material. All matter has been used before and will be used again. Every thing and every body is partly composed of the dead-but-not-gone, which in turn will decompose and be shaped into new forms of matter. (Poole, 1997: ix)

Waste, in contrast, is dust-consummate, a polymorphous, multifaceted, specified and separated materiality, inhabiting a world of exactly divided objects and materials, where life and death, being and non-being *are* certainly sorted:

> Marian and I saw products as garbage even when they sat gleaming on store shelves, yet un-bought. We didn't say, What kind of casserole will that make? We said, What kind of garbage will that make? Safe, clean, neat, easily disposed of? Can the package be recycled and come back as a tawny envelope that it is difficult to lick closed? First we saw

the garbage, then we saw the product as food or light bulbs or dandruff shampoo. How does it measure up as waste, we asked. We asked whether it is responsible to eat a certain item if the package the item comes in will live for a million years. (p. 121)

We saw 'products as garbage' on the shelves of the store, says Nick Shay. But the garbage is not the product itself, it is not the materiality of the desired object that comprises the waste. It is, instead, the packaging around the object or what the object *will become*. Whereas Dickens seeks to expose the essential dustiness of life's packaging, DeLillo asks 'what kind of garbage that will make', not 'what kind of garbage that *always-already is*'. In Nick Shay's world there is an absolute separation between garbage and non-garbage, dust and life which is precisely why he is so obsessive about the act of sorting garbage into its multiple forms of value — the paper, the plastic, the glass, the tin, the aluminium, the yard waste. Nick Shay lives in an unsorted world that he has to sort manually and mentally. Harmon lives in a world that is manually and mentally already sorted as far as it can be: every fine distinction of manner, labour and status is a point on the circumference of life's recycling. Nick Shay has to do the recycling himself and through the diligence of that task he can arrive at fine distinctions of manner, labour and status. This is why Nick Shay longs 'for the days of disarray', the 'days of disorder … when I was alive on the earth, rippling in the quick of my skin, heedless and real' (p. 810). The 'days of disarray' refer both to Nick Shay's youth and to the 'youth' of American culture, to a time when connecting to the past — either by reverently and meticulously preparing the garbage-Pharaoh for its burial or by chasing across a continent to find the 'authentic' baseball — mattered so much less than anticipating and preparing for the future. Whilst Harmon's dust is a material progenitor, a source of life and value — and, thus, is to be revered — Nick Shay's garbage is a cultural terminus, the end of life and value — and, thus, is to be revered. The reason why Nick Shay sorts obsessively is because he must distinguish between the 'product', the value, and the 'waste': the surplus that inevitably persists *alongside* the object of desire and wraps it in a valueless double. The latest transformation in the rubbish aesthetic is laid out clearly by DeLillo: waste is life's ever-present, haunting shadow.

# 3 Rubbish Industries

We glibly dismiss waste as rubbish.

(Frederick Talbot, *Millions from Waste*)

Waste is rubbish.

(United Kingdom Environment Agency, 'Managing Waste')

In Chapter 2, I outlined four stories about waste or, rather, four ways in which waste has been imagined in key works of literature and poetry. Between the late nineteenth and the late twentieth century there have been four clearly different articulations of this rubbish imagination: waste as an elemental foundation of life, waste as a loss or deficiency of life's value, waste as a menacing threat to life, and waste as life's ever-present and inevitable shadow. There are, of course, other ways of imagining waste. I am not claiming that these four imaginary constructions encompass the entire spectrum of modern society's understandings but I think that they are particularly important because they map onto wider industrial and social changes. They refer to and make sense in terms of particular social contexts and societal relationships with waste. The imagination of waste does not exist in a social vacuum: it references what is done with waste, what roles it plays in social life, what values are extracted from or imputed to it and how those values are realised. In this chapter I will extend this line of inquiry by outlining some of the crucial services that waste has supplied to modern industry and the central role that waste has played, and continues to play, in technological development. I will show that without some kinds of waste the modern, scientific and technological world would never have emerged — or, at least, that it is impossible to imagine what it would look like had those wastes not been used in industrial development. The chapter will also reveal some features of the social contexts that gave rise to the four imaginary constructions of waste explored in Chapter 2.

## RUBBISHING THE SCIENTIFIC REVOLUTION

Since the previous chapter was concerned with stories, it is appropriate to remind ourselves of a familiar narrative about the scientific and technological flowering of European civilization. It is recounted in several different ways but the core message is almost always the same. The message is that the Enlightenment paved the way for the scientific revolution, which, in its turn, paved the way for the industrial revolution, which in turn paved the way for the social revolution, which in turn paved the way for the modern world order. To read the history of these revolutions is often to read a history of extravagant discovery and not a little bravery, of resolution and action, of Great Minds and startling inventions. It is rarely, if ever, to read a history of the material means by which such revolutions were made possible. It is even rarer to read a history of the grinding, daily supply of those material means. What kind of progress could have been made if the ideas and opinions of the Great Minds could not be easily communicated with each other, if new ideas and outlooks could not be widely disseminated? What would have happened to the scientific revolution without paper, for example? How could treatises and discourses, books and pamphlets, newspapers and periodicals have been used to spread new scientific ideas if there were no paper upon which to write them? Where did this paper come from? The fact is that the scientific revolution, and the ensuing industrial and social revolutions, were dependent on waste products. Without them they would either have remained the isolated ponderings of small groups of proto-scientists and reformers or may even now have failed to ignite European society to the radical upheavals that gripped the later eighteenth and nineteenth centuries. The reason for this is that the raw material for paper manufacture in Europe until the second half of the nineteenth century was a very valuable waste. Without this waste, materials on which to write would have remained a luxury item available only to a selected few. Europe's literacy might have been set back by decades, at the least, and the scientific establishment would have continued to comprise a few isolated Newtons. A key ingredient of the scientific revolution consisted of rubbish. A brief history of paper making in Britain illustrates this fact clearly.

Paper has been made in Britain since at least the reign of Henry VII (1485–1509). But the first successful *white* paper-mills — producing paper of significant quality to be used as a durable medium for the written word — were built near Dartford in 1588 by an immigrant German named John Spilman. In the following year, Spilman was granted monopoly powers for buying and dealing in rags.

The significance of these powers can be grasped by understanding that the primary raw material for paper manufacture, until its displacement by wood pulp, was rags. Rags were necessary to paper production because the latter consists in bonding together cellulose fibres — and cotton and linen rags provided an excellent source of good length and density of fibres for making paper. Ever since its inception, however, the paper industry was plagued by a shortage of this raw material. As paper-making technology developed, the industry consumed more and more rags. At first, paper-makers obtained rags from within the country but across the eighteenth century, as the industry's appetite became more voracious, rag imports grew relentlessly. In the period 1725–30 Britain imported 192 tons of foreign rags but by 1796–1800 this had grown to 3405 tons — greater than a seventeen-fold increase in imports alone. At first, the Low Countries and France were Britain's major suppliers, but these countries later prohibited rag exports so that after 1750 America, Germany, Scandinavia and Eastern Europe became more important as suppliers (Hills, 1988: 54).

After 1780, key inventions like Hargreaves's spinning jenny, Arkwright's water frame and Crompton's mule increased both the production of textile products and — directly and indirectly — the production of rags. Demand for paper, however, grew inexorably, ensuring that paper's raw material was in constant short supply. As early as 1803, placards were erected in many Northern towns pleading with 'Genteel women' not to discard their old rags on the fire but to save them for supply to the paper industry because 'so doing will prevent £60,000 being annually exported to foreign countries for the importation of old rags to make paper, and which in consequence will become cheaper.' The larger paper mills used agents dedicated solely to organizing steady rag supplies from developing industrial centers (ibid.: 127).By the mid-nineteenth century, the export of rags was prohibited from France, Holland, Belgium, Spain and Portugal in order to supply their own paper industries. By this time, Britain was importing rags from Germany, Italy, Austria, Egypt, the East Indies, China, the Channel Islands, Australia, America, and Scandinavia, amongst others, showing that the global trade in ostensible wastes has a very long pedigree. Indeed, Hamburg had a rag market of truly international proportions and importance.

The exceptional value and role of rags in Britain's economy can be glimpsed in the widespread circulation of a proverb:

RAGS make paper
PAPER makes money
MONEY makes banks
BANKS make loans
LOANS make beggars
BEGGARS make RAGS

(Anon. Circa late eighteenth century. Cited on frontispiece of Hunter (1957).

Their value can also be gauged by the desperate search for a reliable and plentiful alternative to rags as a raw material for paper-manufacture. An advertisement carried by *The Times* newspaper of 1854 offered £1000 reward 'to any person who shall first succeed in inventing or discovering the means of using a cheap substitute for the cotton and linen materials now used by paper-makers' (Hills, 1988: 144).

Once the rags arrived at the mill, 'Hems were unpicked, buttons removed and heavy thicknesses reduced with a jagged blade. Then the rags were beaten out, washed, dried and heaped into a tank or steeping vat where they fermented for more than a month, so as to soften before they were shredded. After shredding, they were mixed with more or less water according to the thickness of paper desired in stamping-troughs, where they were then kneaded for one or two days to form a pulp the consistency of whey' (Teynac *et al*, 1981: 215). The sorting and treatment of rags was carried out largely by women and was a hazardous occupation, mainly because of the transmission of infectious diseases via the rags.

Considerable labour had already gone into the rag industry prior to the rags' arrival at the mills. Henry Mayhew describes in some detail the activities of the bone-grubbers and rag-gatherers and the social changes that were affecting their occupational structure. Apart from the specialist agents who acquired rags in bulk from the old clothes exchanges and the marine stores, England's capital city was home to a small army of tightly differentiated street occupations, amongst whom were those who specialized in gathering rags from the streets and dustpiles of Victorian London. The occupation of rag-gatherer was at one time dominated by women, who were known as 'bunters' ('bunting' originally referring to rags) and who would search the alleys and back streets for this waste. Whilst the women would collect rags of any colour, those which were clean, white and made of linen were considered as a prize find. White rags in good condition fetched around 2d. to 3d. per pound whereas coloured rags fetched only around 2d for 5lbs (Mayhew, ND: 301–6).

The rag industry was a huge, complex undertaking, global in its reach and significance; a form of waste-management that was of crucial importance to the spread of writing throughout the Western world. Without the rag industry, the development of newspapers, novels, paper money (and, thus, the National Debt), the means to codify law and statute and all other forms of written information and communication would have been much slower to develop and scientific and philosophical advances could not have circulated with the ease and rapidity that marked post-enlightenment Europe. Even the first electronic communications revolution, the telegraph system — named by Tom Standage as *The Victorian Internet* — which itself revolutionised communication at a distance — depended on a steadily increasing supply of paper, a fact which appears to have passed by Standage as this requirement for a successful telegraphic communications structure is barely mentioned. A Victorian internet it may have been but, like the 'paperless office' of today, it consumed more and more paper as time went on.

In spite of the insatiable demand for paper and in spite of the long standing search for more efficient means of producing it, the Victorian attitude to its disposal was possibly even less enlightened than our own. True, used paper of all descriptions (including newspaper) was made to serve a variety of different purposes — as wrapping for all kinds of consumer goods, including food and items of hardware, for example, as a single-use cleaning implement to wipe away grime, as a polishing implement for kettles, cutlery, blackened stoves, windows and mirrors, as a substitute carpet for a 'room not in constant use' and as an extra blanket inserted between quilts. But the vast bulk of it was either burned on the open fire, carted away by dust contractors to lie buried in dust mountains or simply discarded carelessly on the streets or into the waterways where, added to all the other abandoned refuse it contributed to clogging up the drains, waterways and streets of towns and cities. Some sense of the callous disinterest in the afterlife of this much sought-after commodity can be gained by considering that in 1862 a brigade of children from the London Ragged School, using only four hand pulled trucks, collected just under thirty nine tons of paper in less than nine months. In fact, the tonnage of paper collected was equal to the weight of all the other collected discards combined — which latter included rags, carpet, metal, fat and bones (see Simmonds, 1876: 30–32, 273, 275).

Even if the Victorian attitude to the disposal of paper seems suspiciously similar to our own, it remains the case that rags and the rag-gatherers played a central and irreplaceable role in its production and, consequently, in disseminating the revolution in social and scientific thought that swept the nineteenth century. In fact, the rags-to-paper industry was not only a key player in the dissemination of new scientific ideas, it also acted as a major stimulus to the development of Britain's chemical industry and is partly responsible for the development and refinement of chlorine because this chemical both removed discolourations from white rags and whitened some dyes, making it possible to use coloured rags in the manufacture of white paper and, later, enabling used paper to become a source of new paper. By supplying a ready, and steady, market for the new products of the emerging chemical industry, the rags-to-paper process provided a platform from which the latter was able to develop commercially.

Yet, the significance of rags and rag-gatherers is only one part of a much larger story about how waste of all descriptions helped to take forward the burgeoning 'knowledge economies' of nineteenth- and early twentieth-century Europe. Another occupation commented upon by Mayhew comprises a different but related plot-line in the story of Victorian social and industrial change. This is the role of 'pure' and the occupation of the 'pure-finder': 'pure' being the name given to dogs' dung. Dogs' dung acquired the name 'pure' because of its use in the tanning trade. Due to its astringent and alkaline character it acted as an effective scouring and purifying agent, especially in the manufacture of moroccos and roans from the skins of old and young goats. Here, the dung would be rubbed into the flesh (interior) and grain (exterior) of the skin — which latter would then be hung up to dry whilst the dung removed all remaining moisture.

In the early part of the nineteenth century, the occupation of pure-finder was not distinguished from that of 'bunter': old women tended to gather rags and pure at the same time. From the 1820s onwards, however, men increasingly took an active role in the occupation until, by the time that Mayhew published *London Labour and the London Poor* in 1851, pure-finding was a male-dominated occupation. The reason for this gendered change was the growth of the London tanning industry and the consequent increase in the value of 'pure'. As higher earnings became possible, men muscled in on the trade and pushed women to the margins of what had once been seen as unsuitable work for men.

Those tanneries with the greatest demand for pure tended to be involved in supplying specialist leathers — such as, significantly for the unfolding story, here, those used in the book-covering trade. Pure was also used in the tanning of thinner leathers — such as calf-skins — but the market here was more erratic because pigeon-droppings sufficed for the same purpose. Some tanneries — especially the larger ones — used regular pure finders. Mayhew recounts the case of Leomont and Roberts of Bermondsey who used twenty-three regular pure-finders, but the normal number was far less than this and some only took pure on an as-needed basis so that at times the finders would have to hawk their products around different tanneries in order to make a sale. Mayhew calculated there to be approximately 240 pure-finders regularly operating in the capital, each averaging an annual income of some £13. Swelling their ranks were numbers of destitute and starving Irish men (who had fled the potato famine) but they were irregular operators and earned very little. So profitable was the occupation that some pure-finders subcontracted to these starving immigrants and paid a fraction of the value they themselves would later realise at the tanneries.

The pure-finders were easily recognisable to anyone knowing the many occupations of the metropolis. Where the bone-grubbers and rag-gatherers carried sacks and often sticks, the pure-finder was equipped with a basket (usually covered) and some had a black leather glove on one hand. Many, however, dispensed with the latter because they found it easier to wash their hands than to keep the glove in a fit condition to be used. The women who pursued the trade generally had a large pocket in which they could store any rags they happened to find. But, Mayhew points out, they would only pick rags of the finest quality and certainly would not make any special effort to search for them. Whereas, also, the bone-grubbers and rag-gatherers tended to wander the alleys, yards and back-lanes where much

of the waste accumulated, the pure-finders were as likely to be seen on the main thoroughfares since the dogs tended to wander wherever they liked.

Mayhew comments that, among the potential means of earning a living on London's streets, the pure finder was relatively high-up the occupational ladder because:

> The pure-finders meet with a ready market for all the dogs'-dung they are able to collect, at the numerous tanyards in Bermondsey, where they sell it by the stable-bucket full, and get from 8d. to 10d. per bucket, and sometimes 1s. and 1s. 2d. for it, according to its quality.' (Mayhew, *op cit*: 306)

Among the pure-finders there were men who cleaned out the kennels of dog 'fanciers' but the dung there collected was generally of very poor quality — the dogs being 'fed on just about anything, to save expense' (ibid.: 308). Pure-finders in the know took the precaution of mixing kennel dung with street dung before offering it for sale because the tanneries would reject the former if they recognised it. Quality dog-dung was in much demand but kennel-dung had to be doctored to make it more appealing. This kind of mixing was not the only form of tampering that experienced finders used in their price-war with the tanneries. Since tanneries paid a higher price for the 'dry limy-looking sort', finders adulterated what they had by mixing mortar broken from old walls with the piles of collected dung and even rolled the mortar into small balls so that it resembled the dung they had really collected. 'Hence,' notes Mayhew, 'it would appear that there is no business or trade, however insignificant or contemptible, without its own peculiar and appropriate tricks' (ibid.: 306–7).

From the inner material upon which words of wisdom were written to the protective outer shell that kept the words of wisdom intact, rags and pure were two components of a waste management machine that enabled nineteenth-century Europe to materialise a revolution in scientific and social thought. Without these 'wastes' the burgeoning literacy of Europe's populations would have been set back by half a century or more and would have had to await the development of paper-making processes from esparto grasses and wood pulp that only became feasible with the development of the chemical industries that the rag trade had itself helped to stimulate. In an even wider sense, rags and pure demonstrate beyond any doubt that the incorporation of so-called wastes into social and economic life has impacts on international trade, government policy, industrial innovation, occupational structure and the gendering of labour relations. Waste has been the spur and the means to industrial and social change and from the second half of the nineteenth century onwards it came to figure more and more importantly in the development of new industries. Whereas mid-Victorian industry relied on a complex scavenging structure that orchestrated the

retrieval of raw materials from unseparated dustpiles, by the end of the century different sources and different kinds of rubbish raw materials began to take an increasingly central position in industrial development.

## RUBBISHING THE INDUSTRIAL REVOLUTION

With paper, in relative abundance, upon which to write the mathematical equations and record the experiments, design the engines and machinery of efficient production, conduct rational public debate across time and space, record the 'statistics' of population composition and change, the scientific and industrial, and the administrative and political, revolutions could all be expanded, buttressed and fervently applied.

Through the second half of the nineteenth century up to the Great War, an unprecedented rubbish revolution occurred that transformed forever the scientific and industrial conception of waste. Tied to other burgeoning political philosophies of efficiency in international economic struggle, waste was no longer understood as the life-giving dust of Dickens's London. From now on rubbish became *the* acknowledged key source of industrial innovation and its transformed management created a massive upheaval in the relationships between 'wastes' and raw 'materials': an upheaval that would displace the comparatively democratic value of nineteenth century dust and relocate it in the workshops and manufacturing plants of European and American industrial and military structures. The population of rag and bone, and related, collectors dwindled and the values of the goods they could supply diminished (sometimes, as in the case of 'pure', to zero) as industrial innovation and political regulation discarded the social and economic functions the collectors once performed. As the world progressed toward the Great War, less and less value was 'recovered', in its nineteenth century sense, and more and more of it was synthesised in a topsy-turvy world of waste and worth.

Take the example of petroleum spirit. For several decades, this highly unstable and explosive compound was considered to be a dangerous 'by-product' of the paraffin refining industry. Simmonds (1876: 386), discussing the distillation process, makes not a mention of it, noting only that:

> When the distillation of petroleum is carried to the full extent, there is left a residuum of compact coke. As an article of merchandise, this coke is at present valueless; but many refiners use it as fule, for which purpose it is tolerably well adapted.

Indeed, he busily and lustily extols the value and many uses of paraffin whilst ignoring the liquid residue that remains. Refineries applied as much efficiency in the extraction of paraffin from the crude petroleum as they could and became extremely ingenious at extracting greater and greater

quantities through the refining process. But to get at the paraffin they first had to deal with the much lighter and more volatile substance — petroleum spirit. Although fractional quantities of this were used in the burgeoning laundry and dry-cleaning businesses, its commercial value was effectively zero. So volatile was the spirit and seemingly so resistant to industrial application that often it was piped or transported to large pits — a safe distance away from the refineries — whereupon it was unceremoniously burned. Then along came Nikolaus August Otto who, in the same year that Simmonds had been extolling the virtues of paraffin, invented the first workable, petroleum driven, four-stroke internal combustion engine, later patented as the 'Otto Cycle'. The relative status of paraffin and petrol was about to change.

It is important to realise that Otto did not invent the internal combustion engine itself. That particular honour belongs to the Dutch physicist Christian Huygens who, in 1680, designed an internal combustion engine fuelled by gunpowder — although the engine was never in fact built. The first vehicle to be powered by an internal combustion engine was designed by Francois Isaac de Rivaz in 1807. This was fuelled by a mixture of hydrogen and oxygen and its descent into the forgotten annals of history indicates that it was not a great success. Later, in 1858, Jean Joseph Étienne Lenoir developed a version that ran on coal gas and whilst this vehicle worked, and included the first electric spark ignition process, it, too, was neither commercially nor technically viable. The problem with the internal combustion engine had always been how to design a means of powering a vehicle that could use a fuel that was plentifully available and use it in a manner sufficiently efficient to make the venture viable. The search for a fuel had been going on for over 180 years when, in 1863, Lenoir realised that the explosive character of paraffin refinery waste — i.e., petroleum spirit — could meet both requirements and redesigned his engine to use this 'by-product'. From then on, the competition was between petrol and gas as the motive force of the automobile revolution with, as we now know, the winner eventually creating a Western dependency on Middle Eastern oil supplies and, according to some, a current (at the time of writing) Anglo-American war against Iraq.

What had been the dangerously useless waste product of an industry devoted to generating paraffin now began to swing round and overturn which product was dominant and which subordinate. Instead of paraffin being seen as the industrial objective and petroleum spirit its dangerous by-product, petroleum spirit moved to centre stage in industrial development and paraffin became the by-product. Frederick Talbot acknowledged the changeover in most appropriate terms as early as 1919 when he observed that: 'A petroleum boom has reverberated around the world, eclipsing in intensity any stampede identified with the search for gold' (Talbot, 1919: 17).

Something that, at one time, was burned by the millions of gallons in pits is now considered an absolute necessity in industrialised nations and has provided modern cities with grid-lock, ground-level ozone and road rage — amongst many other 'benefits'. The incorporation of the refinery waste into automotive industrial development probably also signalled the beginning of the end of the British Empire since this had been built on the motive and industrial force of coal — a fuel that, slowly but surely, diminished in imperial significance across the following century, particularly as it was intrinsically unsuitable for powering aircraft.

Indeed, the story of early air transport itself bears many of the hallmarks of the story of the automotive revolution. Although aircraft also came to depend on the same raw material as the motorcar for their fuel — refined oil — some of the earliest aircraft were of a distinctly different kind from their modern counterparts and depended on a different kind of waste for their aeronautical prowess. In particular, the invention (and relatively short life) of the airship was a function of the waste material that it used to attain lift: hydrogen. The development of the airship in Germany was instigated by Graf Ferdinand von Zeppelin. Following a visit to America, Zeppelin returned to Germany with a scheme to produce a rigid balloon that could transport both persons and goods. He acquired the use of a site near Friedrichshafen in 1899 — which became the Luftschiffbau Zeppelin Ltd. Eleven years later, on July 3, 1900, after much experimentation and determination, a Zeppelin took off for its first flight. Yet, the story of the Zeppelin's development is as much a story about waste recovery as it is about von Zeppelin's ingenuity and resolution. For, the gas used to lift the airship, hydrogen, was a waste product of heavy industries and manufactures.

The waste gases that arose out of German manufacturing processes were considerable. For example, the production of one ton of pig iron resulted in the release of 150,000 cubic feet of waste gas. A considerable proportion of this total (around 20%) consisted of carbon monoxide — a gas with a high heating value. Consequently, German industry turned its attention to the recovery of this raw material and, eventually, the blast-furnace gas engine, making use of the waste product, was developed. If waste carbon monoxide could be recovered and used as a raw material, what about the other gases released during industrial production? The generation of hydrogen in German industry was significant, and continued to grow throughout the second half of the nineteenth century, but no ready market existed for its use. The encouragement given to Zeppelin can be attributed, at least in part, to the potential that his invention held out for giving a value to an almost valueless substance. The lifting properties of hydrogen were well known before Zeppelin's development of the airship (it had been used for ballooning) but airship manufacture offered a regular and steady market as well as promoting other industries and services allied to it. For example, realising that convenient transport of hydrogen would be necessary to facilitate the uptake of airship travel, Zeppelin began to manufacture high-pressure steel bottles so that the gas could be easily transported (and easily transferred) to airships requiring it. The high-pressure bottle industry, and its concomitant impact on steel manufacture, thus derived from the airship industry which itself depended on the abundant existence of a 'waste' (hydrogen) that would make the airship viable. Of course, the very agent that enabled the Zeppelin to be successful also caused its demise. At Lakehurst, New Jersey, on May 6, 1937, the Hindenburg airship ignited and, in a searing ball of hydrogen-fuelled flame, thirty-six crew and passengers died. The incident marked the temporary termination of airship travel and research but should not detract from the remarkable ingenuity demonstrated in recovering and reusing a waste product to achieve transcontinental flight.

Similar stories can be told for countless 'wastes': the seemingly disposed and discarded remnants of industrial production incite the invention and development of new products, services and industries — many of which have further ramifications for social and industrial organisation. Two further examples suffice to demonstrate the validity of this claim. The examples are coal tar and glycerin.

Like petroleum spirit, another seemingly useless 'by-product', and one which had been considered, for a very long time, dangerous and injurious, was coal-tar. Coal tar is a thick, black, liquid waste product of the process of coal gasification (that is, producing gas by the distillation of coal). According to Talbot (1919: 33), this substance was once 'waste in its most compelling form'. It was 'most compelling' because it was difficult to handle, difficult to destroy and deleterious to health. However, the discovery of medicines and dye-stuffs from processed coal tar changed its value significantly. No longer a 'compelling' waste to be discarded freely, coal tar was regarded as a virtually cost-free, industrial gold mine. From it were manufactured thousands of products, including antiseptics, synthetic aspirin, veronol, sulphanol, and phenacetin, chemicals for use in photography and leather processing and countless others, producing a boost to the German economy alone in the region of £150,000,000 annually. Quoting a certain Dr. Edmund J. Mills, F.C.S., Simmonds (1876) sums up the sense of wonderment and reverence in which this most compelling waste was held in the second half of the nineteenth century. 'Within the memory of many of us,' writes Dr. Hills:

> tar was a repulsive nuisance which had sometimes to be stealthily removed at night under apprehension of legal proceedings. It is now, if not the king, certainly the viceroy of manufactures. (Simmonds, 1876: 369)

It should be noted in passing that Simmonds here (and elsewhere) reveals that callous 'fly-tipping' is not at all a modern phenomenon but an ordinary solution to unwanted stuff that has been practised for a very long time.

The status of coal tar as the 'viceroy of manufactures' blossomed as coal tar products quickly displaced their natural counterparts and this displacement had some drastic impacts. When German supplies of coal tar-based medicines dried up during the Great War, for example, 'doctors were forced to polish up long-forgotten or rusty knowledge concerning the herbaceous drugs which had been displaced by those deriving from coal-tar' (Talbot, 1919: 33) and the price of aspirin, for example, rocketed (see Spooner, 1918: 7). Not only medicines but synthetic dyes, again developed and patented in Germany, were also derived from coal tar — first synthetic mauve and, later and crucially, indigo altered millennia of trading patterns between East and West. Whilst India had held virtual monopoly on the supply of vegetable based indigo since before the Roman Empire, the synthetic version — deriving from a seemingly limitless supply of an essentially free raw material — rapidly displaced India's role in world indigo supply. As such, it not only altered historical trading patterns between India, China, Japan, America and Europe — instead of flowing East to West, indigo now flowed West to East (as well as West to West) — it also represented a significant blow to the British Empire since an important source of colonial income was quickly reduced to a fraction of its former value.

As with coal tar so with fats. The candle-makers and soap manufacturers of nineteenth-century Europe were well aware of the useful properties of their own particular by-product — glycerin. Glycerin, meaning 'sweet oil', is produced when animal or vegetable fats are subjected to heat and pressure or are treated with solvents, such as benzene, in order to clarify the tallow. Expansion of the soap and candle trades resulted in the generation of increasing amounts of glycerin as the century progressed. Like chlorine, glycerin became a staple resource for the chemical industries and was put to very many uses. It was used as a moisturising agent for textiles and leather, as a lubricant for clocks and guns, and as a medium for cosmetics and inks, amongst other things. By the end of the Great War, no end was in sight for its potential applications. Spooner (1918: 217) observed that 'Its uses are constantly increasing, and its applications in pharmacy are almost endless.' But its most valuable application was as a base for a very different kind of product. In 1847, Ascanio Sobrero combined glycerin with nitric acid — a combination that resulted in a highly unstable compound that he named nitroglycerine but for which he could see no commercial application. However, in 1863, according to Miller (2000: 46):

> a Swedish munitions maker, Alfred Nobel, figured out what nitroglycerine could do, and thereby made possible New York subways and skyscrapers, the Panama Canal, and World War I.

As an aside, it should be noted that the synthesis of a volatile and explosive material from an unwanted by-product was not a peculiarly modern phenomenon. Nitroglycerine's predecessor, gunpowder, which had served much the same type of military and industrial purpose since at least the battle of Crecy in 1346, was also partly dependent on a waste product, although of a somewhat different kind. The gunpowder used at the battle of

Crecy consisted of a combination of potassium nitrate (saltpetre), sulphur and charcoal. Although the recipe had altered by the time Nelson fought the Battle of Trafalgar in 1805, the ingredients were the same. All fertile soil naturally contains quantities of nitrogen with which to make explosives, but soils that are liberally soaked in urine and dung are exceptionally rich sources. Given the sanitary arrangements of London at the turn of the nineteenth century, and given the widespread practice of keeping pigeons — whose wastes provide an excellent boost to the nitrate crystallisation process — England's alchemists had no trouble supplying more than sufficient quantities of gunpowder to Nelson's fleet. In fact, it was not only the earth outside London's houses that was used to supply nitrate rich soils. So rich were the internal floors in nitrogen that, during the Tudor period, Wylie (1959: 28) notes, it had been illegal to pave over the those floors and licensed diggers were allowed to enter houses without permission and extract the soil upon which the occupants and their furnishings stood.

By the time of the Great War, glycerin was as crucial to the war effort as gunpowder had been to Nelson's fleet. In consequence, between 1914 and 1918, no effort was spared in all European nations in the attempt to squeeze every drop from any available source. In Germany, a systematic recycling system was put in place and in the major cities householders were required to put out their refuse ready for early morning collection on a daily basis. The regulations governing domestic waste management were stringent in the extreme and dereliction of recycling duties was punishable under law. So strict were the regulations that: 'It was criminal for the housewife or maid to permit the grease clinging to the plates and dishes from the table to escape down the sink' (Talbot, 1919: 29).

Whilst less fanatical in its regulatory zeal, Britain pursued a similar policy and, in particular, systematised the collection of fats from the waste foods at army camps, attempting to find ways of collecting and processing every last ounce, and even establishing a quasi-private enterprise in the guise of Army Waste Products Ltd to handle the swill along orthodox business lines. In order to process army wastes as efficiently as possible a portable waste recovery plant was developed that could be assembled and dismantled with ease in order to facilitate its movement between regimental camps. Anything that could be reprocessed in any way was reprocessed and the effort resulted in some, now very familiar, products — such as cream cheese, which was first manufactured by mixing cheddar cheese, including the previously discarded rind, with waste animal fats — and 'Oleo' margarine — produced by the application of a dry steam rendering process for the recovery of high-grade animal fats from crude animal refuse. Kershaw (1928: 169) points out that, as a whole, the recycling effort had produced almost 2000 tons of glycerin for the manufacture of explosives. Adding all of the benefits together, Talbot calculates that the overall income generated by the various savings and reprocessings amounted to £5,626,000 and, in addition, the specific recovery of waste fats and their transposition into nitro-glycerine supplied the army with an additional '18,000,000 eighteen pounder shells' with which to blast the enemy into oblivion (Talbot, 1919: 62).

The experience of the Great War in particular, coming as it did after a period of intense inventiveness and innovation in waste recovery, persuaded many commentators to anticipate a happy, efficient and prosperous future founded on the recovery and reprocessing of industrial and domestic 'waste'. The seemingly endless industrial and commercial applications of refinery wastes, mining wastes, and manufacturing wastes, not to mention the new rich source of raw materials that would become available if householders could be persuaded not to burn their refuse on the open fire, offered the prospect of unlimited industrial and economic expansion because, as Talbot asserted, 'waste creates wealth' in its own right and also generates useful employment (ibid.: 12, 23).

## 'THE GREAT CURSE OF GLUTTONY'

Up until the 1930s, research, policy and industrial development had been riding the rubbish revolution. So inventive and ingenious were the improvements in waste-utilisation that it seemed, for a time, as if synthesised waste resources might eventually supplant a major portion of virgin raw materials in industrial production. Frederick Talbot specifically looked forward to the 'age of electrification' because it meant the demise of the kitchen stove and the factory furnace and, thus, the destruction of the valuable raw materials that would enable British industry to become ever more efficient and ever more cost-effective. A super-confident chemical engineering sector appeared to be overhauling the dependence of manufacturing industry on virgin raw materials for the generation of products. Not only did petroleum spirit, coal tar and glycerin, for example seemingly lead the way towards an economy of newly synthesised materials from what had once been seen as useless by-products of industry, they also pointed to the multi-functional character of those by-products. What were once refinery and mining discards were transformed into fuels, building materials, medicines, cleaning agents and thousands of other products that, today, are taken absolutely for granted in many parts of the world.

The optimism, however — the belief that the industrial world was pulling itself, by its own boot-straps, out of the waste-land of the post-Great War period and entering a new age of innovation and progress — was short-lived. By the early 1930s the 'machine age' was re-generating intellectual disquiet in ways not dissimilar to Karl Marx's original analysis of proletarian enslavement (see Mumford, 1934). By the 1940s, the apparently unprecedented efficiency of European and American industry as a whole was striking some morally discordant notes. What had been seen as a potential cornucopia of rubbish-to-riches industrial development began to turn back on itself as the 'consumer society' appeared destined to swamp the quality of life with the over-production of inessential goods.

Here is born the modern moral critique of consumerism and its association, not with efficiency, but with gluttony and pointless 'waste' in what would later be termed the 'throwaway society'. Far from being an absence or loss of value which scientific and technological progress could counter, the burgeoning critique of over-production and over-consumption construed waste as an excess of values. 'For it is the great curse of gluttony,' wrote Dorothy Sayers in her 1941 essay 'The Other Six Deadly Sins', 'that it ends by destroying all sense of the precious, the unique, the irreplaceable' (Sayers, 1948: 74). Modern over-production and over-consumption, far from extracting the last traces of value from every 'waste' by the best scientific and technical means, was intent on generating waste, on destroying all true values and substituting the pointless, and unsustainable, desire to possess and revel in 'all the slop and swill that pour down the sewers over which the palace of Gluttony is built' (ibid.).

The essay is part of a theologically inspired collection published as *Creed or Chaos?* (1948). The collection consists of a series of laments on the moral decay of mid-twentieth century society, where no-one has the right attitude to each other, to the community at large, to work, to religion, or anything else. They comprise an intemperate tirade against Keynesian demand management and, in Sayers's opinion, the excesses of the burgeoning welfare state. Rooted in Western Christian dogma, the essays condemn almost the entirety of social and industrial development since some (unspecified) mythical age of craft, community and thrift. For Sayers, the modern industrial world is a world of artifice and pretence whose earthly span must surely be near its end, as she suggests in the 1942 essay 'Why Work?':

> A society in which consumption has to be artificially stimulated in order to keep production going is a society founded on trash and waste, and such a society is a house built on sand. (Sayers, 1948: 47)

This polemical blast against the entire edifice of Keynesian economics appears as the frontispiece of Vance Packard's celebrated text *The Waste Makers* (first published in 1960). Given the widespread popularity of the vulgar version of Packard's thesis — that manipulative advertising and marketing strategies are tools for the expansion of an unsustainable consumption-led economic system — it is surprising that its right-wing, dogmatic, theological roots are not the subject of more sustained, reflective commentary. That there are more connections between Packard's thesis and Sayers's tirade beyond the valedictory frontispiece is evident on even the most cursory comparison between the books.

For example, 'We need not remind ourselves of the furious barrage of advertisements by which people are flattered and frightened out of a reasonable contentment into a greedy hankering after goods which they do not need; nor point out for the thousandth time how every evil passion — snobbery, laziness, vanity, concupiscence, ignorance, greed — is appealed to in these campaigns' wrote Sayers in her 1942 essay (Sayers, 1948: p. 71). Packard, describing the alleged 'need' to stimulate growth in the American economy, appended: 'What was needed was strategies that would make Americans in large numbers into voracious, wasteful, compulsive consumers' and 'The way to end the glut [of commodities] was to produce gluttons' (Packard, 1967: 34, 37). In her (1940) essay 'Creed or Chaos?' Sayers complained that, in the modern age, people have lost a sense of personal worth and of the value of service to the community, of work for the sake of contributing to social well-being and for its own intrinsic reward. Thus, people only work to earn money with which to purchase things they do not need, with the consequence that 'the result of the work is a by-product; the *aim* of the work is to earn money to do something else' (Sayers, 1948: 44). Packard repeated the complaint, claiming that 'The lives of most Americans have become so intermeshed with acts of consumption that they tend to gain their feelings of significance in life from these acts of consumption rather than from their meditations, achievements, personal worth and service to others' (Packard, 1967: 292).

The point, here, is not to engage in an extended critical interpretation of Sayers or Packard but to show that, at a societal level — in Britain and America, at least — the economic and social values of waste were undergoing important changes. The question is: what are the reasons for the changes? What had happened to the early century optimism and confidence in the industrial recovery and remanufacture of all things discarded?

It is certainly not the case that industrial reclamation of wastes had failed in its objectives, or that there had been some dulling of the inventiveness with which ostensible wastes were remanufactured into new products. Nor was it the case that the reclamation, recovery and re-synthesis of 'used' products had resulted in economic losses or depleted incomes. On the contrary, Charles Lipsett, writing in 1951, provided an extensive overview — in sixty-five chapters — of the remarkable growth of salvaging, reclamation and recycling, particularly from the 1930s onwards. In the 1963 edition of the book he includes a postscript on 'Research in Waste Recovery' in which he notes that the value of salvaged industrial wastes to the American economy was of the order of $5–7 billion dollars annually. Between 1935 and 1962, the reclamation and recovery value of agricultural products alone had increased by a factor of 25 — from $100 million dollars to $2.5 billion dollars. During the same period, the recovery and salvage of scrap plastic had become a global industry. Scrap plastic was (and is) transformed into 'inexpensive housewares, novelties and toys, wire and cable covers, all injection moulding, packaging, and a certain amount of bottles and other blow mouldings, pipe, garden hose, electrical plugs and some sheeting' as well as combs, seat covers, and rainwater goods (Lipsett, 1963: 12).

Although the development of synthetic fibres — including viscose rayon, acetate, nylon, and acrylic polyester — was one of the major reasons why rags were abandoned as a source of paper, contributing to the decline of the rags-to-paper industry (which now accounts for only around 5% of global paper production), these synthetic fibres themselves proved amenable to recycling and reprocessing. On recovery, sometimes in combination with wool and other textile wastes, they were (and are) transformed into 'stockings, lingerie, foundation garments, shirts, overalls, rainwear, dresses, carpets, sweaters, underwear, tights, ropes, fishing and laundry nets, conveyor belts, tire cords,' amongst other things (ibid.: 265). It is instructive to realise that, potentially at least, the underwear you put on today could have been someone else's underwear yesterday or that, but for a simple twist of fate, you might be wearing what would have been your carpet. Lipsett's book addresses all of the familiar waste-to-commodity industries — including brewery wastes, ferrous and non-ferrous metal wastes, and oil and grease recovery, for example — and includes recovery operations that were not viable or possible when Talbot, Spooner and Kershaw produced their early century surveys. These processes include automobile salvage, paints and solvents salvage, and reclamation of foam rubber scrap. The book also acknowledges the continued inventiveness with which the recovery and reclamation industries operate. For example, the postscript notes that, amongst uncountable other inventions:

> Experiments have produced a milk substitute from wool rags, plastics from tung oil, paperboard from sugar cane waste, vitamins from citrus peel and pulp, energy from sound, chemicals and drugs from wood — and still only a beginning has been made. (Lipsett, 1963: 355)

In industrial terms, then, the post-war period continued along much the same lines as had been laid down from the late Victorian era onwards: continuing research into, and continuing reclamation of, industrial wastes with ever-greater efficiency. Yet, as has been noted, discordant — and strident — voices were being raised about the consequences of the inventiveness, efficiency and productivity of industrial societies. Some people, and their numbers increased over time, did not like what was on offer. The dislike, originally, was not directed at the gross inequalities of the capitalist industrial system, nor at the fraud and corruption by which industrial conglomerates effectively robbed ordinary people of a fair share of the profits of technological and industrial development. The dislike was rooted in a rejection of so-called 'consumer society' and the moral degradation it bestowed on an unwitting populace. A new 'war on waste' was declared but it was not Talbot's, or Spooner's, or Kershaw's war. It was not the determined effort to extract the last ounce of value from the 'triflings', as Spooner called them, of societal-wide wastes. It was a war on over-production and over-consumption — a war on throwing things away in the first place! It was a war against the early century dream of grabbing everything that was discarded for remanufacture into new goods. It was a war, in short, on the very production of 'waste' itself and, in consequence, it was a futile and unwinnable war, a war of principle without practical means of engaging its declared enemy. Thus, in his conclusion Vance Packard could only appeal lamely to Americans to guard their spirits against the encroaching consumer society:

> Americans must learn to live with their abundance without being forced to impoverish their spirit by being damned fools about it. (1967: 302)

An early proponent of the terminology of war was a certain Arthur Jones, MP. In a short Conservative political pamphlet, published in 1967, he encapsulated the growing sense of unease with which the post-war baby-boomers, reaching maturity in the late 1960s, viewed economic growth in industrialised societies. An unimaginative, election-oriented diatribe backed by dubious evidence, Jones's *War on Waste* nonetheless touched the essence of the critique that Packard had borrowed from Sayers. He railed against the extravagance of local government and its abandonment of any principles of efficiency. Cumbersome, over-bureaucratised departments were duplicating each other's work, excessive spending by excessive numbers of committees, and lack of accountability, transparency and audit, he claimed, was resulting in untold financial losses and squandered resources. The political system, he (unknowingly) implied, was like the economic system sketched out by Packard: no-one cared any longer for efficiency and resource management — spending and output reigned supreme. Excessive production and consumption, excessive bureaucracy and regulation, excessive and wanton resource misuse were overburdening both the individual and the social system. Waste was reaching 'crisis' proportions and all of its manifestations demanded urgent attention.

At almost this precise point in time, however, the war on waste took a decisive turn. Rather than a simple problem of excess and mismanagement, some wastes were exposed as menacing threats to life whose production was embedded in the very system that synthesised and re-synthesised the 'excess' commodities. The super-confident chemical industries, whose seemingly alchemical conversions of rubbish into profits had enthused an earlier generation of industrial and social forecasters, found itself under attack. Waste may create wealth, as Talbot had claimed, but it also appeared to create more waste. Rather than reducing the stockpiles of industrial rubbish by efficiently converting them into desired goods, the industries expanded and intensified the problems they had seemed set to solve. The transformations of dirt into gold generated by-products of its own: toxic drums of dangerous chemicals found their way to the roadside, into landfills, rivers and seas. At first, the problems this created seemed to be purely national — Britain's chemical industries appeared to be poisoning Britain, as America's were poisoning America, and so on. Whilst this observation was itself troubling, it represented nothing substantially new. Environmental deposits of lead, arsenic and a range of other hazardous substances have been occurring since at least the time of the Roman Empire (see Rathje and Murphy, 1991: 123–7). What seemed to have altered was the scale and toxic mix of the depositions, and the routes by which they were reaching the environment. It was not merely the industrial processes themselves that were causing the pollution menace: the products they generated, and which consumers purchased and used, were similarly hazardous. A bottle of nail polish, for example, might contain the poisonous and carcinogenic substances xylene, dibutyl phthalate, and tolulene and, as with nail polish, so with all of the objects of consumer desire in developed industrial societies. As Rathje and Murphy (ibid.: 122) point out, if consumers bought these substances in large drums rather that tiny bottles they would be subject to special waste licensing arrangements.

Very quickly it became apparent that the movement of toxic wastes was not just a national problem but was in fact global in scale, threatening the 'environment' as a whole. Rachel Carson's (1962) *Silent Spring* was a watershed in the changed outlook on waste. It told a story of species extinction, pollution of waterways, a carcinogenic and poisonous atmosphere and the resistance of the insect world to the chemicals that were killing the world's animals and plants. The unregulated dispersal of toxic chemicals comprised a recipe for environmental and human destruction. The impact of the book cannot be explained in terms of new awareness or new scientific knowledge. The perilous properties of some industrial wastes have been the subject of research and debate since the flowering of the chemical industries in the nineteenth century (see Colten & Skinner, 1996, for example). What was different about *Silent Spring* and the critique of industrial society that it epitomised, was that it rejected the idea that wastes could be made to go away by the further application of scientific and technological development and, specifically, rebuffed the proposition that for every problem there was a chemical solution. It opened the door to a barrage of research on global toxic trading (the latter well-summarised by Clapp, 2001; and Moyers, 1991) and on the environmental impacts of polluting industrial production and consumption.[1] It also signalled a growing sense of mistrust in the capacity of the modern 'technological coalescence', as Theodore Roszak named it in his aptly titled treatise on politics and consciousness in post industrial society, *Where the Wasteland Ends*, to provide anything other than 'artificial environments' by means of a 'teratoid technocracy' that combined a total disregard for nature with a racist 'megalomania' (Roszak, 1972: 25, 47).

Where, once, waste had been seen as a resource that had the potential to generate limitless benefits, it transformed, almost overnight, into a source of potentially limitless social and environmental costs. A necessary vision, perhaps, but the 'crisis of waste' outlook — in both its 'excessive' and 'polluting' guises — diverted attention from the dependence of modern industry on wastes of all kinds. It provoked storms of protest over the unregulated release, shipment and dumping of hazardous rubbish and, for a time, tarred all waste with the same toxic brush. For almost twenty years, in the UK at least, in spite of the efforts of many Green campaigners, the economic, technological and industrial significance of waste was virtually ignored in the research, policy and scholarly establishments.

## FISHCAKES ARE ENVIRONMENTALLY FRIENDLY

The sense of impending catastrophe generated by the 'crisis of waste' outlook still circulates today. But slowly, from the late 1970s onwards, the doom-mongering has been joined by other voices that signal something of a return to the optimism of the late nineteenth and early twentieth century. For example, Joy Palmer's book *War on Waste*, which has exactly the same title as Arthur Jones's (1967) political pamphlet, suggests that 'waste may actually be a valuable resource' rather than simply an enemy to be defeated (Palmer, 1988: 3). Robin Murray (1999) once more seeks to create wealth from waste by the application of 'smart' design and planning, whilst James Womack and Daniel Jones (1996) propose to banish waste and create wealth by the use of 'lean thinking'. There is no suggestion, here, that this re-evaluation of rubbish dismisses or overturns the sense of menace and threat that blossomed from the 1960s onwards. Rather, alongside an awareness of rubbish risks, it recaptures the sense of innovation and dynamism with which Talbot, Spooner and others had invested the wasting process in the period on either side of the Great War. Paying attention to rubbish is seen, in these re-evaluations, not simply as a means of combating the hazards it represents, but also as a means of stimulating technical advancement, industrial reorganisation and social restructuring. My concern here is not to engage in a debate about the merits or otherwise of these various re-evaluations but to provide some context for the altered thinking about rubbish by showing that what is true historically is true in the present day: significant innovations and inventions, as well as patterns of social organisation, are dependent on and driven by waste — even where those innovations and inventions may seem unpalatable to contemporary tastes. The relationship of contemporary society to its wastes is no less important in industrial and economic terms than was the relationship between Dickens and his contemporaries and *their* wastes. The precise character of the relationships has changed but it is not the case that the industrial and economic significance of those wastes has diminished. From the greatest technological advances of space travel to the most intimate desires for health and beauty contemporary societies are inextricably bound to the wastes they produce.

Take the space programme, for example. Since October 4, 1957, when Sputnik 1 achieved the first successful, human-created satellite orbit of the earth, countless objects have been hurled into space from all over the world. Some of these have remained in orbit for decades; some have broken apart with pieces re-entering the atmosphere; and some have left trails of technological and human detritus encircling the earth. In fact, there are millions of leftover items from space missions whizzing around the earth at incredible speeds. The vast majority of these are far too small to track at present. They consist of flakes of paint and dust-debris from the daily drudgery of space-work. Their number is swelled by minute pellets of frozen urine and faeces left over from earlier space missions. The majority of these items could never return to earth. Being so small, they would burn up within seconds of re-entering the earth's atmosphere. But if a full toilet bag ever lost its orbit and made it through the atmosphere, it would give an entirely new twist to the feeling of being shat upon from a great height.

As a consequence of this revolving scrap-yard, tracking space junk has become a highly skilled and technically sophisticated enterprise. About 8000 items of debris are tracked every second of every day in order to monitor their risk of re-entry or of colliding with functioning satellites. Indeed, the world's space agencies time the launch of their rockets and design flight paths in order to avoid collisions with these 8000 larger items of junk. In fact, there are a further 70,000 to 150,000 items between 1cm and 10cm in size — with potentially catastrophic impact risks — circling the space lanes around the earth. The orbiting debris has encouraged the formation of a body called the Inter-Agency Debris Coordination Group who advise the United Nations, amongst others, on potential solutions to the problems posed by the junk. Apart from creating randomly moving rings to outdo Saturn's staid orbitals, and apart from influencing the flight paths of space-craft, these debris have led directly to refinements in tracking technology and in computer warning systems that are also useful in monitoring meteorites and comets and in long-range, hyper-sensitive object-tracking systems. The more sophisticated becomes the technology, the more possible it becomes not only to track the debris, but also to *capture* it. The person who figures out, at the right time, how to harvest all this junk will become a space scrap-yard billionaire — and the time is not far off. Indeed, recycling decrepit and defunct satellite parts is already an element of the orbiting labour process.[2]

The study of space junk has been christened 'exo-garbology' and it represents a growing field of research and development. Its polar opposite might be christened 'endo-garbology' in homage to the increasing economic and industrial significance of human bodies, body parts and body products. For example, there are interesting parallels between the legal framework for the disposal of waste objects and the legal framework for disposing of corpses. In both cases there is no right of ownership: there is no property in abandoned goods. Waste-objects and corpses are treated as if they have been abandoned and once they are outside a waste- or corpse-management system no-one 'owns' them. A useful illustration of this state of affairs was provided by Castle Morpeth Council, Northumberland, UK in 1998. In a dispute over funeral costs for a deceased resident of a private care home the Council refused to make funeral arrangements on the grounds that deceased residents constituted a waste product of the care industry. 'Without wishing to appear insensitive', a Council spokesman suggested:

> one could argue that from a commercial viewpoint residents of a home are its income-producing raw material. Ergo, from a purely commercial view, deceased residents may then be regarded as being the waste produced by their business. (Brindle, *The Guardian* 7/8/1998)

The general state of affairs signalled by the ambiguous status of the deceased has resulted in some odd, if predictable, consequences that have been the subject of considerable debate in the legal press. The 'scandals' at Alder Hey and Bristol hospitals in the UK — where the organs of dead children were kept for research and teaching purposes — figure high in that debate. Yet, as important as the retention of entire organs is the buying and selling of human tissue. This latter, international, trade is worth hundreds of millions of dollars per annum. A single human body that has been 'abandoned' to medical research or over which no-one claims possessory rights of disposal is worth in excess of $70,000 to the cosmetic surgery industry. Corpse tissues are used in lip-enhancement, breast-augmentation, penis-enlargement and in treating wrinkles. Ounce per ounce, human tissue in this industrial complex, is as valuable as diamonds. In order to perfect the techniques required by the cosmetic surgery service, the heads of cadavers are subjected to nose-jobs, face-lifts, and a range of other cosmetic enhancements before being incinerated. Whole cadavers are used as crash test dummies in developing improvements in car safety, forensic science, and ballistics research whilst arms, limbs and torsos are regularly smashed, cut, burned, boiled and injected with uncountable substances in order to test industrial products of very many kinds. There may be no property in abandoned goods, but there is money and industrial innovation in abandoned bodies (see Roach, 2003; Mims, 1998).

It is not only abandoned bodies and their tissues that generate contemporary industrial innovation and financial gain. The waste products of the human digestive system similarly encourage some weird and wonderful new products. For example, Charles Leadbeater observes that an American organisation called Genetics Institute Incorporated owns the patent on a substance called erythropoietin, or EPO. EPO is a protein made of 165 amino acids that simulates the activities of red blood cells, thus enhancing the uptake of oxygen, and is now a multibillion dollar global industry (Leadbeater, 2000: 173). EPO is a valuable pharmaceutical aid in treating a variety of blood disorders but its power to boost oxygen uptake has made it a highly desirable performance-enhancing substance in a variety of sports. The Winter Olympics in Salt Lake City saw 100 positive tests for EPO, whilst the 2000 and 2001 *Tour de France* witnessed an EPO scandal that rocked the entire sport. The 1998 winner of the competition, Marco Pantani, was given a suspended jail sentence in 1999 after testing positive for EPO and whole cycling teams (as well as the Italian football club Juventus) have come under suspicion of boosting their performance by using the banned drug. The twist to the story is that EPO is distilled and compounded from a base of human urine. This 'waste' — urine — that is discharged by people as an inevitable by-product at the end of a chain of uses of raw materials and products, is itself a raw material that leads to the production of a good, which in turn provides both legal and illegal services to the people who (potentially, anyway) provide the raw material. If making a fortune from urinating is not the height of ingenuity in waste reclamation then nothing is.

Recycled body parts and recycled body products are the tip of a very large heap of human and industrial waste that is reused and reprocessed into valuable goods in contemporary society. They are no more than illustrative of the continuing role played by wastes in industrial development. Almost every object encountered potentially either has been, at some stage, a by-product of some productive process or is destined to enter into another productive process. This is also true of much of the food consumed in industrial societies. The groceries that sit invitingly on the supermarket shelf or the fast food meal that satisfies the carbohydrate cravings of fattening westerners are pumped full of all manner of unpalatable substances. Or, as Schlosser (2000: 197) puts it in characteristically direct terms: 'there is shit in the meat.' In fact, there is much else in it besides. Given that the regulations governing what can and cannot be fed to livestock and what can and cannot be used as fertiliser are confused in the extreme (and continually changing), it is little surprise to learn that sometimes-injurious wastes find their way into the food production process.

For example, during the summer of 1999, amongst many other scary food stories, the Belgian food crisis — in which dioxins were found to be embedded in the agricultural food chain — hit the headlines in many European newspapers. The story took up such a lot of space that it displaced news of a similar phenomenon known to be occurring in France and, undoubtedly, in every other nation of Europe. *The Guardian* newspaper (17/8/1999: 9) reported this story in the following terms.

> The French government admitted at the weekend that some of its animal-feed production plants have been using untreated sewage, residues from septic tanks and effluent from animal carcasses in the preparation of feed for pigs and poultry.

A report, prepared for the department for consumer affairs, competition and the prevention of fraud, noted that water used to wash down lorries was also channelled into the animal-feed production process. The story made the headlines partly because of its affinity to the Belgian food scare but more importantly because the use of effluent 'has been banned in EU animal feed since 1991'. In other words, this particular process was in contravention of EU protocol — but only since 1991. However, and here is the most telling aspect of the entire story, 'some other substances, including motor oil, appear to have slipped through the regulations'. It is not likely that anyone would support the use of untreated oils or excrement or contaminated water in feeding animals, yet the story indicates clearly how widespread is the use of all forms of waste in agricultural, as well as industrial, production.

Even if it can be assumed that there would be no support for such uses of untreated effluents, what about the use of treated effluents and organic by-products? The industrial race to develop appropriate effluent treatment technologies is already well-advanced and has resulted in some odd and innovative inventions. A UK company called Bioplex Ltd has developed a portable anaerobic digester — the 'Portagester'. Anaerobic digestion is a method for converting organic waste products — including 'farm manures, biomass, sewage sludge and the organic fraction of food processing and municipal solid waste' (*New Review*, 1999; issue 40: 11) — into usable raw materials. Anaerobic digestion works by exposing organic wastes, in the absence of oxygen, to bacteria that eat them. The process results in two products: methane, produced during bacterial digestion and which can be burned to supply energy, and a 'solid digestate' with a number of different uses.

> These include processing it by composting it into an organic fibre-rich fertiliser, similar to traditional compost or peat but including nutrients such as slow-release nitrogen. It can also be used as landspread material or as a petrochemical feedstock' (ibid.).

The idea of using flora and fauna to gobble up the pollution caused by human societies before returning it cleansed and decontaminated for human consumption is a dream of many environmentalists and a staple ingredient of the garbology futures literature. Sim van der Ryn, for example, in his DIY earth-closet manual *The Toilet Papers* (1978), envisages a future in which ponds of crayfish wolf down human excrement suspended in water before returning the latter for domestic use and serving up the gorged and fattened crayfish at the family dinner. Sim van der Ryn got only three things wrong in this futurology. The first is that the process is not in any way futuristic. The second is that the effluent is not confined to human excrement. The third is that the species of choice for the food recycling industry is not crayfish, but carp.

The use of carp in pollution abatement schemes is part of a burgeoning world aquaculture industry. This industry grew from around 7.5 million tonnes of fish produced per annum in 1985 to over 26 million tonnes produced in 1996. In just over a decade it almost quadrupled in size. In an industry of this magnitude and exhibiting such a growth pattern there is, not surprisingly, intense interest in finding efficient, effective and economic ways of enhancing fish productivity and growth. As any angler will tell you, if you want to catch a lot of fish, look for a sewage pipe; as any aquaculturalist will confirm, carp are to be found shoaling in significant numbers around any sewage (and often other pollution) outlet. They are efficient at consuming, digesting and processing all kinds of polluting substances and growing fat on the filth of human society. In fact, human and animal excrement, organic by-products of animal husbandry and chemical and industrial effluents are all used as feed-supplements in carp production.

The problem, however, is that carp — whilst efficient and effective pollution-processing machines — are not very palatable. The meat is not very tasty and they are packed with intramuscular bones, making their ingestion and digestion less pleasant than many other fish species. In consequence, two researchers from the Punjab Agricultural University (Sehgal and Sehgal, 2002) developed an experiment to test some processed carp products. They composed a panel of six judges and presented for their delectation samples of fish patty, fish fingers, deboned fish salad and fish pakoura — all made from effluent-munching carp. Each dish was cooked with a mix of herbs, spices, flour and other flavouring products. Their results indicate that processed carp dishes significantly increased the palatability of carp in the Indian diet. Thus, they demonstrated that fishcakes are environmentally friendly and invited readers to write in for the recipes. The recipes they refer to comprise those for making the fishcakes rather than those for feeding the carp. In the words of the authors:

> there is a good scope for the processing of carp flesh into value-added products, which is important for boosting the production of these species for the continued expansion of fish culture ponds which can efficiently recycle wastes into nutritive human foods. (Sehgal and Sehgal, 2002: 292)

George Soper (1909: 7) asserted that '[it] is a rule of sanitary science that what is once rejected and cast off by the body shall not again be taken into it.' If he were alive today, it is not clear whether he would be shocked or impressed by the ingenuity with which this rule has been broken.

It matters not where you live or who you are. Everyone on the planet is surrounded by waste: a highly visible, intricately organised assemblage of rubbish encircles the living and the dead. It encourages incredible technological innovations, it provides the materials to beautify citizens dissatisfied with their appearance, it (legally and illegally) serves as a nutrient to nourish the soil and fatten the animals that end up on the dinner plate, and it enhances the performance of athletes. No wonder the modern imagination represents waste as the shadow of life — it feeds us, beautifies us and makes us better at sport. It is everywhere and, at least potentially, in everything we produce and consume.

# 4   Rubbish Households

Waste or rubbish is what people throw away because they no longer need it or want it. Almost everything we do creates waste and as a society we are currently producing more waste than ever before. (http://www.wasteonline.org.uk/topic.aspx?id=20)

Those who condemn our own era for its conspicuous consumption and conspicuous waste should at least bear in mind that throwing away perfectly good objects seems to be one of those inexplicable things, like ignoring history, that human beings have always done. (Rathje & Murphy, *Rubbish!*)

In spite of waste's central place in modern production and consumption, it is commonly asserted, in 'developed' countries at least, that there is a 'crisis' of waste and a failure of waste management policy. Moreover, the crisis is said to arise from the fact that contemporary consumer societies have developed a 'disposable' mentality in a 'throwaway' culture, and now discard items that, once, would have been reused, recycled or held in 'stewardship' by our ancestral make-do and menders. These claims are so commonplace, so much a part of the commonsense of public and private life, that few have examined whether or not they are true and, with some exceptions (see Rathje & Murphy, 1991, for a rare discussion), little evidence has been provided to test their veracity. In fact, these claims, for the United Kingdom at least, have less evidential foundation than might be expected. They have the effect of misrepresenting what is happening in relation to waste in the contemporary world and they also gloss the past. In the simplest terms, it is not proven that contemporary consumers waste more than their historically miserly counterparts. Nor is it true that, in the past, our grandparents and their grandparents 'stewarded' objects and reused, recovered or recycled more than happens today. Instead, the available evidence appears to show that contemporary consumers waste little more than their historical counterparts. This fact goes against the grain of both public and expert opinion but there are two sets of questions that can help to clarify why the consumerism = waste crisis argument stands in need of a critical assessment.

First, there is an important conceptual difference between talking about what people throw away and talking about what people waste. If one society deposits more unused materials on the environment than another one, does this mean it is more wasteful? Or does it mean that it processes more in the first place — so that there is simply a greater quantity of materials passing through its various industrial and domestic sectors? Is paper or plastic in a landfill more wasteful than offal or ash on the street, for example? It is far from clear that, as a proportion of what is produced and consumed, present-day consumers squander significantly more than any historical society has ever done. This is not to say that larger and/or more toxic depositions have no greater environmental impact but that is a rather different proposition to the claim that contemporary consumers are inherently more profligate. Second, with few exceptions, the claim that contemporary societies are unusually wasteful compared to the past is based on an analysis only of municipal wastes and their relation to consumer discards. The time-frame for the analysis has tended to be short — where any time-frame is referenced at all, less than a decade is typical. However, comparing the historical record with contemporary waste statistics suggest that today's consumers are not necessarily as profligate in relation to the past as contemporary commentary tends to imply.

An important part of the problem with the throwaway society thesis is that it is rooted in a family of ideas about the 'crisis of waste' that confuses a moral critique and a sociological analysis of consumerism. The moral critique pays attention to escalating demand, high product turnover, and built-in obsolescence in a society increasingly oriented towards convenience. The sociological analysis pays attention to economic and cultural changes (particularly in the post-war period) relating to levels of affluence, patterns of taste and industrial innovation. As we have seen in Chapter 3, the family has a respectable intellectual lineage in its recollection of Denis Gabor, Vance Packard, Dorothy Sayers, and others. It is widespread both in popular commentary and in the social sciences generally and has a particularly strong presence in the literature on municipal waste. It lays the blame for contemporary wastefulness at the door of voracious consumers and implies a seemingly democratic response to that wastefulness since, in so far as we are all responsible for the crisis, we should all share in its solution. For some, including Hans Tammemagi (1999), the crisis has made it necessary to develop new infrastructures and technologies for managing waste disposal. For others, including Robin Murray (1999), it is preferable to concentrate on redesigning the 'waste economy' to encourage zero waste generation. Whichever solution is proposed there remain some basic questions about whether or not the evidence underlying the moral-sociological analysis is sufficient to support the conclusions. The questions are especially pertinent in relation to claims that wastefulness is a product of the peculiar characteristics of post-war social development.

Tammemagi (1999: 25–6), for example, whilst acknowledging that waste-generation has been an urban problem for several centuries, argues that two developments following World War II have caused a significant escalation in the amount and kind of wastes produced in contemporary society. The first of these, 'consumerism', he notes, has resulted in an increase in the number and variety of goods entering the home, as well as an increased amount and variety of materials leaving it post-consumption. Here, a consumer-oriented, throwaway culture has created huge increases in the amounts of municipal waste requiring management and disposal. The second development comprised the birth of the 'chemical age', an age characterised by increasingly toxic municipal and industrial waste arisings. Here, scientific and technological innovation has altered the nature of the products that people consume and, as a consequence, it has also altered the nature of discards. It has rendered these discards more toxic and generally more hazardous — resulting in the need for increasingly specialised technologies for their disposal. The twin problems of quantity and hazard have combined to make post-consumer waste a critical problem for all industrialised societies.

Of course, degraded environments and the careless disposal of toxic wastes are not new phenomena. The poisoned towns, contaminated rivers and filth-strewn highways of Victorian England serve as a reminder of the toxic continuities of industrialised societies. Yet it is valid to observe that there has been a proliferation in the variety of hazardous ingredients that make up contemporary consumer products and in the routes by which these ingredients reach the environment both during and after consumption. Post-war industrial development has indeed been characterised by increases in the toxic mix and hazard of the ingredients of consumer goods and post-consumption wastes.

Granting, for a moment, that the post-war period can thus be characterised as an atypically 'chemical age,' the dangers posed by contemporary industrial production are real enough and it is right that attention be drawn to them. However, the nature of these dangers is not the crux of Tammemagi's assessment of the crisis. That argument is basically rooted in issues of quantity — particularly in the over-consumption of goods and the over-production of post-consumption wastes. It shares kinship with Matthew Gandy's earlier assessment of urban wastes and the social and cultural triggers that have instigated their growth. In a paragraph that the two authors might have shared, Gandy (1993: 31) claimed that:

> The post-war period has seen a dramatic increase in the production of waste, reflecting unprecedented global levels of economic activity. The increase in the waste stream can be attributed to a number of factors:

rising levels of affluence; cheaper consumer products; the advent of built-in obsolescence and shorter product life-cycles; the proliferation of packaging; changing patterns of taste and consumption; and the demand for convenience products.

In turn, Gandy's assessment draws inspiration from earlier generations of social critics for whom contemporary society is an improvident aberration from the normal course of civilised history. Like Tammemagi and his predecessors, Gandy acknowledges the existence of industrial and other wastes but retains a focus on municipal waste on the premise that this waste indicates most clearly the profligate and deleterious impact of post-war consumerism. Post-consumer waste represents a symbol of social degeneration in so far as it expresses a collective disdain for the objects and services that people use and for the environmental consequences of their extravagant lifestyles.

Sometimes, however, the commitment to a critique of consumerism can lead to excessive zeal in the presentation of the evidence and the critical evaluation becomes top-heavy in relation to its empirical foundations. A good example of such zeal — and a clear indication that the waste 'crisis' is grasped as a crisis of post-consumption, urban waste — is provided by Tammemagi. In a general discussion of the rising quantities and changing qualities of post-war wastes he claims that 'packaging represents more than one-third of the entire waste stream' (1999: 25). In reality, of course, packaging does not make up anything like a third of the entire waste stream. What he means is that packaging makes up a third of the *municipal* waste stream — which itself comprises around 5% to 8% of total waste arisings. In the UK, for example, if non-household sources of packaging are extracted, household packaging discards make up less than a quarter of the municipal waste generated each year or approximately 1% to 2% of total UK waste. Another example is supplied by Murray (1999: 30) where he claims that disposable nappies contribute 730,000 tonnes annually to the household waste stream. On closer investigation it transpires that the figure of 730,000 tonnes arises from a conflation of disposable nappies together with all other household sanitary wastes (sticking plasters, dressings and tampons, for example) and that, in reality, disposable nappies contribute only around half of this total.

Argument and evidence, then, are not always as strictly separated as they ought to be and to understand why this might be the case it is necessary to grasp why the contemporary 'waste crisis' is represented in terms of a moral critique of consumerism. A classic example of this contemporary critical fusion is Richard Girling's *Rubbish!* Writing under the auspices of the Eden Project, Girling lambasts the callousness of contemporary post-consumer discards even whilst attempting a more subtle and politically conscious critique of the apparently ever-looming waste 'crisis' (Girling, 2005: 177). He nonetheless gets caught up in the demonisation of contemporary wastefulness and its planetary consequences. While he drinks Pinot

Noir and Sauvignon Blanc in a Norfolk farmhouse, it occurs to him that government should 'lead by example' and 'do all the obvious things' — like recycling and conservation (ibid.: 355, 389). 'Ranting' (ibid.: 388) he may be but the moral lesson is clear enough and has been declaimed by many an author with an avowed interest in waste. For Girling and Tammemagi, and Gandy before them, post-consumption waste is the democratic hazard par excellence. It is an expression not of the sectional production of environmental problems by groups with vested interests but of contemporary industrial society's *collectively shared* failure to manage its relationships with the natural environment. It arises through each individual's separate activities — in buying too many things, discarding too many things, carelessly ignoring the mounting evidence of the hazardous impacts of those discards — and affects both widely dispersed communities around the globe and natural environments. Thus, Tammemagi suggests, 'we are all to blame' (1999: 17) for the critical impasse represented by post-consumer waste. The consequence of sharing in the blame is that consumers must be persuaded to share in the solution. In particular, the populations of industrialised societies need to be convinced of the need for replacement disposal facilities in order to get rid of the visible signs of their profligacy. The challenge for contemporary waste management, then, consists in finding ways of:

> ... introducing new technologies such as incinerators and underground disposal. Communities need to be persuaded to accept these facilities. Environmental assessments and public hearings will need to be held, and there will be the inevitable NIMBY arguments. (Tammemagi, 1999: 253)

Tammemagi's appeal to invest in new technologies for waste disposal is heartfelt and well-meant and it is shared by other commentators on contemporary municipal waste problems (see Alexander, 1993: 204–6). It does, however, portray a somewhat idealised understanding of how democracy works. For, even if it is true that 'we' share equally in the blame for growing quantities of municipal waste, there is no sense in which the distribution of disposal technologies is shared in the same way. The democratic question is not *how* to persuade communities (although see below) to accept incinerators but *which* communities will be targeted by the persuaders? Will San Francisco's super-rich, gated communities be persuaded to build municipal-scale incinerators in their midst? Or will the impoverished of America's urban sprawl be the target of the persuaders? Or will regional landfills become the favoured option and upon whose land will these be built? Even if the idea that waste production is democratic were true, it is still the case that *waste management* is not democratic in any meaningful sense of the term. Recent research shows a clear link between 'race,' class and proximity to hazardous waste disposal sites, for example (see Lynch et al, 2001; Pearce & Tombs, 1998; Stretesky & Hogan, 1998). Similarly, although the data are more ambiguous, research has also suggested that there is a link between low income and proximity to hazardous waste generation sites (see Atlas, 2002).

I am also given to wonder how it is that communities are to be 'persuaded' to accept waste disposal facilities. Since consumers have, allegedly, been brought to purchase things they do not need by the marketing firms targeted by Vance Packard in his critique of over-consumption then presumably the most effective way to win over communities to the need for new disposal technologies will be rooted in the same techniques. It is a strange kind of inversion when the critical object of Vance Packard's critique should rear its head in a treatise intended to resolve a situation that the persuaders were said to have caused in the first place. In fact, part of the problem underlying Tammemagi's representation of a better-managed future, replete with sound technological solutions and communities 'persuaded' to face up to their responsibilities, lies in the initial decision to lump together 'consumerism', 'households' and the 'waste crisis.' This triangle of ideas can lead to some serious misunderstandings of contemporary waste since it tends to misrepresent historical levels of waste and disposal and marginalizes the role of production and industry in fuelling the waste stream.

In this chapter I want to assess the merits of the consumerism = waste-crisis thesis by focusing on the available data about household or 'post-consumer' waste in Britain. I will show that, when placed in its appropriate social and economic contexts, the waste generated by contemporary households appears more or less consistent with their historical counterparts, rather than a gross aberration from them or, at least, that the historical evidence does not clearly support the view that post-war households are grossly more profligate than their earlier century forebears. In short, when placed in the appropriate contexts, it is far from clear that the post war period has seen a dramatic increase in the production of post-consumer waste. It is similarly unclear that what increase there has been is fundamentally a consequence of consumerism and the available evidence seems to suggest that gross patterns of behaviour are not particularly more wasteful today than in the past. As surprising and, for some, unsettling as this may seem, the evidence does not support the overall proposition that contemporary consumers are an inherently wasteful bunch compared to their not-so-distant forebears.

In order to develop this analysis I will spend some time looking at the numbers — the quantities of domestic post-consumer waste that are used to validate the current 'crisis' outlook. Then I will provide some historical context for these quantities by comparing them to data about waste generation in England across the twentieth century. For reasons that will become clear I will focus the analysis on household waste generation in general and dustbin waste in particular rather than on total municipal waste quantities.

I will make some comment on the latter but my primary goal is to show that disposing of very large quantities of materials via the household dustbin, or by other means, is not a peculiarly post-war phenomenon.

## CRISIS? WHAT CRISIS?

There are several difficulties in providing an accurate picture of household waste both in the present and in the past. The difficulties arise because different waste surveys use different definitions of what constitutes 'waste' and different classifications of what proportions of the defined wastes are attributable to households. Thus, research into contemporary waste generation carried out by DEFRA (2005) and Murray (1999) reach different conclusions about the precise quantities and contents of household waste.

For example, according to Murray (1999: 52–3), in 1999 total household waste generation in the *United Kingdom* amounted to 20.24 million tonnes from a total 'domestic [i.e., municipal] waste' stream of 27.79 million tonnes. DEFRA (2005), on the other hand, calculated that total household waste generation in *England* for the same year amounted to 24.76 million tonnes out a total 'municipal waste' stream of 27.48 million tonnes. The problem of confusing the geo-political areas to which the statistics refer is common in the research on waste, as we shall see below. In this instance, it is beyond the bounds of possibility that households in non-English regions of the UK produce negative quantities of waste so the explanation for the large differences in these estimates may be that DEFRA and Murray are labelling the same geo-political entity differently (but which label is the correct one?) and that they are including and excluding different materials from their estimates of the 'household' contribution to their respective totals. The latter problem is clearly visible in the ways that wastes are attributed (or not) to household sources. So, for example, Murray says that his starting point is 'the amount of material in the household dustbin' but includes garden waste and recycled glass, metal and paper (which are not found in the dustbin) in the totals. Moreover, Murray painstakingly tries to list the total individual contents found in household wastes (paper, glass, metals, putrescibles, etc.) but does not say what proportions of these are in the dustbin and what proportions are recycled. DEFRA calculates the recycling rates for key materials (paper, glass, metals, putrescibles, etc.) but does not say what proportions of these materials are found in dustbins. Nonetheless, it is clear that both DEFRA and Murray include materials that are recycled in their definition of 'waste' even though these materials are not in fact 'wasted'. Another issue is that DEFRA includes street litter in its category 'household waste' whilst Murray excludes it and places it in the overall category 'domestic waste.' As a consequence, each study draws different conclusions about household waste contents in England (or the UK — depending on which geographical label is accepted).

Comparing studies of this kind side-by-side reveals some of the problems of accurately representing the overall situation with regard to contemporary household waste. Apart from providing general sketches of total quantities the research tends to confuse as much as clarify that overall situation. Detailed studies of what dustbins allegedly contain do not, on the whole, improve the quality of the sketch but simply add further confusions. For example, in the same year as Murray's study of household waste generation in the UK, Hampshire County Council established 'Project Integra' — an information resource programme on Hampshire's waste. Based on a regional study of that waste the project produced an information pack including an analysis headed 'What's in your dustbin each week?' In spite of referring specifically to the 'dustbin' the data in fact cover 'kerbside collected waste, recyclables and residuals.' In other words, the definition of 'waste,' as in DEFRA and Murray, includes materials that are not wasted. Whilst Project Integra and Murray have this definitional oddity in common the studies differ markedly in their estimates of some important contents of household waste. Thus, for Murray, each UK household generates, on average, 28kg of metals per annum — which is 3.4% of total household waste. On the other hand, Hampshire's households, according to Project Integra, generate 42.43kg of metals per annum — or 5.1% of total household waste. Similarly problematic, on average, UK households, according to Murray, generate some 70.5Kg of glass per annum — which is 8.6% of total household waste — whilst Hampshire households, according to Project Integra, generate only 34.9kg of glass per annum — or 4.2% of total household waste. Obviously, there are socio-economic, seasonal and other influences on quantities of specific items found in municipal waste streams in different regions at different times but these variations in the calculated quantities of glass and metal are so gross as to suggest that no amount of regional variation will flatten them out. They arise, basically, because the studies counted waste contents differently and used different weighting scales to arrive at their estimates of household waste composition.

In these ways, amongst others, studies of household waste paint highly confusing portraits of the contemporary waste situation and such confusions are germane to the whole business of counting waste. The only things that different studies usually agree on is that households, on average, dispose of between 15.5 and 16kg of 'waste' each week. Yet, even here, there is a tendency to conflate too many different kinds of materials — recycled glass and metal, etc., household jumble, compostible garden matter, and so on — under the inappropriate catch-all category 'waste.' There is also the problem of what '15.5/16kg' of waste means in relation to the alleged waste crisis. Do these numbers represent substantial growth in quantities of waste? If so, what is the baseline for comparison? What quantities of wastes did householders discard in the past and in what sense do contemporary quantities signal *critical* increases? DEFRA's data start in 1996/7, and neither Murray nor DEFRA provide historical comparisons. How, then, can we tell whether contemporary households waste more than in the past?

Official data seem to suggest, and are regularly taken to imply, that household waste generation is growing at an unsustainable rate. Indeed, according to DEFRA (2005) between 1996/7 and 2002/3 total municipal waste (including non-household sources) appeared to increase from 24.59 million tonnes to 29.31 million tonnes. Total household waste generation appeared to increase from 22.55 million tonnes to 25.82 million tonnes although, as I will explain later, this household fraction of the total is not as straightforward as it appears. No explanation is offered for this enormous increase and DEFRA does not provide any commentary on how it has been possible for householders to process close to 3.3 million *extra tonnes* of waste in just six years. Using Murray's calculation of the total number of households (24.6 million) this increase represents an extra 134kg per household per annum or about 5.7lbs per week. From where have householders gained the capacity to consume enough extra goods to generate approaching 6lbs more waste every week? Whatever the numbers appear to show there is something mysterious about this incredible rate of growth and I want to investigate whether the statistics really do paint a picture of relentlessly and rapidly rising profligacy.

The temptation to view with alarm the apparent increase in household waste is understandable but the alarm needs to be tempered with a realistic assessment of what lies behind it. There are several possible explanations for the apparent growth rate, only one of which demonises consumers and their throwaway mentality. The simplest explanation for increased amounts of household waste may be that there has been an increase in the population during the period. In this case, if the rate of growth of the population equalled the rate of growth of household waste there would be no per capita increase in the total discards. Rather, the increased amount of waste would reflect nothing more than an increased number of people disposing of unwanted items. It is true that England's population increased between 1997 and 2003 but by only 3.5% — approximately from 48.2 millions to 49.9 millions. The rate of growth of the population has been slower than the alleged rate of growth of household waste. Even so, however, it is still the case that a proportion of latter's increase derives from a larger population rather than an increase in consumer profligacy.

A second explanation might be that people have become relatively wealthier across the period — either through absolute gains in monetary income or through relative declines in prices. In both cases, increasing amounts of waste might reflect increasing quantities of goods being brought into the house as a consequence of increasing personal wealth. According to the Family Expenditure Survey (2003), average incomes rose by 17% between 1997–78 and 2002–03 with the largest gains being made by lower income groups. However, whilst monetary incomes rose, the evidence on increasing personal wealth is more ambiguous. Certainly, in spite of the gains made at the lower income levels, the inequality gap continued to widen over the same period. Similarly, inflation has eaten away at the real value of the incomes and the rising costs of key items of household expenditure (such as fuel and housing) have had unequal impacts on lower and middle income groups. Whilst there have been some gains in income, on average these have been too small to account for the alleged growth in quantities of municipal waste. The apparent increases in that waste cannot be attributed to wealthier consumers acquiring and disposing of more goods.

A third explanation might be that there has been no change in population, no significant increase in wealth but changes in disposal practices. In this case, without any increased material 'inputs,' households have consumed proportionally less and less, and discarded more and more, of those materials. If this could be confirmed it would indeed demonstrate that the throwaway mentality really had taken hold and in turn would support the moral critique of the effects of consumerism. However, there is not a single shred of evidence to support a claim that contemporary consumers have taken to discarding greater proportions of what they buy.

Although I have been discussing apparent trends in household waste generation, an important caveat needs to be entered into the analysis. The caveat, as I noted above in relation to different waste surveys, is that the statistics include wastes that do not originate in households and materials that are not actually wasted. The bulk of the increase in household waste is accounted for by increases in recycling activity. During the six-year period for which data are presented waste collected via household dustbins — that is, unseparated, unsorted detritus headed for landfill, incineration or other end-of-life management — appeared to increase by around 6%. The quantity of materials collected at civic amenity sites fell fractionally. Rates of household recycling almost doubled and rates of non-household recycling increased by around 1200% — from 68,000kg in 1996/7 to 835,000kg in 2002/3. Other 'household' (including litter) and non-household sources increased by around 35% but from relatively low bases and DEFRA does not explain these increases or from what sources they are derived. According to DEFRA, then, in six years the amount of rubbish that voracious consumers discarded via the dustbin grew by 6% (remember that the population grew by 3.5%) whilst these same wantonly profligate wastrels managed to double their recycling rates.

It could be argued, of course, that increases in dustbin weights combined with increases in recycling demonstrate that householders are processing more and more materials over time and, thereby, provide proof of the ever-expanding impact of consumerism on the amount of waste produced. Oddly, however, after six years of continuous increases in quantities of household waste, DEFRA's preliminary analysis of the 2003–4 municipal waste data suggests that the increase has stopped and even reversed slightly.

Again, there is no comment on why this is the case. What happened in 2003 that reversed a seemingly inexorable trend in household waste generation? England's population continued to grow, gains in income continued to follow the same pattern as previous years, the price of the bulk items in the household waste stream did not rise dramatically.

If there is a 'crisis' of waste in contemporary society an important part of it is a crisis of information about waste and a crisis of inference about wasteful, profligate and lazy consumers who need to be persuaded to sign up to blaming themselves for something that the evidence suggests they may not be doing. The basic data do not provide a solid enough foundation on which to draw conclusions about peculiarly wasteful consumption-driven households. Yet, problems with the evidence do not seem to prevent people from asserting, as does Project Integra, that 'the amount of waste we throw away keeps increasing' or, as does Murray, that since the introduction of the landfill tax in 1996, fly-tipping has become a 'growing problem' (Murray, 1999· 167). In fact, since data on fly-tipping activity before the introduction of the landfill tax is virtually non-existent and since greater commitment to and sophistication in reporting fly-tipping has developed since 1996 it is moot whether there has been an increase in the activity rather than an increase in its bureaucratic visibility. Like the yearly disputes between politicians over the latest crime statistics, apparent increases and decreases in the amounts of waste generated are very dependent on how the waste is counted and to whom it is attributed. These kinds of problems with evidence relating to waste are amplified when contemporary data are compared to data on past practices. But comparisons have to be made in order to say anything sensible about post-consumer waste in present-day society.

## DISPOSABLE HISTORY

As well as the problems of classification and counting that I have mentioned above there is another major difficulty in providing an accurate picture of the post-consumer waste situation over time. That difficulty arises because there is no accepted base-line evidence on historical changes either in rates of household waste disposal or in the ratios of the various discarded materials. What evidence does exist, like data on contemporary waste disposal, is compromised by the use of different classification systems and by attention to different substances found in domestic dustbins. The differences reflect changing understandings of what the waste problem comprises as much as changes in the quantities and kinds of materials that have found their way into dustbins over time. Historical estimates of household waste arisings diverge in their classification systems as much as they differ from contemporary systems. In relation to changing understandings of the character of the waste problem, the available research pays attention to different dustbin contents over time. I will explore this in more detail below, but a useful illustration of the problem is provided by Talbot (1919) who presented research on dustbin contents that included the category 'shells (oyster, etc.)' and the catch-all category 'vegetable matter.' Skitt (1972), on the other hand, presenting data on dustbin contents for 1935, excluded the category 'shells' and produced a composite category of 'vegetable and putrescible' matter. Over time this latter has been given a further nuance by referring to 'garden waste' as well as 'kitchen waste'. Talbot included 'bones,' as does Murray, whilst Flintoff and Millard (1969) and DEFRA have no such category and none of these more recent studies includes 'shells.' The differences in classification — and the emergence of the category 'garden waste' — are worthy of some comment since they indicate important social changes in the contexts of household waste generation and municipal waste management as well as intellectual shifts in grasping the implications of those processes.

As I noted above, recent government statistics (DEFRA, 2003) on municipal waste indicate that a little under 29 million tonnes of municipal rubbish was collected in England in 2000–2001. Of this, almost 3 million tonnes was non-household waste, almost 4.5 million tonnes was collected via civic amenity sites and 2.8 million tonnes was generated by household recycling schemes. In fact, the total waste collected via the dustbin was only 16.8 million tonnes. This figure represents a very small fraction (about 3.5%) of the total (industrial, commercial, agricultural, etc.) annual waste arisings in the UK. DEFRA calculates that, via the dustbin, in 2001 each English household disposed of 15.5 kilograms of rubbish each week. This is equivalent to just over 2.2 kilograms or 4.4 pounds per household per day. If the total English dustbin waste for 2001 is divided by the population of England at 2001 (a little over 49 millions), it transpires that waste-generation per person is 749.6 pounds per annum or approximately 2.05 pounds per day. It is highly instructive to compare this with the figures provided by the National Salvage Council (NSC) for 1918–19 (quoted in Talbot, 1919: 143–4). The NSC's conservative estimate was that, for the year following the end of the Great War, household waste arisings stood at 9.45 million tons. According to Talbot's calculations, this produces a figure of around 1.68 pounds of waste disposed of via the dustbin per *person* per day, or 613 pounds per annum for every person in Britain. In fact, if the total weight is divided by the population of Britain as recorded by the census of 1921 (which stood just under 43 millions) the waste generated per person would be 1.35 pounds per day or 494 pounds per annum. The apparent discrepancy in Talbot's use of the NSC data, like the discrepancies between DEFRA and Murray above, may arise from the fact that although he claims to be analysing the British situation the figures he uses most likely refer to England only. In fact, 613 lbs multiplied by the population of England in 1921 (a little over 34 millions) does indeed correspond approximately to the total of 9.45 million tons.

The population question needs a little further exploration because the population that forms the basis of the calculations has increased by more than a third in the period between 1921 and 2001 (Hicks & Allen, 1999). If the population of England at the end of the Great War were the same as it is today, the conservative estimate of waste arisings collected via the dustbin would have stood at around 13.4 million tons per annum.[1] If we take these figures at face value, and comparing dustbin wastes only, the conclusion must be that between 1919 and 2002 total household waste arisings by weight might have increased by around 20% — although, as we shall see, there are yet more caveats to be entered into the picture.

In fact, by weight, the amount of waste disposed of by households fell consistently across the middle part of the twentieth century, only returning to early-century levels in the 1970s. The UK Department of the Environment (1971) observed that the weight (and density) of household refuse fell from an average of 17Kg (290 kg/m3) per week in 1935 to 13.2Kg (157 kg/m3) per week in 1968 (Department of the Environment, 1971; Flintoff and Millard, 1969). Obviously, there have been several social changes in the intervening period — such as the smaller number of occupants per household — but these national average figures for household waste disposal, like Talbot's calculations of per capita waste disposal, are not markedly dissimilar to the present time. It is tempting to suggest that the weight of household waste fell because of the diminishing proportion of ash and cinder to be found in it. Indeed, this explanation is proffered by the DoE (1971) in the following terms:

> Much of the reduction in weight of refuse has been due to the decline in the domestic consumption of coal and manufactured solid fuel which reduced from 37.5 million tons to 25.5 million tons in the ten years prior to 1967, with a consequent reduction in ash content.

However, the data about the relationships between ash content and weight are contradictory. Skitt (1972: 19) compared waste from households in smoke control areas with waste from households in 'open fires' areas and noted that, in spite of the fact that 'open fires' household waste had more than double the ash and cinder content of the smoke control households, the overall weight of the waste differed by only half a pound. Flintoff and Millard (1972), on the other hand, concluded that the weight of waste produced by households in smoke control areas was almost 25% heavier than the waste produced by 'normal properties' even though the two kinds of households generated roughly the same amount of ash and cinder content. The waste generated from centrally-heated multi-storey flats, on the other hand, was less than two thirds the weight of that produced in the smoke control area. These comparisons of the waste generated in different types of household are interesting in other ways and I return to them below but the point of introducing these data here is to note that whilst ash and cinders did have some impact on the weight of domestic refuse it is far from clear precisely what that impact was.

Some might argue that straight comparisons in terms of weight distort the picture because households in the post-Great War period appeared to dispose of a smaller variety of items overall and the bulk items that they discarded had little value. Whereas today's households, the argument might run, regularly dump useful resources, or items they have over-purchased and cannot use, did not our great grandparents discard only what was finally, utterly useless? After all, according to the NSC, the contents of the household dustbin at the end of the Great War consisted mostly of ash and cinders. In fact, these two constituents accounted for over 90% of the dustbin's contents — the remainder comprising fractional quantities of metal, glass, rags, bones and miscellaneous items (see Table 4.1). Thus, a simple glance at these numbers appears to support the conclusion that, in the aftermath of the Great War, households were indeed thrifty units that discarded virtually nothing other than the dust and cinder of the domestic hearth. What were householders supposed to do with the ash and cinder that accounted for some 90% of their discards? Even if the weight of their dustbin discards was not that much less than our own, the more important indicator, surely, appears to lie in the contents. A study of those contents initially appears to reveal the truth of the proposition that our great grandparents stewarded, cared for, or used up as much as they possibly could before discarding the last, valueless traces of useless rubbish.

However, things are not as straightforward and obvious as they might appear from a cursory glance at the NSC's estimates of the contents of post-Great War dustbins. There are reasons why the dustbins contained these particular materials and, as we have seen in Chapter 3, there were some highly critical voices being raised at the wanton profligacy of householders in discarding or destroying them. On the latter issue, although the complaints were diverse in their tone and targets there was a particular concern over the (mis)use of the domestic fire as a household waste incin-

*Table 4.1* Contents of Dustbin (Talbot, 1919).

| Material | Percentage by weight |
|---|---|
| Fine Dust | 50.98 |
| Cinders | 39.63 |
| Bricks, pots, shales, etc. | 5.35 |
| Tins | 0.98 |
| Rags | 0.40 |
| Glass | 0.61 |
| Bones | 0.05 |
| Vegetable matter | 0.72 |
| Scrap iron | 0.06 |
| Shells (oyster, etc.) | 0.08 |
| Paper | 0.62 |

erator (see also below) and a complaint about the 'waste' of the dust and cinders that householders discarded. The cinders, for example, retained a high calorific value and, instead of unceremoniously dumping them on the rubbish tips, they were candidates for recovery and re-use — either in fuelling domestic fires or in fuelling central power-generation plants or, indeed, in any business that used solid fuel for heating or production purposes. In this way, effective use of the cinder content would substitute for new coal extraction. 'The total conservation of this fraction of refuse,' claims Wylie (1955: 87), 'would be the equivalent of rather more than two million tons of coal.' Moreover, the ash was seen as a good basis for producing fertiliser that could be applied to cropland — by combining it with sewage sludge or other wet fertiliser compounds — and, thereby, act as a substitute for imported guano or dug-up peat, for example. Additionally, both the cinder and the ash could be made into construction materials — especially, but not exclusively, in road-building — and thereby substitute for newly quarried materials. The bulk of the ash and cinder content of the dustbin, far from representing the final and utterly useless remnants of thrifty household stewardship, were construed by some as valuable resources that householders and municipal authorities callously and selfishly 'wasted.'

A related set of issues arises when considering what the remaining contents of the post-Great War dustbin comprised and the set falls into a number of different subgroups. Like the ash and cinder 'waste,' an analysis of these contents does not automatically demonstrate that early century households were less wasteful than present day households. It is notable that Talbot does not say why early-century dustbins contained the materials that they did, or what these materials revealed about household rates of wastage. The first impression gained might be that such fractional quantities of discarded vegetable matter (0.72% of the total), for example, indicate clearly that those households only very reluctantly discarded this material. However, there are several reasons why such an impression cannot be validated. The first problem is that whilst the quantity of vegetable matter as a proportion of dustbin contents is provided the most crucial datum — the ratio of vegetable matter productively used to vegetable matter discarded — is not. If we take the NSC's figure of 613 lbs of waste generated per person per annum and apply to it the ratio of vegetable matter found in the dustbin it emerges that each person would have been disposing of 4.6lbs of vegetable matter every year or 0.09lbs per week. At that rate, a family of five would be throwing less than ½ lb of vegetable matter per week into the dustbin. But this number says nothing about how wasteful that family is. If the family brought, say, 50lbs of vegetable matter into the house weekly, then ½ lb does appear to represent a very low wastage rate. On the other hand, if the family brought only 1lb of vegetable matter into the household weekly, then ½ lb represents a significant amount of wastage. Since we do not know what the ratio of input to output is, then we cannot draw conclusions about

Table 4.2 Average Representative Samples of House Refuse from Towns in Britain for the Year 1935 (DoE, 1971: 23)

| Material | Percent | Weight (lb) |
|---|---|---|
| Fine dust & small cinder — 1/2 in AND cinder – + 1/2 in — 13/4 in | 56.98 | 21.4 |
| Vegetable & putrescible | 13.71 | 5.1 |
| Paper | 14.29 | 5.4 |
| Metal (ferrous & non-ferrous) | 4.00 | 1.5 |
| Rag (including bagging & all textiles) | 1.89 | 0.7 |
| Glassware (bottles, jars & cullet | 3.36 | 1.2 |
| Unclassified debris (combustible & incombustible) | 5.77 | 2.2 |
| | 100 | 37.5 |

whether early century households were more or less profligate than our own in their dealings with vegetable matter.

Another subgroup of questions arises if we ask whether the dustbin was the only means of disposing of unwanted quantities of matter. The question is thrown into sharp relief if the NSC's figures for 1919 are compared with figures provided by the Department of the Environment for 1935 (see Table 4.2).

There are several remarkable things about the data for 1935. They include the changed proportion of ash and cinder — down from 90.61% to 56.98% in just sixteen years — and the relatively large proportion of glass (compare the 1935 ratio of 3.36% with Project Integra's calculation of 4.1% for 1999). Of particular interest, given the preceding discussion, is the enormous increase in the proportion of vegetable and putrescible matter — from 0.72% to 13.71% of the dustbin's contents. Obviously, not all of this is attributable to the extra vegetable matter itself. Some of the proportionate increase is a consequence of the changing overall contents, in particular the reduction in ash and cinder content. However, the DoE data indicate that the total weight, as well as the ratio, of vegetable matter in the dustbin had grown very rapidly since the end of the Great War. The first reaction to the stark contrast between the amount of vegetable waste in dustbins in 1919 and the amount found in 1935 might be to reason that either a) households in 1919 consumed much smaller quantities of vegetable matter or b) that they were much less wasteful of what vegetable matter they did consume. In other words, it may be taken as evidence of the growing profligacy of householders under early impact of a nascent consumer culture.

However, there is something puzzling about Talbot's initial claim about the quantity of discarded vegetable matter. Given the glaring difference between the 1919 weight (less than half a pound for a family of five) and the 1935 weight provided by the DoE (an average of 5.1 lbs), it must be asked what it is that the NSC's and the DoE's data represent. Do they represent the total quantities of vegetable matter disposed of by households or only the quantities disposed of via the dustbin? If the former then, at least in respect of the waste of vegetable matter, the period following the Great War might be characterised as the most rapidly developing throwaway society imaginable (in the region of a 1000% increase in this waste in just sixteen years), putting contemporary consumers in the shade when it comes to rates of profligacy. Alternatively, they may represent the fact that the British diet had improved hugely and the amount of vegetable waste in the dustbin reflected nothing more sinister than a better-provisioned population who were not proportionately more wasteful than their 1919 counterparts. Alternatively again, the separate collection of vegetable matter by Local Authorities and independent traders diminished in the period following the Great War and, in consequence, increased amounts of vegetable matter in the dustbin may have reflected changing waste management practices rather than changing household wastefulness.

An illustration of the importance of this latter issue is provided by Soper (1909: 72). Referring to London only, he observes that, in the year 1905, 51,572 loads of house and trade refuse were collected and '31,915 loads of street sweepings and slop.' In other words 'street sweepings and slop' that were not thrown in the dustbin were equivalent to almost 62% by weight of the total house and trade refuse collected annually. Soper does not define specifically what is meant by 'slop' in this context but, in an earlier section discussing common terms for rubbish in the United States, he says that 'garbage, swill and slop' all denote kitchen waste (ibid.: 31). Assuming consistency of definition, Soper provides a plausible reason for the absence of vegetable matter in the 1919 dustbin: it is not that householders discarded very little of it but that they disposed of it by means other than placing it therein.

Soper's observation about sweepings and slop alerts us to another dimension of early century household waste generation. Extrapolating from his (1905) figures for London, if the NSC's national calculations for 1918–19 had included street sweepings and slop then it might be suggested that the total amount of what is now termed 'household' waste collected would have been in the region of 15.3 million tons; and if the population were the same as that used to estimate contemporary waste generation then total annual household waste arisings for 1918–19 would have been around 20.4 million tons. It is true that these calculations of weight may not represent an accurate picture since Soper does not indicate the relative weight of street sweepings and slop compared to house and trade refuse — but this only reinforces the need to ensure that equivalent data are used when comparing waste generation in the past and in the present, especially if claims are made about a consumption-driven, post-war waste 'crisis.'

All of the studies referring to early- to mid-century household waste note high proportions of dust and cinder in the dustbin. It is tempting to think of this material as merely the remains of the solid fuel that provided householders with heat for cooking and comfort but that would be to miss the crucial role of the domestic fire as a waste management technology. As Talbot, Wylie and others had noted, the domestic fire was as important a waste disposal method as the dustbin itself; in general, if it *would* burn it *did* burn. The waste incinerator that was the open fire not only consumed paper, cardboard and wood it also devoured rags and putrescible matter including waste fats. In fact, as Wylie (1955: 87–8) observes, householders had for long been encouraged to burn putrescible materials 'in order to simplify disposal difficulties and reduce collection costs.' Spooner (1918: 259), discussing ways of economising by productively utilising wastes in the household, confirms what Wylie anecdotally acknowledged by providing specific instructions on the matter:

> Rubbish, leaves, potato and apple parings, tea-leaves, orange peelings, paper, cardboard boxes, and animal and vegetable refuse of every kind and description should be burnt in the kitchen grate, and on no account be placed in the dustbin. Burning the rubbish at home will reduce the coal bill and relieve the Borough Council of a great deal of unnecessary expense, amounting to thousands a year, in collecting and destroying the refuse.

It also needs to be remembered that metal dustbins provided another means of incinerating waste in the past whereas the spread of rubberised bins from the 1960s onwards has closed off this important waste disposal option. These comments are significant because the tendency to burn wastes did indeed have a dramatic impact on the contents of the household dustbin, an impact that is sometimes visible in studies of the seasonal variations in the proportions of its assorted constituents. Drawing on data from the City of Edinburgh for the year 1949–50 Wylie notes the huge differences in the amount of food and paper waste found in domestic refuse. During the summer months, those dustbins contained five times more vegetable waste, three times more paper waste and double the amount of bones compared to the winter months. Some of these differences would be explained by variations in diet but more significantly — as the case of paper suggests — they were a consequence of how often the fire was lit and what could be consumed in its flames. No exact figures are available to specify how much the domestic dustbin would have weighed (or what the volume of household waste would have been) if a considerable proportion of its contents had not gone up in smoke but it is clear that household waste incineration had a major impact on those contents. Interestingly, *all* categories of materials that today would be considered candidates for recycling — including glass and metals — were more commonly put in the dustbin in the summer months compared to the winter months. The proportion of what Wylie categorised as 'combustible materials' found in the dustbin — including wood, leather and straw — was over six times greater in summer than in winter. On the other hand, 'incombustible materials,' which Wylie considered to be valueless — mainly stones, bricks and ceramics — were discarded via the dustbin at roughly the same rate across the seasons.

Wylie's concerns about the quantities of materials going up in smoke are partially confirmed by Skitt (1972) who undertook a comparison of dustbin contents in a smoke control area and an open fires area in the late 1960s (see Table 4.3). Just as Wylie had claimed, the more it was possible to burn rubbish on the open fire the more dramatic was the impact on the contents of the household dustbin. In the smoke control area, 23.65% of those contents consisted of vegetable and putrescible matter and a further 23.62% consisted of paper. In the open fires area, on the other hand, only 6.23% of the dustbin's contents comprised vegetable matter and an even smaller proportion (3.91%) comprised paper.

Further corroboration is supplied by Flintoff and Millard (1969: 11) who provide a comparison of domestic refuse from multi-storey, centrally heated flats, households in a smoke control area and 'normal properties' for the year 1965. Their data purport to show that 80% of the refuse from the flats consisted of paper and vegetable matter whilst only 40% of the refuse from 'normal properties' was made up of these two types of material. In Flintoff and Millard's study, 'normal properties' generated around 27 lbs of waste per week and the flats around 20 lbs per week. More importantly, where householders had no access to a fire, the combined weight of the paper and vegetable discards came close to 16 lbs per week, whereas in areas where the open fire was regularly used these constituents accounted for around

*Table 4.3* Comparison of Dustbin Contents in a Smoke Control Area and an Open Fires Area Circa 1969 (from Skitt (1972) p.1 9).

| Dustbin Contents | Smoke Control Area | Open Fires Area |
| --- | --- | --- |
| Fine dust & small cinder (under ½") | 27.61 | 50.61 |
| Cinder content (between ½" & 1 3/4") | 1.82 | 17.25 |
| Vegetable & putrescible | 23.65 | 6.23 |
| Paper content | 23.62 | 3.91 |
| Metals (ferrous & non-ferrous) | 6.51 | 6.03 |
| Rags (inc. bagging & all textiles) | 0.87 | 1.37 |
| Glass (bottles, jars & cullet) | 10.83 | 8.40 |
| Unclassified debris (combustible & incombustible) | 4.27 | 5.41 |
| Plastics | 0.82 | 0.79 |
| Yield per house per week (lb.) | 28 | 28.5 |

only 11 lbs per week. On the other hand, in Skitt's analysis, the difference in the total weight of the household discards is only half a pound. According to Skitt's data, 'open fires' households were discarding less than 3 lbs per week of paper and vegetable matter whilst households in smoke control areas were discarding over 13 lbs per week of the same materials. These various historical snapshots of the contents of household dustbins do not constitute 'proof' of past wastefulness but they do at least suggest that some scepticism needs to be applied to the claim that contemporary consumers are uniquely improvident or that the waste 'crisis' is a consequence of ever increasing discards blighting a throwaway society. It is true that the variety and proportions of discarded materials in the dustbin have changed over time but it is not clear that these changes ought to be laid unproblematically at the door of consumerism. As important have been changes in waste management practices — changes that have encouraged the trend towards sending more and more discards to landfills instead of destroying them at home. The ash content of the domestic dustbin, far from comprising merely the remnants of the solid fuel used for heating and cooking, represents a profligacy in waste management that contemporary critics of the post-war 'throwaway society' have ignored entirely.

Bearing these comments on household incineration in mind, an examination of the trends in domestic waste disposal appears to show that householders have been discarding ever-increasing quantities of materials. Although Table 4.4 and Table 4.5 list somewhat different quantities for dustbin discards, and although the percentage constituents are not identical, they both sketch a similar picture of the trends in the generation of this waste.

Both studies appear to show that there have been steady increases in the amounts of paper, vegetable matter, metals and glass in English dustbins across the twentieth century. What they in fact show, however, is the chang-

*Table 4.4* 'Typical Analysis of Domestic Refuse by Weight' (Flintoff and Millard, 1969: 8).

| Constituent | 1935 % | 1955 % | 1960 % | 1965 % |
|---|---|---|---|---|
| Dust (under 1/2 in) | 39 | 45 | 43 | 24 |
| Cinder ( 1/2 in to 1 1/2 in) | 18 | 8 | 8 | 12 |
| Vegetable and putrescible | 13 | 12 | 12 | 17 |
| Paper & cardboard | 15 | 15 | 16 | 23 |
| Metal | 4 | 6 | 6 | 7 |
| Textiles | 2 | 2 | 3 | 3 |
| Glass | 3 | 6 | 6 | 8 |
| Unclassified Debris | 6 | 6 | 6 | 6 |
| Yield per house per week (lb.) | 38 | 33 | 32 | 27 |

*Table 4.5* 'Average Representative Sampling of Refuse from Various Towns in Britain. Domestic Refuse Only' (Skitt, 1972: 16).*

| Constituent | 1935–6 % | 1963 % | 1967 % | 1969 % |
|---|---|---|---|---|
| Fine dust & small cinder — under 1/2 in | 56.98 | 27.95 | 22.66 | 15.24 |
| Cinder content — 1/2 in to 1 3/4 in | – | 10.88 | 8.29 | 1.98 |
| Vegetable and putrescible | 13.71 | 14.07 | 15.50 | 19.45 |
| Paper content | 14.29 | 23.03 | 29.50 | 38.03 |
| Metal (ferrous and non-ferrous) | 4.00 | 8.02 | 8.00 | |
| Rags (including bagging and all textiles) | 1.89 | 2.61 | 2.10 | 2.28 |
| Glassware (bottles, jars, cullet) | 3.36 | 8.56 | 8.10 | 10.45 |
| Unclassified Debris (combustible & incombustible) | 5.77 | 4.88 | 4.70 | 1.50 |
| Plastics | – | – | 1.15 | 1.36 |
| Average yield per house per week (lb.) | 37.50 | 31 | 28.50 | 28.10 |

* The column for the year 1968 has been removed from Skitt's original table.

ing *proportion*, rather than the changing *amounts*, of the contents of those dustbins. In reality, the only component that witnessed significant weight increases across the middle part of the twentieth century was paper which, according to Skitt, increased from 5.4 lbs per week in 1935 to 10.6 lbs in 1969, although Flintoff and Millard put the figure at a much lower weight of 6.2 lbs in 1965. It is interesting to note that Murray (1999) calculates the weekly weight of paper in the dustbin to be around 8 lbs — or somewhat lower that Skitt's calculations for 1969. The weight of some of the other constituents has risen only very slowly or remained stable over time and, in more recent times, may actually have fallen. For example, according to Flintoff and Millard, in 1960 householders binned around 1.9 lbs of waste metals weekly compared to 1.52 lbs in 1935. Yet, forty years later, according to Murray, households generated only 1.2 lbs of metal waste weekly, a significant proportion of which was recycled (16% of steel cans and up to 33% of aluminium cans. Murray, 1999: 50; 85). In 1969, according to Skitt, households generated a little under 3lbs per week of waste glass compared with 1.26lbs in 1935. In 1999, according to Murray, households generated a little over 3lbs per week of this material with, again, a significant proportion being recycled (30%; ibid.: 85). Returning to the theme of food waste, note that the actual weight of vegetable and putrescible matter in the dustbin barely changed at all across thirty years of a developing consumer culture, being roughly 5 lbs per week in 1935 and roughly 5 lbs per week in 1969. Again, these numbers need to be set alongside Murray's (1999) calculations which put the weekly weight of kitchen waste at around 6.3 lbs at the end of the twentieth century. In terms of metals, glass, food and, to a lesser extent, paper, the suggestion that post-war consumerism has produced a rabidly wasteful culture in which mindless householders callously waste ever-increasing amounts of materials that our grandparents stewarded does not stand up to scrutiny.

But what of all the other refuse and detritus that contemporary house-holds produce? Surely, the hugely increased variety of goods entering the house has had an impact on contemporary dustbins? At least here the proposition has some evidential basis but it is not the case that contempo-rary households generate significantly greater amounts of miscellaneous waste. According to the DoE, Skitt, and Flintoff and Millard, the weight of 'unclassified refuse' in the dustbin in 1935 was a little over 2 lbs per week. In Murray's study, as well as a greater variety of constituents (nappies, plastics, drinks boxes, and so on) the total weight of the 'other refuse' is also larger — at just under 7 lbs weekly. Here, the weight of the discards has certainly increased — by around a factor of three — but from a very low initial base to a not very high final total. More than half a century of a consumer culture, then, has caused households to generate an extra 5 lbs (or less) of miscellaneous household refuse weekly some of which (like engine oil, for example) often does not find its way into the dustbin.

It may be that some readers will dispute an analysis that focuses on the contents of the dustbin, excluding other elements of the municipal waste stream. However, if claims are to be made about a consumer-driven waste crisis, based on comparisons between waste arisings in the past and in the present, then equivalent data must be used. Since the historical data quoted in the literature relate to domestic waste collected via the dustbin it is only proper that contemporary data relate to the same source. There is no value comparing dustbin data from the past with all municipal waste data in the present because they refer to different things. The NSC's data for 1918–19, for example, excludes the millions of tons of horse manure and horse carcasses, litter and street scrap, building and demolition debris collected annually by the municipal authorities or simply dumped wher-ever it was convenient by what we now call 'fly-tippers'. Neither Skitt, nor Flintoff and Millard include non-dustbin waste in their analysis and the DoE (1971), observing the stability in the vegetable content of the dustbin comment, separately, that 'there has been an increase in the quantities of garden refuse collected' — in other words, garden waste was not included in their analysis of household waste. Murray's study, on the other hand, places garden waste within the category of household waste. This 'waste' accounts for fully 18% of the total household waste generated annually — about 326 lbs per household per year. If this material is subtracted from the total, for the purpose of comparing like with like, we find that in 1999

English households disposed of around 1485 lbs of waste per week. In 1969, according to the DoE, households disposed of 1518 lbs per week.

What can be concluded from this brief foray into twentieth century patterns of domestic wastage? On the basis of the available evidence, and comparing like with like, in Britain, at least, the claim that the period following the Second World War has been an anomalously wasteful era is somewhat dubious. It is questionable whether the waste crisis is a feature of profligate post-consumption disposal. It is not proven that contemporary consumers are more wantonly wasteful than our predecessors. It is certainly not true that, on the basis of consumer activity, we can contrast our own 'throwaway society' to our grandparents' age of stewardship, carefulness and frugality. Notwithstanding the longer-term historical trends discussed in previous chapters, the evidence indicates that our grandparents were as likely to discard reusable items as we are. They were as wasteful — *in the social and industrial context of their time* — as we are. Even if, to us, our grandparents and their grandparents before them appeared to be more frugal and careful, gross habits of waste and disposal exhibit continuity, not radical change. Indeed, in line with the general argument being advanced in this book, the evidence on urban domestic waste supports, rather than undermines, the proposition that throwing lots of things away and only partially (although often inventively) managing the throwing away process is an intrinsic element of all kinds of social organisation and is not a peculiarity of our putatively wasteful post-war era.

# 5    Rubbish Relationships

With a sort of faded enthusiasm he would finger this scrap of rubbish
or that — a china bottle-stopper, the painted lid of a broken snuff-
box, a pinchbeck locket containing a strand of some long-dead baby's
hair — never asking that Winston should buy it, merely that he should
admire it. (George Orwell, *1984*)

In Chapter 3, I showed that waste has been, and remains, crucially important to industrial development in the modern world. Not only did it make a
significant contribution to the scientific and industrial revolutions, it plays
a continuing role in technological development — from the high technology of the space programme to the cosmetic surgery industry and the recycling of wastes 'into nutritive human foods'. In Chapter 4, I showed that the
proposition that contemporary society is gripped by a uniquely throwaway
mentality is not supported by any evidence. On the contrary, the evidence
shows that, when placed in the appropriate contexts, contemporary patterns of household waste disposal are not markedly dissimilar to past patterns of household waste disposal. At least in these two cases there is a
hint that the core claim of the throwaway society thesis — that post-war
consumerism has generated a profligate disregard for the material world so
that modern consumers now callously discard what would have been saved
by our not-so distant forebears — fails to grasp the central importance
and complex roles that waste plays in industrial and social organisation.
Neither the numbers nor the evidence of disposal practices add up to the
profligate conclusion.
   I suggest that the general problem with the 'throwaway society' thesis — both in industrial and domestic terms — is that it is too simplistic.
It presents a highly complex and intricately organised social scheme as a
one-dimensional moral problem. It has certainly become embedded in the
popular, as well as academic, imagination and this has deflected attention away from the very many different relationships that people have with
wastes of all descriptions. If callousness, profligacy and wanton disregard
do not describe accurately how modern citizens relate to their waste then
what does? In this chapter I explore some of the different understandings of

and relationships with waste that characterise the consumer society. I will show that there are tensions and contradictions in these differences and, in particular, that how waste is valued and handled in personal, familial and communal contexts is different to how it is valued and handled in institutional and commercial contexts. Waste is pulled in several different directions in contemporary society, it is located at the intersection of different interests, and releases different kinds of values in these contexts and for these interests. I begin with accounts of some of the personal and communal values of waste before presenting an example of how waste is made to release commodity values.

## ADVENTURES IN SCROUNGELAND

In December 2001, Jeff Ferrell, urban ethnographer and cultural criminologist, resigned his tenured professorship at an Arizona University and spent the next eight months supplementing his meagre income by living off the discarded debris of the citizens of Fort Worth, Texas. The resulting account of this immersion in the world of scrounging, trash-picking and dumpster-diving, *Empire of Scrounge* (Ferrell, 2006), is organised as an assemblage of vignettes and personal reflections on the art and technique of second-hand living: retrieving the lost and discarded objects of consumer society and reinvesting them with value, utility and meaning. At the same time, it is also a lamentation on excessive consumption and the cultural and social forces that underpin the (allegedly) wasteful materiality of contemporary urban existence. In this, the book is both a celebration of the scrounger's life and a critique of consumerism. Thus, the moral thrust of Ferrell's critique is inspired by the familiar 'throwaway society' argument and I will make some comment on this moral critique below. On the other hand the ethnography is inspired by the 'appreciative' tradition in (primarily urban) social inquiry in which the purpose is to reveal an outsider or marginal world from the point of view of its members.

In the latter case Ferrell's vignettes are used to record a 'meandering series of scattered situations' that punctuate the urban landscape: an assortment of 'little theatres of the absurd' in which the 'ebb and flow' of discarded goods reveals a 'constellation of values and preferences negotiated quite literally by the give-and-take of the streets'. Like Strasser (1999) before him, Ferrell adopts an intellectual stance equivalent to the urban ragpicker or 'prospector', sorting through the material and symbolic dimensions of trash to expose something of the qualities of individual and collective life in a consumer society. Here, studies in human character and the situational dynamics of scrounging portray a vibrant world of urban reinvention through which the scroungers and street-scavengers survive, but hardly prosper, on the discarded bounty of post-consumption waste (Ferrell, 2006: 14, 32, 34, 45, 167).

In this shopping mall of excessive debris, Ferrell learns the essence of Michael Thompson's thesis when he notes that 'the process by which [discarded objects] and their meaning move about matters more than the objects themselves' and that today's trash can be tomorrow's collectible (ibid.: 98, 100). In Thompson's hands, as we shall see in Chapter 6, the 'delightful consequence' of this insight is that 'in order to study the social control of value, we have to study rubbish' (Thompson, 1979: 10). Ferrell takes the thesis rather more literally — as *actual* as well as *symbolic* movement — and sets off on a set of urban wanderings that generate unexpected, unplanned and unregulated encounters with the denizens of Scroungeland. On these wanderings many seemingly exotic characters and situations are encountered — the guy who 'comes out of the old garage carrying a rifle', the 'weathered, white, middle-aged homeless guy', the 'older white woman, worn down, darkly tanned, wearing a big cowboy hat', the 'beautiful working class woman' in the scrap yard, the 'elderly black man' pushing a 'cart full of bottles', among many others. The encounters, and the fundamental humanity of the scrounger's life, encourage Ferrell to propose a 'philosophy of scrap that I'll refer to as democratic essentialism': a philosophy that contradicts and counteracts the regulation of everyday life that he sees as a hallmark of the 'class war of city capitalism'. As in his earlier work (see Ferrell, 1996; 2002), Ferrell finds on the margins of urban existence those little bits of anarchy and subversion that point to something other than the mundane rhythms of modern existence; something other than doing what the respectables of modern American society get up to in their consumption-driven public and private lives (Ferrell, 2006: 62, 85, 119, 121, 124, 144, 178–9).

As well as salvaging and selling bottles, aluminium cans, cast iron and copper piping, books, clothes, and miscellaneous video and audio recordings, Ferrell recounts how he collected tools, stencils and artwork, children's toys, jewellery, money and furniture, among countless other useful and valuable objects. So rich was the bounty that Ferrell sometimes struggled to make his way through it, a struggle that led him to conclude that the sheer quantity and variety of urban discards expose 'one trash pile and Dumpster at a time, a cornucopia of material culture' that offers 'all the benefits of shopping with none of the bills'. As a consequence of the abundance, the city teems with a rag-tag army of 'prospectors' who 'mine' the trash piles 'for treasures that otherwise would languish in the landfill' (ibid.: 45, 176). But, for Ferrell, life amongst the debris is not only a process of acquisition, it is simultaneously a set of practices of reconstruction or reconstitution. Furthermore, the 'complex alternative economy' of scrounging is not a limited, insignificant endeavour. Instead, it is a 'widespread enterprise of everyday survival' engaged in by homeless and/or impoverished marginal populations and also by the more settled and relatively more affluent citizens of (primarily) urban America. This widespread enterprise generates many different kinds of relationship with the cast-offs of consumer culture

— including everything from 'scrap art' to homes fabricated entirely from scrounged materials destined for the dump.

In between these poles on the conversion continuum persists a vast array of labours through which waste objects and materials are reprocessed, refashioned and reinserted either into the industrial economy or into the domestic arena where they take on another useful life. So, at the same time as describing the second life of retrieved cupboards and filing cabinets, writing materials, photographic equipment, lighting fixtures, tools and time-pieces, Ferrell details the 'little configurations of skill and practice' that are required to work scrounged goods into usable or profitable forms. Here he uses the language of workmanship to convey both the intimacy and the craft that underscore the scrounger's relationships with material waste. Items that are not immediately usable or sellable are subjected to 'skinning and harvesting, stripping and ripping' as the skilled scrounger separates the objects into different gradations of value. Doorknobs are 'skinned' to detach the valuable brass shell from the much less valuable steel or tin interior. Television antennas are 'ripped and clipped' using wire cutters to harvest their extruded aluminium components from their steel mounting plates and bolts. Wire is 'stripped' of its plastic exterior to reveal the shiny, valuable copper by pushing a knife blade along a taut length of cable. Among many other effects, these labours result in an intricate assortment of objects and materials that require organized sorting and storage systems — different receptacles for copper, steel, tin, aluminium, plastic. Different drawers and shelves hold handles, springs, glassware, sockets, valves and so on (see ibid.: 86–7, 114).

For Ferrell, the Empire of Scrounge is an artisanal economy involving an 'organic', 'do-it-yourself' relationship with the scrounged objects. It is as much about the material interaction with those objects as it is about their pecuniary values. In this regard, the labours, skills, tools and even the style of the work environment where they are applied shadows masculine experiences of craft labour in other sectors of the economy. Like the mechanics in Tim Dant's study of 'car care' culture (Dant, 2005), the committed scrounger learns to routinise and sequence his (all of Ferrell's artisan examples are men) labour according to the characteristics of the materials on which he is working. He 'lets materials speak' (Ferrell, 2006: 155) and works within the limitations and opportunities they afford. Although Ferrell only touches upon it in passing, and derives no analytical insight from it, the Empire of Scrounge also comprises a developed network of formal and informal institutions — scrap yards, junk stores, yard sales, charity outlets, glass and bottle recycling centres, among many others — to co-ordinate the flow of scrounged materials around the economy. Every urban environment teems with these waste transfer stations — they are on the high street, in the industrial estates, in school and church buildings, on housing estates. They are, in short, a normal feature of the social arrangement and social processing of material surplus. The Empire of Scrounge, then, is not a precarious social framework but a well-developed arrangement through which what is once cast-off comes to take on new forms, new meanings and new values as it is reworked, reclassified and reappropriated and offers the real promise of turning 'social scrap into some sort of social change' (ibid.: 135).

Leaving aside the highly integrated character of the social framework of scrounge, Ferrell finds in the Empire's rich complexity of characters and behaviours, situations and interpersonal relationships, labours and skills that renegotiate post-consumption waste an immanent critique of consumerism. In spite of acknowledging that the trash-picking and dumpster-diving denizens of Fort Worth are effectively engaged in forms of consumption (shopping, collecting, valuing, trading and exchanging), he still suggests that there is a moral lesson to be plucked from the rubbish. 'Where consumer society spawns waste', he writes, 'the empire of scrounge offers recuperation'. This moral disjuncture bears all the hallmarks of the morality play penned by Sayers (1948) and expanded by Packard (1967) that was discussed in Chapter 3. Here, contemporary consumer society is 'awash in its own waste' because people have been transformed into rapacious desiring machines. The 'culture and economy of consumption,' writes Ferrell, 'promotes not only endless acquisition, but the steady disposal of yesterday's purchases by consumers who, awash in their own impatient insatiability, must make room for tomorrow's next round of consumption'. This 'programmed insatiability ... creates and sustains among its adherents a sort of existential vacancy — a personal void, a material longing promoted by the same corporate advertisers whose products promise its resolution' (Ferrell, 2006: 28, 111, 162, 169).

Ferrell's moral critique of his fellow citizens connects clearly with a large body of critical work on the ravenous appetites of, particularly American, consumers (see, for example, Young, 1991; Durning, 1997; Cooper, 2005). It is a critique that accuses ordinary citizen-consumers of a callous disregard for the material world they inhabit. Whether this disregard is fundamentally a consequence of corporate advertising and persuasion, as argued by Packard (1957; 1967), or of an expanded culture of emulation and conspicuous consumption, as proposed by Veblen (1961), it nonetheless clearly targets the gullibility and/or self-interest of those citizen-consumers. But, as in Ferrell, the wider critique largely ignores what people, in fact, do with their waste and ignores other kinds of relationships in which waste is invariably socially and economically entwined. When viewed through the lens of the Empire of Scrounge 'ordinary' consumers may very well look like ravenous wastrels whose professed concern for the state of the world is contradicted in their pitiless and remorseless disposal of valuable materials. But such a critique only really works if the embedded normality of recycling, refashioning, re-using consumer objects is disregarded or treated as a marginal activity. Recent work on disposal practices and hand-me-down (around) economies suggests that the critique is not as all-encompassing as it seems at first sight and that ordinary citizen-consumers, and not only marginalised scroungers, are central players in the recirculation, revaluation and refashioning of those material objects.

## CAREFUL DISPERSAL

Ferrell portrays the Empire of Scrounge as a peripheral economy populated by marginalized social outcasts or self-styled drop-outs whose motivations for participation range from basic survival needs to a commitment to building alternatives to mass consumerism. In reality, however, the scrounge economy — as the resale, reuse or refashioning of post-consumption objects — is an enormous undertaking, global in its reach and scope and touches the lives of people all over the 'developed' and 'developing' world. Although it is not the purpose of this chapter to expose the grand scale on which this economy operates some sense of its socio-political centrality, rather than peripherality, can be intuited from its extreme variability and transnational organisation: from systematic bartering and auctioneering over the internet — such as the scheme operated by *Profit From Waste International,* based in Sheffield, UK, and the increasingly popular *ebay* service — through high street charity shops, such as *Oxfam*, garage sales and community jumble sales, to specialist, international used clothing industries — such as *General Waste Trading Ltd*, based in St. Louis, Missouri, or the *Humana People-to-People* NGO, currently headquartered in Denmark and Zimbabwe, which came under police investigation in the late 1990s for misappropriation of funds. These latter organisations are the direct descendants of those nineteenth century pioneers — such as the Salvation Army and Goodwill Industries (both of which continue operations in the present day) — that recognised the value of sorting, re-processing and trading useable discards from the municipal waste stream. Referring specifically and only to the world of second hand clothing, Karen Tranberg Hansen details the billions of tonnes and billions of dollars generated by an industry that 'begins in private households and homes' (Tranberg Hansen, 2000: 100). In other words, at least as far as discarded clothing is concerned, the empire of scrounge is deeply embedded in the international economy and is utterly dependent on the *non-callous* disposal of these used materials.

Moreover, where Ferrell's urban wanderings and experiences connected intimately with the social arrangements of traditional masculine labours ('skinning and harvesting, stripping and ripping'), the wider economy and social practice of trading, using and discarding post-consumption goods is much more subtly gendered and built into dense webs of social relationships and personal biographies. Over several years Louise Crewe and Nicky Gregson (see Gregson and Crewe, 2003) have been investigating aspects of 'second hand cultures'. Whilst they have been able to engage with only a fraction of the intricate variety of these cultures — charity shops, car boot sales, retro-traders and jumble sales in particular — they nonetheless paint a richly textured portrait of how practices of second hand consumption are woven into deeper understandings of the values of things and how these values connect with 'the links between people' and with personal constructions of past, present and future selves (Gregson & Crewe, 2003: 142, 143).

Like Ferrell, they observe that trading used objects is rooted in 'different principles of exchange' to those found in 'first hand', mainstream shopping environments (ibid.: 56, 58). In second hand sites both sellers and buyers are brought into negotiations around the utility, transformation, repair and combination of objects that rarely feature as elements of first hand purchase and sale. They also confirm that engaging with these sites involves renegotiating the everyday spaces of city life into 'new geographies of second hand exchange' (ibid.: 33). But, unlike Ferrell, Gregson and Crewe do not propose that such principles and relocations provide models of 'democratic essentialism' that point immanently to alternative or resistant relationships with consumerism. Instead, a more complex interaction between first and second hand consumption emerges in which trading used objects persists alongside and helps to make sense of practices of first hand consumption. Indeed, this recirculation of discarded objects is not an automatic practice of 'recuperation' but an intrinsic element of the process by which objects are acquired, used and moved around second (or third, fourth, fifth, and so on) circuits of value.

Such circuits of value are characterised by traditional gender relations. Noting that shopping has been traditionally, and largely remains, women's work, Gregson and Crewe suggest that second hand acquisition can be defined in terms of 'social reproduction' that makes sense 'when seen in relation to what goes on elsewhere in these women's lives'. The second hand sites act as both a source of household provisioning for which the women are primarily responsible and at the same time as a 'means of redistribution within communities' (ibid.: 87, 96) by redirecting the flow of money spent on those provisions away from the high street towards independent or charitable traders. The objects acquired and what is done with them also signal gender relations in second hand consumption. Whilst men might typically purchase tools or electrical goods that can be repaired, the women in Gregson and Crewe's study recounted finding clothes and other textiles that could be altered, transformed into other uses or repaired, or 'bric-a-brac that needed a bit of care and attention — a bit of repairing and a good scrub and polish up' (ibid.: 61, 162–66). Where Ferrell's artisans strip, rip and skin materials to harvest their values Gregson and Crewe's bricoleurs scrub and polish, sew and repair.

The general point to be derived from this brief description of second hand cultures is that ordinary consumers are far from callous when it comes to discarding objects they no longer need or desire — indeed their lack of callousness is evidenced by a multi-billion dollar global industry devoted to the trade and exchange in used objects, as well as by the dense and intricate worlds of second hand consumption described by Gregson and Crewe. At the same time, it is not only marginalized outcasts and drop-outs who participate in this economy of used values. Instead, the economy thrives on the boundary between first hand, mainstream consumption and second hand, third hand (and so on) circuits of exchange and distribution in which millions of 'ordinary' consumers are engaged. Moreover, practices of disposal themselves — that is those acts that distribute no-longer desired objects around these (and other) circuits — are also far from callous or profligate.

Following on from their study of second hand cultures, Gregson et al (2006) examined such practices of disposal across a twelve-month period in a group of householders in Nottingham. What they found was that whilst these households did indeed discard large numbers of objects, the overwhelming majority of them were not disposed of as 'waste'. Only 29% of the total discarded over the period of the research was placed directly into the waste stream. The remainder was carefully moved into alternative sites where they could take on a second life. In other words, in spite of the popular rhetoric surrounding the 'throwaway society' and the attendant critique of consumerism, Gregson and colleagues found that householders took remarkable care to dispose of objects through conduits where they might be revalued, reused or refashioned. Moreover, these efforts on the part of householders were connected with the intimate relationships that many of the objects signified to their owners. For the objects retained traces of memory, residues of lives lived with and through them — of marriage (or divorce), of children growing up, of key points of change in the life course. In many instances they were not simply 'dead' objects for which their consumerist owners cared nothing. They held a rich repertoire of sedimented meanings that obligated their owners to care for their disposal.

Where objects were perceived to be beyond repair or had simply deteriorated into shabbiness these were often, indeed, discarded straight into the waste stream even though they might still retain some use value to someone. But the reasons for such disposal decisions are rarely callous. Gregson et al (2006: 14) describe the case of a mother who replaced her son's shabby wardrobe precisely because its shabbiness seemed to signal a lack of love and care for her child. Acquiring a new object, and discarding an old one, in this instance, they suggest, amounted to a display of continued love, care and affection rather than profligate disdain for the material world. In other cases, the purchase of new objects that duplicated those already owned was undertaken precisely in order to pass on the old to those perceived to be in need of them. In this case, the acquisition of the new and the disposal of the old amounted to a form of social assistance most often, in the first instance, to friends or relatives (ibid.: 11). Where objects could not be passed on directly to those in need of them they were taken to charity shops, gifted to jumble sales, sometimes sold through newspaper classified advertisements or yard sales or, when moving house, bequeathed to the next tenant or owner who might make use of them. In other words, the bulk of items 'disposed' of were treated with significant care and attention either because they held important meanings for their owners or because they continued to hold use values that could be appreciated by others. Far from expressing a 'throwaway' mentality, the households in Gregson et al's study invested the majority of their discards with sentiment and value and worked hard to avoid their gratuitous wastage.

## COPING WITH JUNK

What Gregson et al's study points to is that the desire to keep objects, to steward them, hold them in trust or reinvigorate their usefulness by channelling them to new users or new sites of revaluation is at least as strong, and possibly stronger, than the 'programmed' urge to dispose of them in endless cycles of renewed consumption. Their research shows that, when paying attention to what people actually do with the material discards of their lives, it is far from clear that ordinary consumers are lost in an existential void or are necessarily consigned to acts of wanton destruction. Instead, there is care, love, sentiment and value attached to the material objects that fill our lives. Of course, it may be countered that such sentimentality can be actualised only in relation to objects that endure or which have forged a lived connection with the circumstances and life transitions of their owners; that the bulk of the remaining discards really do represent the void of consumerism. When speaking of the mundane detritus of everyday life — the packaging, the obsolete technologies, the cheap knick-knacks, the paper, and so on, that are regularly routed into dustbins — surely there is no sentiment or value attached to these surpluses of consumption?

But even here it is not clear that ordinary consumers are in dereliction of their duty to the material world. On the contrary, here too is angst and desire aplenty; here too is a realistic assessment of the place of waste in everyday life. O'Brien (1999a; 1999b) reported very similar constructions of waste to those exhibited by Gregson et al's later respondents but not in relation to furniture, white goods and other bequeathable objects. Instead, the focus of the analysis was on precisely those mundane items that do regularly enter the waste stream directly — the packaging, the plastic containers, the 'junk' of life that is really at the heart of the throwaway society critique and that is used to sound alarm bells about the unsustainability of consumer society. Note Alan Thein Durning's warning, for example, that the sheer quantities of discarded materials represent a peril in themselves. 'The world makes and tosses away at least 200 billion bottles, cans, plastic cartons and paper and plastic cups each year', he writes:

Single-handedly, Tetra-Pak — the largest manufacturer of multilayer paper-foil-and-plastic drink boxes — made 54 billion cartons world-wide in 1989. (Durning, 1997: 72)

This is a truly gigantic quantity of stuff; it is a statistic that appears to offer an immanent threat to civilisation as a whole. But ordinary consumers do not need these kinds of data to develop their own critique of waste. Our understanding of the problems and potentials it represents are intimately bound up with our own experiences and our own strategies for managing the transmission of objects through our lives.

'Look at this bottle', remarked one of the respondents in O'Brien's (1999a) study in the sociology of waste management:

> It's a beautiful thing, really, all these things [*household 'waste' items on a table*], colours. It is designed to look beautiful, attractive to buy it, sell it, what's in it. It's such a shame to throw it away because of my son [*i.e., who will grow up in a world of discarded objects*] and it is a nice package and well presented and when I am throwing it in the bin I feel so guilty about it. (272–73)

Like Gregson et al's (2006) respondents discussing the material objects of their lives, there is here the sense both of appreciation for the object itself and for the contexts in which it exists as a 'waste' item. The seeming senti-mentalism is not merely a fleetingly guilty reaction to the bare fact of dis-posal. It is built into the structured relationships that consumers have with the daily management of material culture. 'Sometimes I cook', continued the same respondent:

> I feel like crying because I keep on throwing this, throwing this. One time I kept them and my house was full of bits and I had to throw them all away. People do not take me serious but it gives me a serious head-ache. (O'Brien, 1999a: 273)

The same plastic bottle that is a waste object, one of the 200 billion con-tainers 'tossed away' annually, is also a nice, beautiful, attractive cultural form; an object that inspires guilt and headaches and induces tears. It exists in a network of related objects (the 'bits') that consumers are required to manage and it carries meaning not only in terms of its own attractive form but also in relation to what can be coped with inside the home and what it implies socially and environmentally, here in relation to a child's future. Thus, the plastic bottle that exists as a callous discard amongst billions of other callous discards is, at the same time, a means of beautification: it is a vehicle for beautifying waste, for appreciating its material forms and mourn-ing the loss of its attractive presentation. But the 'beauty' of the bottle is not its only everyday quality and its existence in networks of dependent objects renders its status in the household ambiguous. It is one of the beautiful bits that regularly pass through households but its passage is, at least partly, a consequence of its displacement by 'junk'. 'I think everybody's got a junk drawer or a junk cupboard', remarked a different respondent:

> I know we have. You think it might come in handy and you put it in the drawer and it gets so full you can't open the drawer. (ibid.)

Far from the reckless dissipation of material objects through their 'wasting', ordinary consumers fill drawers and cupboards with junk for which they seek uses. Even if the imagined use never materialises, in fact, the relationship to those objects remains one of imputed value and utility. The filling of the drawers and cupboards, lofts and cellars, garages, sheds, shelves and under-stair spaces with potentially useable and potentially valuable items means that decisions have to be made about how much stuff householders can store. The sadness and guilt at the discards is driven precisely by the fact that there is neither room to keep them nor any place where they can be converted into useful objects. The storage and management of household junk extends not only to bottles, tins, string, screws, boxes, wallets, old keys, curtain hooks, pictures, ornaments, redundant lamps and other electrical equipment but also to paperwork, music and audio equipment:

> I've got a sort of cupboard which is sort of, which has got my old files and information cupboard and I mean I do move bits of paper around the house from downstairs to upstairs to this cupboard and try and file it and try to keep it organised but I'm aware I'm always doing that and the older I've got, thinking about old things that you don't use, … brought to mind things like videos and I mean this is sort of new technology. I mean we tape things from the telly and say "Oh, must keep those", that set of Victoria Woods, or whatever, . . . I mean we have got loads and loads of videos that some of them we would want to keep and others we don't know what's on them because you haven't looked recently or you haven't got the time to keep finding what's on them. (ibid.: 276)

The respondent here notes a fact of household junk management: that it is perpetual, he is 'always doing it' and even though his household is filled with things he may never want to use or experience again he nonetheless 'must keep' them. So germane to ordinary life is this perpetual junk management relationship felt to be that some express it is a law of junk, a law that parallels Rathje and Murphy's (1992: 25) law of garbage — that garbage 'expands to fill the receptacles that are available to put it in'. In the same way, junk fills the spaces available to store it: 'If you had a big house with four bedrooms' asserted a different respondent, 'you would have a junk house.'

In these reflections junk is a foundation of life, giving meaning, memory and substance to personal, familial and social change. It is a kind of material sediment whose changing constituents provide social (and industrial) markers of personal history. Thus, observed another respondent:

> My son's bedroom . . . always looked reasonable on the surface but underneath there was masses of stuff in drawers and in cubby-holes and masses and masses of stuff and since he has left home it is largely still there because when he left he just left it behind him on the whole and occasionally we think we ought to clear it out, we've thought of it. (O'Brien, 1999a: 274)

'Clearing it out', then, is not at all a disinterested divestment of 'stuff' in order to make room for more 'stuff'. It is a difficult challenge, fraught with emotional dangers and threats, admissions that the *status quo ante* cannot be redeemed. 'My son' has gone and the house will never be the same again but there he still lurks in the cubby-holes and the drawers, in the 'masses and masses' of stuff that persists as a marker of who he was and who he became over time as he grew up. This emphatic bond between people and seemingly useless junk is not only a matter of domestic nostalgia, of memories rooted in the love of children. It can also express a personal longing for fixity and stability, for a meaningful link with past actions and relationships, an attempt as Don DeLillo (1998: 31) puts it, to connect to 'the dusty hum of who you are'. 'You still, if you've enjoyed a book or something on TV or whatever', observes one of O'Brien's (1999a) respondents:

> ... you still do want to keep it. It is a strange thing and even though you probably know you might not do it again, read it or see it again, you still have this desire, you try to resist it sometimes, but ... (ibid.)

Like the beautiful bottle that opened this discussion of the intimate entanglement between consumers and material objects, the junk is neither waste nor not waste, or it is both at the same time. It is simultaneously doubt-inspiring and virtuous all in one go:

> Well you usually think of them [*little bits of junk*] as waste because we don't use them again, it's there and what are you going to do with them? It's not waste. I don't know.

> And, in fact, that's almost a virtue [*keeping junk*] if you are interested in the environment, isn't it? ... Once you realise you should be trying to reuse a lot of things [a vice] becomes a virtue. (ibid.: 273)

Junk, thus, refers to things that belong, at least in part, 'in a spiritual category', claims another respondent, 'I wouldn't want to throw them, I wouldn't regard them as waste, they may not be useful on a day to day basis but I want them around me in my life'. In utter contrast to the core of the throwaway society thesis, these consumers exhibit anything but callousness about the material objects that fill their lives. They precisely do not want to 'make room' for the next round of consumption; they do not want to jettison the 'debris' of their lives. On the contrary, they want to keep it, treasure it, refer to it, even if only in acknowledgement that they will probably not 'do it, read it or see it again'. The debris, in fact, is a strange object of desire that is simultaneously valueless and valuable. These wastes of life are 'beautiful', 'spiritual' and 'virtuous' because they are closely linked with personal networks that include 'my son', 'my life' and 'getting older' rather than bare numbers of bottles, boxes and cans. They are located in familial, communal and historic contexts that define the kinds of personal relationships that people have with wastes of many descriptions.

## CREATING COMMODITIES

So far in this chapter I have concentrated on the dispersion of post-consumption objects around interpersonal, familial and communal networks and how, in these networks, the meaning and material status of such objects are translated into an abundance of different forms. These include the sedimentation of personal memories and stories in household junk, the beautification and spiritualization of waste objects, the careful donation or resiting of objects to reinvigorate their utility or value, and the committed craftsmanship applied to transform urban discards into useable and/or exchangeable goods. In each of these cases what people do with the debris of material life exposes intimate personal relationships with the objects themselves or with the materials out of which they are fabricated. Objects that were once commodities, purchased by consumers, used, then stored, discarded or donated take on second, third, fourth, and so on, lives as they are revalued, restored or refashioned. But to construe these objects as 'ex-commodities' whose pecuniary values have been exhausted in acts of consumption and whose redemption is entirely a matter of personal or communal commitment is mistaken. Wastes are, in fact, commodities or, rather, they display something elemental about what commodities are. They do not represent the end of value. Instead, they reveal important processes by which all objects attain the status of 'commodities'. This is because individual consumers, families, and communities are not the only entities that enact a complex series of relationships with the discards of contemporary society. The same is also true of political institutions and commercial organizations. In this case the kinds of relationships established with waste and the translations of its status and meaning are of a very different order. Each of the formal means of managing post-consumption wastes institutionally — recycling, landfill and incineration, primarily — is embedded in an intricate web not of personal, familial or life-course relationships but of institutional relationships. In this final part of the chapter I will explore some of the political and economic processes by which waste is translated not into forms of beauty, virtue or spirituality but into forms of commodity.

A useful way of grasping how putatively valueless economic objects can be transformed into tradable and profitable commodities on a grand scale is provided by Arnan Appadurai's (1986) discussion of 'commodities and the politics of value'. In this essay Appadurai notes that a commodity is a 'thoroughly socialized thing' and proceeds to explore the definitional question: 'in what does its sociality consist' (Appadurai, 1986: 6). Arguing that commodities are 'things with a particular type of social potential' he outlines three interrelated dimensions of an object's commodity status. The first is the object's commodity 'candidacy' — that is, whether it meets the 'standards and criteria (symbolic, classificatory, and moral) that define the exchangeability of things in any particular social and historical context' (ibid.: 14). The second is the object's commodity 'context' — that is, 'the variety of social arenas' that determine a 'regime of value' through which the exchange of the object transpires (ibid.: 15). The third is the object's commodity 'phase' — that is, the temporal and social limits within which 'certain things are seen as moving in and out of a commodity state' (ibid.: 13). For Appadurai, a commodity 'is not one kind of thing rather than another, but one phase in the life of some things' (ibid.: 17). In this case, he treats commodities:

> ... as things in a certain situation, a situation that can characterize many different kinds of thing, at different points in their social lives. This means looking at the commodity potential of all things rather than searching fruitlessly for the magic distinction between commodities and other sorts of things. (ibid.: 13)

In concrete terms, Appadurai's account implies that a commodity cannot simply spring into being of its own accord — commodify itself by its own bootstraps, as it were. Rather, the translation of an object into a commodity depends upon contractual bargains, legal specifications, institutional alliances and political projects rather than interpersonal sentiments and communal commitments. These formal conditions are, effectively, the contexts that enable the commodity value of objects, including 'waste'objects, to be realised. But this also implies that the 'social situation' prescribed by Appadurai actually refers to an incredibly complex array of political and economic negotiations, agreements, conflicts and contradictions. The sociality of the commodity 'waste' stretches out in tangled tentacles across very many different settings and, indeed, exactly what 'thing' is being commodified is fundamentally ambiguous. An important reason for the ambiguity is that waste is neither a 'singular' nor 'homogeneous' commodity — that is, neither one indistinguishable example *from* a class of objects (Appadurai uses the example of a 'perfectly standardized steel bar') nor a unique example *within* a class ('a Manet rather than a Picasso', for example) (ibid.: 16). Instead, it is a 'whole indefinite, disintegrated mass, thrown hither and thither', as Marx said of the lumpen proletariat (see Chapter 7) and its commodification depends precisely on divesting its objective contents of any exemplary or unique character.

O'Brien (1999b) uses the example of the construction of a waste-to-energy plant (hereafter the Plant) in London in the early 1990s to explore some of the processes through which waste is 'contextualised' and 'phased' as a commodity. The Plant, now operational, takes municipal waste from the surrounding London Boroughs, incinerates it and uses the heat generated to drive turbines that contribute a small amount of electrical power to the National Grid. The main sponsoring Borough Authority is responsible for supplying the (waste) fuel to drive the turbines, the private company is responsible for reducing the volume of waste by incinerating it. The negotiations and settlements that underpinned the construction of this Plant is a neat illustration of some of Appadurai's main claims.

Like all such major projects, the Plant was required to undertake an Environmental Impact Assessment (EIA) before construction work could begin. An addendum to the EIA included a discussion of its financial feasibility. It opened by proposing that 'It is not for this statement to comment in specific on financial aspects'. There then follows a page of comment on such aspects, including the observation that:

> Landfill is the only alternative for some types of waste, e.g., inert building waste and incinerator ash and the plant will help to preserve the increasingly scare commodity of landfill. (O'Brien, 1999a: 271)

In assessing the plant's financial feasibility, then, it is necessary to take into account the kinds of commodities and services with which it interacts. That is, the commodity context of the plant's operation is a necessary datum in evaluating its viability. Further on, the addendum notes that, as well as being attractive in terms of preserving 'scarce' commodities, the plant will also benefit from the price inflation of other commodities:

> The plant will create energy from waste. Energy as a commodity may rise substantially in price in the medium to long term. (ibid.)

The addendum deals with landfill and energy as commodities, in part, because the thrust of environmental legislation enacted by successive governments has encouraged the privatisation and commodification of waste services both by legislating for the introduction of private waste contractors into Local Authority waste management arrangements (see the Environmental Protection Act, 1990) and by driving up construction and operation costs or, as the addendum points out:

> Suitable landfill sites will become a scarce commodity in the future ...
> as [existing landfill sites] become exhausted, new ones, driven by Legis-
> lative controls, will become increasingly expensive to purchase, license,
> operate and comply with aftercare requirements. (O'Brien, 1996: 94)

In the previous section of this chapter, the waste, junk and discarded
items of material life connected with personal, familial and communal contexts. The 'beautiful' bottle, the 'little bits of junk', the 'masses of stuff'
in a child's bedroom held nostalgic, spiritual and virtuous meanings for
their possessors. In contrast, these same items are here divested of their
intimate individual and collective meanings and are connected to landfill
and energy — that is, to economic contexts in which their pecuniary values might release profits to private enterprise. But it is already apparent
that the context does not consist only in other commodities themselves.
It also comprises a network of institutional relationships designed to situate the exchange and use of these commodities in cognate markets and in
appropriate political structures — in a 'regime of value', in Appadurai's
terms. The practical scaffolding for these situating strategies consists of
legal redefinitions of waste as a specific *kind* of commodity and permissive
political arrangements enabling its exploitation.

In the first case, 'waste' is an attractive kind of commodity because, as
members of the sponsoring Borough's Environmental Services Committee
were informed:

> Electricity privatisation has ushered in a new method of subsidising
> renewable energy projects and waste is considered a renewable fuel. In
> future, such waste to energy projects as [the Plant] would be supported
> by a levy on all electricity users, known as the non-fossil fuel obligation
> [NFFO]. (O'Brien, 1999b: 288–9)

In the second case, the sponsoring Borough is *legally* required to discharge
its waste management functions but *politically* enabled to extract their
operations from certain forms of scrutiny and control. Thus, the sponsoring Borough agreed to a:

> maximum equity investment indicated at 18% i.e. £900,000 in order
> to exclude [the Plant] from local authority company control provisions
> of the Local Government and Housing Act 1989. (ibid.: 289)

It is not my intention, here, to comment on whether these manoeuvres are
good or bad, right or wrong; on whether waste should or should not be
defined as a renewable resource or whether public monies ought to be used
in such a way as to avoid certain provisions of Government Legislation.
Rather, I want to point out that, at least in the case of waste, a 'commodity
relationship' is not primarily a relationship between an individual and an

object, nor between an individual consumer and producer. It is crucially a relationship between political and commercial entities, between different kinds of legislation and authorisation (taxes or levies and privatisation policies, Local Authority controls and energy subsidies, and so on). It is, in short, a complex social negotiation of legal and political, as well as economic, conditions to create or substantiate waste's commodity candidacy — that is, to translate its status into the 'standards and criteria (symbolic, classificatory, and moral) that define the exchangeability of things'.

However, given the vagaries of commodity markets and their potential impacts on Public bodies that get involved in them, the sponsoring Borough involved in the Plant stipulated a condition on its acceptability. The plant would only get the go-ahead if the private business agreed to:

> not expose the authorities to unacceptable risk and offer flexibility/protection from market forces. (O'Brien et al., 1996: 97)

Whilst 'market forces' and commodity chains offer attractive vehicles both for managing waste and releasing its pecuniary values to private enterprise, they also present potentially 'unacceptable' risks and can threaten the integrity and viability of those very bodies charged with responsibility for providing waste services. Hence the Borough agrees to provide the commodity 'waste-fuel' to the private company in exchange for protection from 'the market' during the operational phase of waste-throughput — which comprises a financial life of twenty years in the first instance (with an initial five-year renewal option). Not only is the commodity *candidacy* of the waste-fuel thereby made conditional on market protection, the commodity *phase* is established temporally (the phase lasts for twenty to twenty-five years) at the same time. For up to a quarter of a century, then, the plastic bottles, the little bits of junk and the 'masses of stuff' that contained the sediments of personal meanings and familial histories are transformed, en masse, into exploitable commodities.

Finally, it needs to be noted that just as waste exhibits several different kinds of personal relationships, so it exhibits several different kinds of commodity relationships. For, even *qua* its status as commodity, waste is not one thing — it is not one 'singular' or 'homogeneous' object. In the example I have been discussing here, the commodity phase of waste is divided into three discrete, albeit connected, units. These are construction and operations contracts (private members of the company), sale of electricity (Electrical Supply Industry), and supply of refuse (sponsoring Boroughs). Each of these groups holds different responsibilities for and has different interests in those commodities. The 'commodity' of waste-fuel is not a unique or exemplary object enclosed in a unified social situation. It inhabits, at least, three commodity contexts whose parameters must be aligned in order to enable waste to release its optimum economic values. Waste, here, is an operational commodity, a service commodity and a fuel commodity *because* the enabling contexts upholding its 'regime of value' are legal, political and commercial rather than personal, familial and communal.

Thus, paradoxically, the wastes that underpin the 'throwaway society' thesis, far from representing the end of value or the transition to negative value, exhibit an enormous array of positive values. These are situated in intimate everyday contexts and impersonal commercial and political contexts and it is the contextualisation that determines the specific set of values that waste releases. To transform wastes into objects of personal desire, love for a child, cherished symbols of the life course expresses an intricate set of relationships between people and the material stuff of life. To transform waste into a fuel, an energy commodity or a service commodity is no less intricate even if it is profoundly less intimate. Waste in modern society is not one thing and one thing only. It is many different things in many different contexts. Surely, any social analysis of a 'throwaway society' should *begin* by exposing the multifaceted meanings and values that waste represents rather than reducing these to the moral shibboleth of programmed insatiability and disposability.

# 6   Rubbish Idealisms

Coming up for air! But there isn't any air. The dustbin that we're in reaches up to the stratosphere. (George Orwell, *Coming Up for Air*)

Mary Douglas's *Purity and Danger* is one of the most important books on dirt and pollution ever written. It bears this accolade because for forty years it has held formidable sway over the sociological imagination of unclean things. Its claim, that dirt and pollution are cultural categories rather than physical realities, has inspired some of the finest scholars to dig into the cultural articulation of uncleanness and persuaded some, as we shall see, that what is true for dirt is true also for waste. In fact, the claim that dirt is 'matter out of place' might be said to reflect dimensions of mid-twentieth century understandings of the discarded and degraded in much the same way that Dickens's 'dust' reflected mid-Victorian conceptions. As Rachel Carson and others had portrayed the toxic terrors of misplaced chemicals and industrial detritus, so Douglas's book served as a lesson that all integrated, non-pathological cultures paid careful attention to the perils of pollution. When it was first published in 1966, however, the book received something of an ambivalent reception. Some of the ambivalence arose from perceived misinterpretations in the text, especially in Chapter 3 'The Abominations of Leviticus' — a situation that persuaded Douglas to include an apology and explanation in the preface to the Routledge Classics edition (Douglas, 2002: xiii–xvi). Some of the ambivalence arose because the book appeared 'to be praising structure and control' in the middle of an intellectual and alternative culture that emphasised freedom and love (Douglas, 2002: xvi–xvii). Perhaps some of the ambivalence arose merely because the book was very much a product of its time and as such vulnerable to the vagaries of the intellectual currents in which its thesis floated. Its intellectual heritage in functionalist anthropology, its debt to Durkheim and Mauss and its mission to step beyond Frazer's legacy in the interpretation of primitive ceremonial set the book historically and intellectually in a very particular landscape.

That landscape comprised an (imagined) liberal tolerance towards and acceptance of cultural diversity, resistance to quasi-scientistic rankings of racial characteristics and qualities, an affirmation — driven, importantly, by the realities of a rapidly post-colonialising world — that cultural difference is not evidence of racial inequality. In this regard, the book's line of descent is to be found in the anthropological humanism of Douglas's Oxford mentor, Evans-Pritchard, and in the comparative humanist anthropology of Mead and Benedict. Armed with a Durkheimian notion of social evolution (from primitive/undifferentiated to modern/differentiated), Douglas sought to use comparative anthropology to illuminate the cultural divergence but simultaneously psychic unity of the human species. Its underlying thesis, that each 'primitive culture is a universe to itself' (Douglas, 2002: 4), illustrates the relativistic thrust of much mid-century anthropology and the faith that advanced, industrial society could learn about itself by cataloguing and comparing the array of alternative beliefs, rituals and practices by which other cultures imposed a meaningful order on experience. Mary Douglas's notion of 'dirt' only makes proper sense when this context is taken into account.

There is no better place to begin a consideration of Douglas's conception of dirt than her now widely quoted aphorism that:

> There is no such thing as absolute dirt: it exists in the eye of the beholder. If we shun dirt, it is not because of craven fear, still less dread or holy terror. Nor do our ideas about disease account for the range of our behaviour in cleaning or avoiding dirt. Dirt offends against order. Eliminating it is not a negative movement, but a positive effort to organise the environment. (Douglas 2002: 2)

Dirt, she goes on, is an 'anomaly' that disturbs the certainty and pattern of life. It is culturally ambivalent. It is, at one and the same time, an essential element of cosmology and a disruption to that cosmology. Dirt and its symbols intervene in relations of gender, in ritual statuses and in the beliefs and hopes of a culture. Here, of course, is Douglas's famous paradox. 'Dirt' is matter out of place, it is matter that either is yet to be allotted its cultural and political space in the ordered world of a total culture or intrudes to disturb a culture's ordered totality. Yet, it is the very 'out-placedness' that makes dirt a meaningful cultural category. The very fact that dirt is 'out-placed', that it is wrongly or ill-fittingly located, is precisely what generates its unique and inescapable usefulness and worth. It is what enables a culture to distinguish — in its rules, norms, conventions and rituals — between order and disorder, being and non-being, life and death. Dirt is necessary to keep cultures clean. Whilst dirt, then, is 'matter out of place' pollution is the process of defining what its proper place is and keeping it out of the ordered system of life. For dirt, the 'by-product of a systematic ordering' is also 'that which must not be included if a pattern is to be maintained' (2002: 36, 50). Ergo, dirt is an unintended consequence of creating order that *absolutely must* be rejected lest the order disintegrate into chaos. Whilst there may be no such thing as 'absolute dirt' there is, it transpires, such a thing as absolute rejection.

This thesis is the root from which many and divergent conceptions of dirt and waste have branched out in the intervening forty years. As we shall see, it inspires McLaughlin's (1971) dig into historical filth, Thompson's (1979) statement of a cultural theory of value, van Loon's (2002) essay on the abjection of waste, Scanlan's (2005) encounters with the haunting shadow of modern garbage and Inglis's (2002) exposition of the historical emergence of excretory manners. There are, however, two curiosities about the widespread homage to Douglas's thesis. The first is that, in spite of the extensive use of the term 'dirt' — together with a series of synonyms (including uncleanliness, impurity, contagion) — *Purity and Danger* is not really a book about dirt. It is, instead, a book about the role of marginalia in anthropological interpretation and, specifically, a critique of Durkheimian anthropology's focus on the large-scale rituals, ceremonies and customs of other cultures. The second curiosity is that, in spite of extensive praise for Douglas's contribution, her original thesis on dirt is invariably rejected, restrained or modified by those who seek to apply it to the study of modern filth and waste. Ironically, in this intellectual arena, the very thesis that Douglas pursued, and the lessons she thought the book might teach, have been discarded.


## DIRT? WHAT DIRT?

To begin with the first curiosity, it is important to remember that *Purity and Danger* derives from the discipline of social anthropology. That it is necessary to observe this fact may seem strange — but its anthropological orientation is largely glossed in those works that use it as a launch pad for the study of modern waste. Douglas's starting point, and the core debate she engages, is the problem of defining 'culture'. For Douglas the (then) mainstream anthropological definition of culture concentrated on the large ceremonials — the religious rites, marriage ceremonies, fertility rituals, rites of passage, and so on. In her assessment this approach to culture, and particularly the concentration on religion's large ceremonials as its analytical core, excluded the mundane practices and symbols of everyday life and ignored the meaning-generating function of the small sacraments, the daily rules and rites of making the world a symbolically ordered place. The investigation of everyday rites of symbolic ordering, she declared, revealed the porous quality of sacred and profane cultural categories whilst simultaneously exposing the humdrum routines by which people sustained the tidiness and orderliness of their social systems. These routines involve everything from cleanliness rituals, through memory rituals, to 'ritually contracted death' (Douglas, 2002: 84). Many, but by no means all, of them orbit around ideas of dirt and pollution but all of them certainly converge on the central question of the book: is it possible for any culture to confound sacredness and uncleanliness (ibid.: 196); do pollution, and related, rituals, no less than the worship of gods, express cosmological patterns and perspectives?

In responding to this question, the book says very little about what happens to dirt outside of its symbolic and ritualistic functions. There is mention of how some particular categories of polluting substances, such as menstrual blood, faeces and hair, are imbued with various powers and properties that reflect aspects of primitive social organisation. There are comments and observations on the ordering and boundary-defining role of modern housework (ibid.: 85). Yet the *stuff* of dirt and the material, as opposed to symbolic, places it occupies in the systematic organisation of life, is left unexplored. Instead, Douglas concentrates on an *ideal* of dirt as something that arises from the 'differentiating activity of the mind' (2002: 198). She also offers the theory that it is temporally fixed: dirt exists as dirt only in a *phase* of cognitive activity that separates it out from 'its true indiscriminable character' in the undifferentiated background of a culture's distinctive cosmology. Once dirt has performed its social function of challenging a culture's distinctions and disrupting that cosmology, it then returns to the cognitive formlessness from which it had been plucked by the creativity of the human mind. Its function, in true Durkheimian spirit, is to *unite* and *affirm* that cosmology, not undermine or alter it. Like the Biblical undertones of Dickens's 'dust,' dirt is the medium of both creation and destruction (see Chapter 2). Unlike Dickens's dust, however, dirt is not part of the substance of life. It is, instead, part of its symbolic form: in all but representational terms, dirt is wholly immaterial.

A consequence of the idealist definition is that the book does not pursue inquiries into dirt itself, only into the means and processes of its classification. Asking whether there is such a thing as 'absolute dirt', Douglas replies in the negative — because dealing with dirt is an attempt 'to make unity of experience' (2002: 3, see also 209) and since different cultures seek to unify experience differently there can be no classificatory absolutes of any kind. In this regard, the nature of dirt, its universal and fundamental quality, is not to be found in its physical properties or objective effects. Instead, it lies in its cultural impacts. Dirt is certainly a by-product but it is a by-product of a will to cognitive order that is given particular forms in the separate symbolic universes of unique cultures. Moreover, whilst each culture's definition is determined by the peculiar characteristics of that surrounding symbolic universe, no definition has any greater or lesser purchase on the reality of dirt than any other. If there is no such thing as absolute dirt then, logically, there is no such thing as absolute purity either. Indeed, that which might express a culture's concept of purity is always and irredeemably contaminated or, as Douglas (2002: 220) puts it: 'corruption [is] enshrined in sacred places and sacred times'. In other words, dirt and cleanliness are cosmological cohabitees in the beating heart of a primitive culture's worldview.

Whilst Douglas goes to great lengths to dismiss any 'absolute' concept of dirt the same energy is not expended on whether there is such a thing as absolute danger. The 'danger' of dirt lies not in any pathogenic or virulent qualities — in fact, Douglas is at pains to abstract 'pathogenicity and hygiene' from the concept of dirt altogether — but in its symbolically contradictory and cognitively ambiguous relation to cosmological order. Nor does Douglas enquire into whether there is such a thing as absolute pollution since the book's focus is on the 'acts of atonement' that comprise (ritual) 'pollution behaviour' or 'pollution powers which inhere in the structure of ideas itself' (ibid.: 43, 140, 209). Quite naturally, then, the book does not consider whether toxic spills, radioactive leaks and ozone depletion can be grasped through the same cognitive lens as ritual corruption. It understandably bypasses questions relating to the material qualities of dirt and never broaches the physical existence of waste. An important reason why these questions do not arise is because, as Douglas observes of 'all colonial anthropology,' *Purity and Danger* is an example of 'sociology in a teacup' (ibid.: 138). The boundaries of the book's analytical world and the visible horizons within it are constrained by the empirical particularities of cultures predefined as self-referential and matchless cognitive constructs. Certainly, there are advantages to the confined outlook — it encourages greater clarity of detail and greater definitional precision — but always it requires that 'other' cultures are congealed into unique and isolated symbolic universes. This congealment, after all, is what drives the book's analytical motor and, later, gives rise to the Grid/Group map of cosmological types (Douglas, 1978). The *connections between* cultures and the *material implications* of what cultures do are beyond the rim of the teacup. Dirt, pollution, purity, uncleanliness, danger, corruption: these terms are regularly unpicked but not in order to articulate a sociology of dirt or danger. They are unpicked to demonstrate that 'primitive' cultures really are cognitive totalities — that their symbolic universes apply as much to the margins and 'crevices' of their social structures as to their central, core institutions (Douglas, 2002: 169). The anthropological study of the everyday — such as cleanliness rituals — is thus as important in understanding the sense-making and meaning-giving function of culture as the anthropological study of kinship systems, religion or myth.

All of the delving into dirt, then, is intended to specify both the symbolic unity of primitive culture and what it is that is primitive about it. For Douglas, it is not the beliefs or knowledge-stocks — that is, the cultural contents — of such cultures that are 'primitive.' Nor is it the degree of differentiation within either their social structures or cosmologies. In fact, Douglas rejects Durkheim's particular attempt to correlate undifferentiated ('primitive') and differentiated ('modern') social structures with sets of 'collective representations' embodied in religious beliefs. She rejects the correlation because she is unhappy with the vague generality and moral condescension implied in the idea of 'differentiation.' What could be 'more complex, diversified and elaborate,' she asks, than the primitive cosmologies of Samoa, the Dogon, 'or of Western Pueblo Hopi for that matter'? If differentiation can define the distance between primitive and modern mentalities it can do so, she argues, along only one dimension — that of the differentiation of subjective and objective:

> There is only one criterion of differentiation in thought that is relevant, and that provides the criterion that we can apply equally to different cultures and to the history of our own scientific ideas. That criterion is based on the Kantian principle that thought can only advance by freeing itself from the shackles of its own subjective conditions. (ibid.: 97–8)

In 'our own [advanced] culture', knowledge has progressively freed itself from the 'subjective limitations of the mind' and *this* is what distinguishes our culture 'from others which lack this self-awareness and conscious reaching for objectivity'. The primitive world view, she continues:

> ... is rarely itself an object of contemplation in the primitive culture. It has evolved as the appanage of other social institutions. To this extent it is produced indirectly, and to this extent the primitive culture must be taken to be unaware of itself, unconscious of its own conditions. (ibid.: 113)

In this sense, and in this sense only, 'primitive means undifferentiated, modern means differentiated'. However, even if only along one dimension, 'primitive' and 'modern' cultures are symbolic and cognitive worlds apart. Primitive culture is a cosmological totality, modern culture a hotch-potch of 'different fields of symbolic action' (ibid.: 85). So whilst the patterning and ordering activity involved in dirt avoidance occurs in both primitive and modern cultures, the difference is that in the former the patterning works with 'more total comprehensiveness' whilst in the latter it 'applies to disjointed areas of existence' (ibid.: 50). Thus, whilst it is possible to read or interpret the totality of primitive culture through its mundane rituals of dirt-avoidance and cleansing the same does not hold for modern culture. It may be ethnographically interesting, even taxonomically fascinating, to chart such rituals in the modern world but in the end the disconnectedness and disjointedness of modernity means that dirt management says nothing about modern culture as such — only about the diverse arenas in which uncoordinated cleansing practices are made micro-culturally meaningful.

Once some of the intellectual context of *Purity and Danger's* thesis is filled in, it is no surprise that when Douglas turned her attention to the system of cultural goods in modern society (Douglas and Isherwood, 1979) the mis-located and out-placed dirt that had been so central to that early text disappears from view. In the title and thematic structure of *The World of Goods*, dirt recedes to its pre-1966 anthropological invisibility. The world of goods is a world of desires and needs, of cultural systems and social relations, of wants, investments and wishes. Hence, the reader is urged to set 'the very idea of consumption ... back into the social process, not merely looked upon as a result or objective of work. ... Goods, work and consumption have been artificially abstracted out of the whole social scheme' (Douglas and Isherwood, 1979: 12).

In sharp contrast with the centrality of dirt and pollution in *Purity and Danger*, the 'whole social scheme' enunciated in *The World of Goods* no longer has any dirt in it. Dirt has evaporated from the anthropological framework by which Douglas and Isherwood seek to make sense of the practice of consumption and the circulation of values that accompanies it.

*The World of Goods* opens by asking why people want goods (Chapter 1) why they save (Chapter 2) and the uses of goods (Chapter 3). It goes on to consider, amongst other things, consumption technologies, consumption periodicities and consumption classes. There is no chapter that says why (or how) people make dirt or waste goods, nor how dirt and waste enter and/or exit the social scheme of modern society. The book seeks to reorient social science's understanding of consumption behaviour and to redefine the nature of 'goods' in every field from economics to political science yet strangely omits to acknowledge that dirt, pollution and danger are of as much relevance to a 'modern' system of consumption as to a 'primitive' system of ritual.

The omission is not immaterial. It underpins a specific view of human needs and desires and represents the unspoken counterpoint to what a 'good' *is* and *is not* in a modern consumer society. Douglas and Isherwood write that 'Goods that minister to physical needs — food or drink — are no less carriers of meaning than ballet or poetry. Let us put an end to the widespread and misleading distinction between goods that sustain life and health and others that service the mind and heart — spiritual goods' (1979: 72). This rhetorical flourish appears to make immediate sense: personally, I can relate to the need for food and I grant that some people desire poetry. But what of goods that satisfy neither 'physical' needs nor 'spiritual' needs?

For example, Douglas and Isherwood contrast Brillat-Savarin's and Barthes' discussions of the process of coffee making. Brillat-Savarin, we learn, 'preferred coffee beans pounded by hand in Turkish fashion' in a wooden mortar, whilst Barthes was interested in the poetics of bean-crushing and supplied a semiotics of the powdering process (ibid.: 73–4). Yet, neither Brillat-Savarin nor Barthes, nor beyond them Douglas and Isherwood, indicates what happened to the coffee dregs after the brew had been savoured. None of them ask whether the deep brown sludge that remained in the coffee maker goes on to satisfy any physical or spiritual need. Does this mean that the sludge is not a good? Has the act of drinking coffee transformed what the beans are made of from a 'good' to a 'non-good'? Or has it transformed only a cultural representation of the coffee beans from a visible 'good' to an invisible 'bad'? Has the drinking of the coffeed liquid banished the dregs from the perceptible world of goods? What is the sludge, the sediment that Brillat-Savarin's brew leaves behind it: is it a good or is it dirt? Later in the same chapter the idea of a sediment, a trace, a collection of dregs is introduced but by this stage Douglas and Isherwood have left behind them the empirical reality of coffee making and the brown sludge it produces. Now, sediments have become unsedimented: they have transformed into a coral-like structure of cultural supports:

> The stream of consumable goods leaves a sediment that builds up the structure of culture like coral islands. The sediment is the learned set of names and names of sets, operations to be performed on names, a means of thinking. (75)

Brillat-Savarin's brew, then, leaves two sediments, not one. It leaves a first sediment that is crucial to culture and to meaningful social life and it leaves a second sediment that, it must be inferred, is entirely superfluous and incidental to culture and meaningful social life. Whilst the sediment of the coffee-making ritual supports a 'means of thinking', the sedimented sludge of the coffee-making act is left unthought entirely — a *matter* of marginal significance.

In the very last chapter of *The World of Goods*, there is finally an oblique reference to the second sediment — an ambiguous moral judgment in a political polemic for greater economic and social equality — when Douglas and Isherwood accuse the occupants of 'society's top floor' of

> shortening everyone's time perspective for the sake of their own competitive anxiety, generating waste while at the same time deploring it. (Douglas and Isherwood, 1979: 203)

What does this mean? Are Douglas and Isherwood saying that society's 'bottom floor' do not waste? Or that they waste but do not deplore it? Surely, given the thesis of *Purity and Danger*, no social stratum could be understood as existing without a relation to dirt, pollution, muck, waste? Dirt, it appears, does not cement the margins and crevices of consumer culture in the same way that it serves to unify primitive culture. It simply disappears from the consumer's cosmology whilst all around waste tumbles from the top floor.

There are, it appears, two contradictory theses on 'goods' and 'dirt', both of which have been hugely influential in the study of culture and consumption: (cognitively) dirt is matter out of place and (empirically) ritual sediments nurture cultural growth. It is feasible to maintain this contradictory stand on the empirical and cognitive relationships between dirt and culture only from inside the anthropological teacup. That is, only if the material reality of the sediments of modern culture is ignored entirely. But then this is *precisely* the point of Douglas's idealism: to eject the material qualities of dirt and its alleged dangers from the study of pollution; to reject the notion that modern society's rational, scientific concepts, measures and evaluations have greater purchase on experience and behaviour than primitive, 'undifferentiated' ones. The anthropological study of dirt reveals that there are other ways of cleaning up that are not embedded in the technologically-dependent, military-industrial complex of the modern world. These are just as meaningful, just as logical and, within the totality that is the 'primitive' world-view, more culturally coherent than the fragmented and disjointed practices of our own culture. *This* is the core of *Purity and Danger*: it is a core that has been effectively swept away, tidied out of sight in the periodic but regular endeavour to pluck Douglas's thesis from comparative anthropology and make it speak the language of modern sociology. It is an endeavour that inevitably fails because the very reason that Douglas did not address 'dirt' or 'waste' in relation to contemporary society was because the lessons to be learned from her anthropology were located elsewhere — in *other* cultures. The 'modern' mind, remember, has freed itself from 'the shackles of its own subjective conditions' and thus modern culture has drifted away from the undifferentiated symbolic unity that immanently connects the dirty crevices of a primitive culture to its clean cosmological universe.

## RE-VIEWING DIRT

Douglas's thesis has been taken in many directions since its initial formulation in an attempt to transpose it from comparative anthropology into modern sociology — directions that indicate more about wider changes in social science than about the specific value of the thesis to the study of modern dirt. Some have attempted to set the thesis in terms of a history of dirt and hygiene (McLaughlin, 1971; Strasser, 1999). Others have shifted its ontological foundations from the symbolic universes of primitive cultures to the socio-cultural systems of modern societies (Thompson, 1979). Others again have attempted to situate the cognitivist thrust of Douglas's definition in a post-Deleuzian social philosophy of 'technological culture' (Van Loon, 2002), an Eliasian account of civilizing processes (Inglis, 2002) or a postmodern reading of 'Western culture' as a doubled social form, haunted by the 'uncanny' spectre of its material and symbolic leftovers (Scanlan, 2005). Whichever direction is taken, there is dissatisfaction with the original thesis. Its famous dictum that there is 'no such thing as absolute dirt' has provided an anchor or reference point around which to construct a bewildering array of different arguments, but social scientists have been conspicuously loath to explore in detail why Douglas proposed this to be the case or why she did not apply the thesis to the modern world. Whilst it is common to acknowledge Douglas in the study of modern dirt and waste, it is rare to encounter a text that does not bolt onto her case some other proposition(s) intended to secure its relevance to a world beyond the teacups of separated symbolic universes. The reasons for and foundations of Douglas's thesis on dirt have been largely forgotten as have the lessons it purported to teach.

Thus, even Terence McLaughlin (1971), in his wry assessment of changing cultural sensibilities of dirt, acknowledges that dirt 'can be almost anything that we choose to call dirt' and that 'it has often been defined as "matter out of place."' However, for McLaughlin, dirt is already something other than a symbolic artefact and he calls up a different strand of Douglas's book to affirm this other quality. Here, in a very short passage, Douglas (2002: 47–8) uses Sartre's discussion of sliminess to illustrate the power of classification and the importance of anomalous categories in cultural distinctions. McLaughlin, however, treats the same discussion rather differently. Far from dirt being merely a cognitive by-product of the will to order, a categorical anomaly that affirms a culture's main classifications, McLaughlin proposes that it is '... evidence of the imperfections of life, a constant reminder of change and decay. It is the dark side of all human activities — human, because it is only in our judgment that things are dirty' and because, he continues, in a rewording of Mary Douglas's thesis, 'there is no such material as *absolute* dirt' (1971: 1; emphasis in original).

Notwithstanding the nuance and subtlety of McLaughlin's ensuing text, it is clear that two judgments, not one, are made, here. The first is that dirt is a purely cognitive matter — not material matter at all: dirt is dirt not because of what it is but because of what we do with it and how we relate to it. If people take relief hidden behind the locked doors of the toilet, this is because, elsewhere, excrement is dirt. If dead skin is vacuumed or dusted away from carpets and cupboards, then, in these places, dead skin is dirt. If vegetable peelings, bacon rinds or empty containers are thrown into refuse receptacles this is because these all threaten contamination. On one level, of course, not all of these items are necessarily dirt: human waste can be (and is) used as a fertiliser, feedstock or raw material for the synthesis of drugs, vegetable peelings can be composted, empty containers (at least some of them) can be recycled and need not be feared for their dirtiness at all. On another level, however, for McLaughlin they are clearly and inescapably dirty. The reason for this is that dirt is not just any old 'matter out of place.' Dirt, in the second and more telling judgment, is that matter which indicates life's 'imperfections' and 'decay'. So whilst dirt is simply what we say it is, it nonetheless stands as mute evidence of something else, something elemental about the condition of life: its degeneration and decomposition. On the one hand '...dirt is an entirely relative concept and [...] there is no limit to the strangeness of people's attitudes to it'. On the other hand, '...

every new advance in our technological standard of living seems to provide new waste products to foul our water supply' (ibid.: 5, 163).

Between these opening and closing statements on the nature of dirt McLaughlin paints a richly disgusting portrait of the habits and worldviews embedded in our ancestors' soiled experiences (see Chapter 1). Thus, the seventeenth century 'was a dirty age' in which 'the streets between the fine houses were mud tracks littered with garbage, dung, and offal, and the rivers were open sewers' (1971: 68, 69). Nor was the eighteenth century any cleaner; it improved on its predecessor only in the scale and efficiency of its polluting practices:

> Not only chamber pots were emptied into the streets, although there were enough of these. Offal from butchers' slaughter-houses, waste from tanneries, trimmings from vegetables and meat, fish heads, eel skins, and any food which had decayed too far even for those robust stomachs, all was shot into the kennel, or gutter that ran down the middle of each street. Unless a scavenger found some part of the rubbish useful, it might lie there for days, rotting, until rain came to carry it away, or at least transfer it from one street to another. (1971: 100)

So it goes on. The Victorian era — especially, but not only, in the cities — was a bug-infested, disease-plagued, stinking Hell (1971: 155). Filthy living conditions, polluted water supplies, open sewers and begrimed streets and thoroughfares created a struggle for survival in which, for many, life was indeed nasty, brutish and short. The twentieth century saw the development of all kinds of cleaning agents appealing to 'a very deep human need, the need for decontamination.' Yet, McLaughlin says, like their careless forebears, people paid too little attention 'to the effects of the cleaning products when they went down the sink' (ibid.: 158–9). Multiplied a thousand fold by the pollutants and discharges of industrial processes the twentieth century has remained faithful to a long-standing tradition by continuing to foul its own nest (ibid.: Chapter 12) with substances that really are 'dirty.'

This interweaving of relativism and realism is a theoretical world apart from Douglas's initial formulation of the problem. Gone are Douglas's tolerant idealism and her underlying proposition that are no classificatory absolutes. Gone is the sociological teacup in which the separated symbolic universes of world cultures make their own unique cosmological sense. Gone is the cognitive creativity that plucks dirt from the formless surfaces of a culture's cosmological edges. In their place are sensual and passionate grounds for judging the dirtiness of the world, substantial and real qualities of things that inspire danger, disgust, fear, and discomfort. McLaughlin's particular interest concerns bodily excretions — 'saliva, mucus, excrement, semen, blood, lymph' — and he suggests that we feel 'helplessness' and 'horror' when we encounter these slimy substances. Invoking Sartre's *Being and*

*Nothingness*, he argues that these feelings arise because the slime 'clings to us,' we 'cannot get rid of it,' its stickiness blurs 'the boundary line between ourselves and the slime' and we fear for our own dissolution into its cloying viscosity (McLaughlin, 1971: 2–3). For McLaughlin, then, that which is dirty reeks (literally) of decay: not of the cyclical transitions between formlessness, ritual danger and formlessness again but of the inevitability of the end. Dirt is no longer the behavioural or ritual manifestation of a world view — a symbolic 'crevice' in which a culture's larger cosmology is refracted. For McLaughlin, it is a sticky reminder of mortality and a socially produced menace to health and life.

Where McLaughlin invoked Sartre's existentialism to escape the particular constraints of Douglas's idealism, Michael Thompson (1979) took a very different tack. He opened his eloquent survey of the creation and destruction of value (*Rubbish Theory*) by reminding his readers of an old riddle, viz: what does a rich man keep that a poor man throws away? Answer: snot. The riddle depicts a difference between the 'docker's hankie' which spreads far and wide beneath the poor man's feet and the rich man's silken cloth secreting his private phlegm from public scrutiny. Thompson used this riddle to alert his readers not to the cosmological crevices that interested Douglas, nor to the sensual 'hell' that is (other people's) dirt (McLaughlin, 1971: 6) but to the socio-cultural systems that give meaning *and* substance to rubbish. Muck, garbage, trash, snot, filth or waste are not incidental ephemera either of societies' (re)productive activities or their unique cosmologies. Rather, they are themselves at the centre of any meaningfully co-ordinated social activity at all.

The reason for this centrality, for Thompson, is that the 'social landscape' is divided into three interacting realms of value against which worldly objects are judged. These realms or categories Thompson labels durable, rubbish and transient. 'Durable' objects — like certain items of antique furniture or works of art — are those whose value increases over time. 'Rubbish' objects — like certain items of domestic waste, perhaps — are those without value or, rather, whatever value they have is 'covert.' 'Transient' objects — like modern computers — are those whose value decreases over time (Thompson, 1979: 9–10). Thompson's goal, however, is not to draw up a taxonomy of objective values but to expose the cosmological precariousness of the social categories themselves. Objects in the social landscape do not inhabit the different realms because of their intrinsic qualities. They are assigned to these realms as a consequence of social pressures that arise partly from the micro-activities of individuals creating, ignoring or demolishing the values of objects (through their purchase and sale, display and concealment, collection and disposal) and partly from broader collisions between world views that connect the value of worldly objects to the value of ideas about objects.

The two social pressures exist in an uneasy tension so that objects may find themselves traversing the boundaries between durable, rubbish and transient and it is the rubbish category that enables such crossings to occur. The commonly quoted example of this process is Thompson's discussion of Stevengraphs (1979: 13–33) — brightly coloured silk pictures woven on a Jacquard loom between 1879 and 1940. Beginning life as something of a manufactured novelty, Stevengraphs retailed at a modest price of one shilling. But, as nothing other than mundane consumer objects, they inhabited the 'transient' category and their value decreased markedly and quickly to zero. For a long period, Stevengraphs were all-but unsaleable: they had entered the category of 'rubbish', were accorded no cultural status and consequently no economic value. Then, beginning 'from a rather vaguely defined point somewhere around 1960' (Thompson, 1979: 18), these decorative objects were classified as historically and aesthetically interesting and their value steadily increased: they had entered the category of 'durable'. Thus, 'value' itself is a cultural category and 'rubbish' is merely value-in-waiting. It is the cultural reservoir from which once-transient objects may be plucked in order to revitalise and replenish the trickle of durables through a consumer culture.

Thompson is aware, however, that his thesis contradicts Douglas's original formulation. Whilst the propositions about the translations between transience, rubbish and durability provide for a theory of rubbish 'at a high level of abstraction' (ibid.: 91) they do not (explicitly, anyway) expose anything about a culture's unique cosmology and nor do they relate rubbish to the intricate details of any given way of life. It is true that Thompson provides many subtle examples of the very different values implied by the categories of rubbish, transient and durable and that, pace Hetherington (2004: 166), these are not at all limited 'within the field of exchange value' — see, amongst countless other non-economic examples, Thompson's (1979: 92, 95–7) discussion of 'dewdrops' and 'dogs' or the entire chapter on 'the geometry of credibility' (ibid.: 152-83). But in offering a generalized theory Thompson is moved to ditch the central plank of Douglas's thesis, namely, that dirt, as matter 'out of place', contributes positively to cultural unification. Far from providing the 'validating framework' for Douglas's 'more readily comprehensible idea', Thompson ejects the idea from his cultural schema altogether. Like McLaughlin before him, Thompson seeks a way out of Douglas's particular idealism by picking up on another short passage from her book. Here, Douglas asks 'why primitive culture is pollution-prone and ours is not' and responds:

> With us pollution is a matter of aesthetics, hygiene or etiquette, which only becomes grave in so far as it may create social embarrassment. (Douglas, 2002: 92)

Thompson interprets this to mean that, instead of positively contributing to the process of order maintenance, dirt or rubbish *in the wrong place* are 'emphatically visible and extremely embarrassing' (Thompson, 1979:

89, 92). Dealing with their out-placedness is no longer a ritualistic performance of social reincorporation — a behavioural affirmation of the symbolic universe shared by a culture — but either a discomfiting blow to an individual's social self or a hidden drama of personal spaces and technologies designed to prevent the public effluence of private secretions. Thompson's rubbish, then, does not complete a cycle from symbolic formlessness via cultural utility to symbolic formlessness, but, instead, bifurcates into a socially positive space of covert values and socially negative displaced detritus. Like McLaughlin before him, Thompson is happy to recommend Mary Douglas but distinctly unhappy with the cognitivist thrust of her analysis: dirt or rubbish (i.e., 'negatively valued things', ibid.: 91) stands for something other than the 'differentiating activity of the mind'. In Thompson's hands this is not the sticky reminder of the inevitability of the end but the socially processed reality of distinctions between public and private values.

More recent forays into modern muck are no happier with Douglas's thesis than McLaughlin or Thompson. For example, citing Douglas's 'famous work on the association between dirt and taboo' and declaiming her 'excellent account' of how 'waste operates as *nomos*', van Loon (2002: 120) proposes that:

> ... the problem of waste is a universal one. It is the problem of selecting what belongs and what does not, that is, it functions as a focal point for a politics of inclusion and exclusion, with waste (as that which is left over and discarded) relating to the latter.

In universal terms, then, the *problem* of waste is the problem of selection — of categorization and ordering, in Douglas's terms — and the *process* of wasting consists in defining 'that which is to be discarded' (ibid.: 107). So far, so Douglas. However, whilst Douglas used the matter-out-of-place metaphor to investigate the cosmological unity of primitive worldviews, van Loon uses the same metaphor to explore the 'abjectivity' and 'contagion' of consumer capitalism. As with Douglas, there is a degree of nominalism about these conceptual distinctions but the two analyses travel in different directions and end up at radically different conclusions. For example, as we have seen, Douglas contends that dirt begins in undifferentiated formlessness, is then transformed 'by the differentiating activity of the mind' into a series of threats to cosmological order before returning once again to undifferentiated formlessness. For Douglas, dirt is *only* a category invented by the mind. It exists symbolically, ritualistically, meaningfully because of the universal necessity to negotiate the cultural boundary between order and disorder and to sustain the former against the threat of the latter.

In contrast, for van Loon, the consequence of particular selections, particular categorisations, is the production of an 'amorphous blob' of 'uncontrolled matter out of place' (ibid.: 106) whose toxic, pathogenic and virulent qualities return 'in a zombie-like fashion ... to haunt the brains of the living' (ibid.: 108). There are two rejections of Douglas occurring simultaneously, here. The first is that Douglas's schema extracted all notions of pathogenicity, toxicity and virulence from the definition of dirt. The entire point of the 'matter out of place' argument was to shift the analytical focus away from the natural sciences, away from the 'real' destructive properties of dirt, and take it 'straight into the field of symbolism' because 'dirt is never a unique, isolated event. Where there is dirt there is system' (see Douglas, 2002: 44). Dirt is never 'uncontrolled' and can never persist as an 'amorphous blob' for that would imply the system destroyed — negating the symbolic power of dirt to be 'ploughed back for a renewal of life' (ibid.: 207).

The second rejection is that, in contrast to Douglas's dirt, van Loon's waste does not complete a cognitive cycle from formlessness to formlessness but a more or less straight line from (primarily) industrial excess to environmental contamination. The origin of waste, in this scenario, lies neither in mental inspiration (as does dirt for Douglas) nor in socio-cultural contradictions (as does rubbish for Thompson) but in 'excess production, excess material, leftover' (van Loon, 2002: 108). In consequence, waste 'returns to haunt the present' but it does not haunt the present as 'waste.' Instead, it haunts the present as 'risk' (ibid.: 120): waste has been transformed from one entity into another in two dimensions. First, it has transformed cognitively and symbolically. The universal problem now is not selecting and representing what is and is not a waste but what is and is not risky *about* waste. In this sense, unlike Douglas's 'dirt', the category 'waste' is in no sense a threat to cosmological order because it is not an entity that fits no symbolic 'system of classification' (Douglas, 2002: xvii). Instead, in van Loon's hands, it is an entity that is classified along a risky continuum and risk, rather than waste or dirt becomes the object of contemplation. In this regard, waste may (or may not) be a threat in some general sense but, unlike dirt, it is no threat to the cultural order. Secondly, it has been transformed ontologically. No longer arising out of formlessness but out of 'excess' waste pre-exists the differentiating activity of the mind and persists regardless of the multifarious classificatory schemes in which it is specified as having this or that particular symbolic resonance and power. In contrast to Douglas's 'dirt,' waste is not a means of gaining access to the independent cosmologies of unique cultures but emblematic of the 'bads that have affected the organization of modern society' (van Loon, 2002: 187) and symbolic of the risk 'perceptions' and 'sensibilities' that characterise a globalised 'technological culture' (ibid.: 101, 205).

Where Joost van Loon's attempt to reinvigorate Douglas incorporated a diversionary sojourn into risk and virulence, David Inglis's study of defacatory technologies and norms crosses into the study of historical habits and manners. 'In the modern West,' writes Inglis (2002: 17) excreta and excretion are regarded as "dirty".' Therefore, 'the sociology of excreta and excretion may be oriented upon the same lines as a sociology of "dirt".'

This bold statement of analytic intent appears, at first sight, as Douglas through and through. But a clue to the distance between Inglis and Douglas is visible in the geo-political setting of the claim. There is no specified culture here: the analysis is not about the Dogon or the Hopi, the Welsh or the Russians, Romanies or Mormons — it is not about the unity and orderliness of a particular culture at all. It is, instead, about 'Western civilisation' as a whole and the slow but certain standardisation and rationalisation of its excretory foibles.

In spite, therefore, of declaring a Douglasian rationale, Inglis's exploration of the excrement of modernity actually flows down a very different channel. Inspired by Bourdieu, in particular, and Elias, in general, he sets off to explore the slow process by which contemporary 'excretory practices' have become culturally sedimented and how the ways of organising and carrying out excretion have become unremarkable and taken for granted. The main argument of the book is that

> ... the genesis of the habits and attitudes characteristic of excreta and excretion in the modern West are explicable in terms of the development and operation of the bourgeois faecal habitus. (ibid.: 113)

In order to develop this argument, Inglis suggests that three historical processes must be understood. These are, first, 'the erection of a set of symbols based on the moral cleanliness of the body, which involved a denial of that body's excretory capacities'; second, 'increasing levels of negative charging of excreta, such that excreta become evaluated as highly dirty in the moral sense'; and, third, 'the progressively greater degrees of repression of excretory practices that had been acceptable in medieval society' (ibid.: 115). In a nod to Marx, Inglis suggests that the aforementioned 'faecal habitus', together with the 'corresponding means of excretory disposal' comprise 'the mode of excretion' (ibid.: 60)

Where Inglis does follow Douglas is in the attribution of behaviour to the power of ideas. Thus, the 'cosmological evaluation of excreta will shape the ways in which acts of excretion will be carried out' and 'the set of evaluations of excreta held by a society shapes the ways defecation can be legitimately carried out in that society'. Fundamentally, then, a set of ideas and evaluations emerge, with an identifiable (bourgeois) class location. These ideas and evaluations form the basis upon which practices are generated, which latter 'conform to the imperatives of the [faecal] schema' (ibid.: 26, 27, 32). Now, although Douglas does associate dirt with power, it remains the case that power has no specific location in the cultures investigated in *Purity and Danger*. Spiritual powers are simply 'part of the social system. They express it and provide institutions for manipulating it' (Douglas, 2002: 140). For Inglis, on the other hand, the cosmology of 'Western civilisation' does not vaguely inhere the system's 'social structures' but derives, rather, from the specificity of its 'class structures' — in particular, the patterning of that cosmology is a consequence of the fact that the 'materially dominant class' in society is always also the 'symbolically dominant class' (Inglis, 2002: 36). Hence, the particular features of Western civilisation's aesthetic rapport with excretory behaviour are tantamount to interpolation into a dominant ideology of defecation

Dealing with excrement, however, involves much more than toilet protocol. It also involves the development of technologies and infrastructures for enabling habits and manners to be carried out. This is as true for dirt in general — that is, dirt considered as something other than a classificatory ingredient of a culture's worldview — as it is for the specific character of excrement. Acknowledging this, Inglis spends some time on the emergence and development of sewerage systems and on the installation of water closets in private homes — although the installation of the latter in workplaces and public buildings is given less consideration. In so far as these technological and infrastructural strategies are dependent not only on ideas and worldviews but on practical developments in science and engineering, it is clear that modern excretory manners cannot be traced straightforwardly to purely ideological roots. Instead, they must be a function of both ideal and material factors and, indeed, Inglis goes some way to accepting this when he describes the 'Janus face' of excrement in the modern period as deriving from both 'socio-cultural factors' and 'developments in the medical and natural sciences' (ibid.: 55). Once again, whilst Douglas had proposed to abandon these factors in the explanation of dirt, Inglis is forced to incorporate their impacts in the account of modern defecation. In spite of attempting to orient the study of excrement 'upon the same lines as a sociology of "dirt"', Inglis finds that Douglas's idealism is insufficiently elastic to expose either the scientific and technological infrastructures of modern excremental manners or their ideological and aesthetic superstructures. It may, or may not, be the case, as Inglis concludes, that:

> The flush of the toilet is thus the music of modern Western humanity, an attempt to drown out sweetly a cacophony of foulness that persistently lurks in the background of consciousness. (Inglis, 2002: 292)

Yet, neither the flushing music nor the cacophony of foulness can perform any cultural function in congealing or reaffirming the cosmological solidity of Western civilisation: if they did they would neither occur behind the locked doors of private privies nor lurk in the background of consciousness because, here, their symbolic and representational utility is collectively unverifiable.

In a, not dissimilar, effort to read Western civilisation through the lens of its ideas about waste, John Scanlan's *On Garbage* attempts a philosophical exegesis of the meaning(lessness) of modern life in a reflection on its discards. 'Garbage', he concludes, 'is [Western] civilisation's double — or shadow — from which we flee in order to find the space to live'. It arises from the 'disappearance of meaning in modern life', a disappearance that is:

> ... covered up by a preoccupation with essentially superficial "things" that are fetishized (endowed with a mystical transforming power) and become the true carrier of radically subjective meaning, but rather than substantially replacing the apparent loss of meaning they only add bulk or clutter to life. (Scanlan, 2005: 176–8)

Unusually among Douglas's idealist interpreters, Scanlan openly argues that the analysis of waste must reach 'beyond the temporal domain of specific cultures' but this is not because of the historical or sociological generality of either the mental categories or material contents of garbage. Nor is it because certain kinds of discard may signal or effect common personal, social or environmental problems. Rather, it is because, in a remarkably accurate transposition of Philip K. Dick's proposition (see Chapter 2), 'everything is eventually reduced to the condition of dirt' (ibid.: 43. Emphasis omitted). This reduction is held to be both a material quality of objects — 'they may have been something once but are now nothing' — and a moral judgment that effects their devaluation — 'the taint of garbage ... has the effect of reducing the value of the thing in question' (ibid.).

　In fact, as we have seen in Chapter 5, this is not really accurate: waste, garbage, discards, junk are all valued and revalued in many different ways, not all of which effect a 'reduction'. But Scanlan's polemical comments on formlessness and value are not the core of his thesis. Instead, expanding on Douglas's original view, he argues that the 'centrality of "garbage" in contemporary life' is a product of the fact that 'the development of knowledge in Western culture seems inseparable from a cleansing or refining impulse; a will to order' (ibid.: 58). It is the cleansing and the refining, the 'disposal and tidying; cutting off, chucking out, and of sweeping away the debris that lies on the territory of reason' that generates the latter's 'spectral double' in the 'uncanny' shape of garbage metaphysics (ibid.: 61, 65, 87). Unlike Douglas, however, this 'spectral double' is not plucked from the background formlessness of a culture's cosmology. Indeed, Scanlan's grasp of modern waste is much closer to van Loon's in so far as garbage has its own existence, independent of a cognitive will to order. 'Materially', Scanlan writes:

> ... garbage represents the shadow *object* world, the leftover of a life, a world, or a dream, created by the voracious speculations of commodity production and consumption. (ibid.: 164. Emphasis in original)

So, whilst 'garbage' is the product of a will to order, it nonetheless persists objectively as a consequence of 'voracious' production and consumption. 'We remain blind to the reality of waste because modern society has almost perfected the means to forget', and because 'absent-minded consumption ... institutes a relentless movement of desire to and fro, effectively creating an economy of ignorance' (ibid.: 129). Like so many others who have been persuaded by the throwaway society thesis Scanlan, here, is uncompromisingly dismissive of ordinary people. Ordinary modern citizens are 'blind', 'ignorant', 'voracious' and 'forgetful'. Of course, ordinary citizens are not any such thing or, at least, we are no more 'blind' than sighted, no more 'ignorant' than knowledgeable, no more 'voracious' than restrained and no more 'forgetful' than attentive. The idealist conception of the 'throwaway citizen' is a long way from the real modern person who copes, sometimes ingeniously, with the material stuff that flows through and around everyday life.

In order to produce an assessment of modern garbage, then, Scanlan begins with Douglas but discovers, like all who went before him, that her thesis does not service the analytical needs of contemporary social inquiry and must be overturned by the addition of an array of theoretical and moral propositions in order to make it speak critically about the contemporary scene. In rejecting the core of Douglas's thesis, however, what is also lost is its fundamental humanism: the recognition that ordinary people are not one-dimensional, programmed ciphers of a static social system but active and knowledgable world-makers; the sense that cultures comprise uniquely united environments where what happens at the margins and in the crevices — be it rituals of cleanliness or of memory — is as important, as meaningful, as useful and as positively *essential* as what happens in its core institutions — of religion, industry or, for that matter, academia.

# 7    Rubbish Materialisms

This is how one pictures the angel of history. His face is turned toward the past. Where we perceive a chain of events, he sees one single catastrophe which keeps piling wreckage upon wreckage and hurls it in front of his feet. The angel would like to stay, awaken the dead, and make whole what has been smashed. But a storm is blowing in from Paradise; it has got caught in his wings with such violence that the angel can no longer close them. This storm irresistibly propels him into the future to which his back is turned, while the pile of debris before him grows skyward. This storm is what we call progress (Walter Benjamin, 'Theses on the Philosophy of History, IX').

Douglas and her followers target the symbolic and representational character of dirt and waste. The power and effect of the detritus of life is explored through its cultural impacts on human behaviour, experience and interaction. Dirt and waste perform the social functions of challenging, channelling, or exposing society's moral and economic values or, more accurately, the relationships between the two. The character of any particular example of dirt or waste is not of interest in itself. The goal is to expose dimensions of ideas about dirt and waste rather than dimensions of their material incarnation in any given societal context. To the question 'why is there dirt or waste?' the idealist's answer revolves always around the conceptual and/or metaphysical functions that they play in human understanding. Thus, dirt is a necessary category of cultural representation because the cultural rules governing its treatment 'serve to settle uncertain moral issues' (Douglas, 2002: 162). Detritus is built into the operations of mind because 'every act of differentiation produces garbage' (Scanlan, 2005: 182). Waste is central to culture because it liberates 'a conception of a beyond, of traces, of unknown consequences, of the hidden, the repressed, the invisible and the different' (van Loon, 2002: 121).

But what of the actual dirt, garbage and waste? Why does this debris exist visibly, tangibly, really in contemporary societies? Where does it come from and what theoretical lenses address the material, as opposed to mental, stuff that is modern waste? To the question 'why is there waste' a very different answer can be provided, one whose focus is not on the cosmological unity of unique cultures nor on the haunting shadows and hidden regions of modern cultural values. Instead, the focus is on the production and consumption of waste or, more specifically, on the socially organised relationships through which that production and consumption is undertaken. Where idealism provides universal concepts of dirt and waste that, at least in theory if not in practice, can be transposed to all cultures in all times and places materialism insists on the particularity of these phenomena in specific social formations under definite historical conditions. The issue here is whether, through a materialist analysis, those organised relationships can be held accountable for the generation of waste or whether materialism finds that waste is too complex a phenomenon to be grasped through the same lenses as production and consumption. To explore this question theoretically I begin with an overview of Karl Marx's contradictory writings on waste before going on to discuss how later interpreters have attempted to develop these into a more systematic analysis.

## PRODUCING WASTE

It is a difficult task to derive a critical theory of waste from Marx's writings directly because he was decidedly ambivalent about the nature and role of waste in capitalist production. Whilst Marx vilified capitalism, often in the most glittering prose, for its rampant exploitation of all social and natural resources he was far less precise, and far less confident, about how to grasp the material wastes that it generated. When Marx explicitly used terms such as 'offal', 'refuse', and 'scum' he was most often referring to social groups — the lumpen proletariat, specifically — rather than the products or by-products of industry and consumption. When he does make reference to these latter objects, he tends to use phrases like 'excretions' or 'so-called wastes' and is, if anything, a little awe-struck by industry's ingenuity in overcoming waste, inefficiency and loss. There is, in short, no coherent theory of waste or of the contribution of waste to capitalist development or degeneration to be extracted from Marx's voluminous output. Instead, there are contradictory hints and unevenly developed propositions about different dimensions of what constitutes 'waste' in a capitalist social formation. Some of these provide for a more or less coherent statement about the genesis and reproduction of social detritus, some ambiguously undermine the general applicability of this statement to different realms of the capitalist system and locate wastefulness in different economic logics, and some, equally ambiguously, oscillate between a critique of technological intensification and admiration for its seemingly limitless inventiveness.

Here, I deal with Marx's contribution through three analytical strands. These are the social production of a class of human 'refuse' (the lumpen proletariat), the overproduction of total capitalist output, and the 'excretions' of production and the technical means of their reconversion in capitalist industry. I begin with an outline of Marx's treatment of the lumpen proletariat partly because it reveals something about the contrast between materialism and idealism and partly because Marx's rubbishing of the lumpen proletariat is occasionally picked up in social science texts on waste (see Scanlan, 2002: 170, for example) but, as with the use of Douglas's definition of dirt that I investigated in Chapter 6, the analytical framework behind it is too often underrepresented.

It is worth noting at this point that whilst Marx and Engels made regular use of 'spiritual' metaphors, the opening line of the *Communist Manifesto* (1981: 78) being a case in point ('A spectre is haunting Europe — the spectre of communism'), they generally had little time for shadows and ghostly hauntings in the practical analysis of capitalist society. Expounding on the materialist conception of history in *The German Ideology*, for example, they lambast the 'idealistic humbug' that seeks to dissolve 'all forms and products of consciousness ... by mental criticism, ... by transformation into "apparitions," "spectres," "fancies," etc' (Marx & Engels, 1976: 298–9). In contrast, they purport to assert a vision of historical change rooted in 'real processes of production' and the 'active life process' of 'men, not in any fantastic isolation or abstract definition, but in their actual, empirically perceptible process of development under definite conditions' (ibid.: 289, 298).

In the *Communist Manifesto*, Marx and Engels specified the 'empirically perceptible process of development' of certain classes of men in the following terms:

> Of all the classes that stand face to face with the bourgeoisie today, the proletariat is a *really revolutionary class*. The other classes decay and finally disappear in the face of modern industry; the proletariat is its special and essential product. (Marx & Engels, 1981: 91)

Later, recalling this passage in the *Critique of the Gotha Programme*, Marx adds that the statement does not imply that all other existing classes must therefore constitute 'one reactionary mass' (Marx & Engels, 1976: 162). Here, he refers back to 'the artisans, small manufacturers, etc., and peasants' who are not necessarily enemies of the working class and, indeed, some of whom already showed signs of becoming revolutionised. In actually existing capitalist societies several classes co-mingled, some were subject to proletarianisation, others to embourgeoisment. The class character of capitalist societies for Marx, is not a simple polarity between bourgeois and proletarian. But there is one class that is missing from this short list and which could not conceivably be included in the 'etc' attached to the small manufacturers. This class is the 'lumpen proletariat' upon whom Marx heaped abuse and scorn aplenty and which he and Engels characterised as:

The "dangerous class", the social scum, that passively rotting mass thrown off by the lowest layers of the old society [which] may, here and there, be swept into the movement by a proletarian revolution; its conditions of life, however, prepare it far more for the part of a bribed tool of reactionary intrigue. (Marx & Engels, 1981: 92)

In *The Eighteenth Brumaire of Louis Bonaparte, Class Struggles in France*, and *The Civil War in France* the proletarian combatants of the Paris insurrection of June 1848, and the Communards of 1871, were praised by Marx for their honour, their principles and their determination. The lumpen proletariat, on the other hand, were castigated as the sub-human 'refuse of all classes', rag-pickers, brothel keepers, dregs, thieves and criminals who live on 'the crumbs of society' (Marx & Engels, 1976: 338, 368, 415 *et passim*) — 'the whole indefinite, disintegrated mass, thrown hither and thither'. Some of this scorn may be due to the fact that they represented the 'holy phalanx of order' whose members made up a significant portion of Bonaparte's 'substitute' army following the Paris insurrection of 1848 (ibid.: 369, 383). On the other hand, it is crystal clear that the term 'lumpen proletariat' is as much a moral as a sociological classification. In scathingly contemptuous prose, Marx compared the French finance aristocracy with the 'scum of bourgeois society'. This class, he wrote, is 'nothing but the *resurrection of the* lumpen proletariat *transported to the heights of bourgeois society*' (ibid.: 326. Emphasis in original). In Marx's view, the lumpen proletariat indicated a collection of social trash that was undisciplined, licentious, retarded and parasitic on the social body. They were disconnected from the organised working class communities and factories and were, to all intents and purposes, a kind waste product 'thrown off' by the wider struggle between bourgeois and proletarian in the contradictory context of capitalist development.

The lumpen proletariat, however indignantly excoriated by Marx and Engels, were not a residual class *outside* the existing capitalist social order, any more than were the small manufacturers and artisans. They were in fact produced and reproduced by it in particular forms. They emerged partly as a consequence of the social disintegration attendant on the ongoing transformation of that social order, partly as a consequence of the degradation and impoverishment of the working class — described in all its soiled murkiness by Engels (see Chapter 1) — and partly by the very struggle between bourgeois and proletarian itself. They were detached from their social class both by the immiserating consequences of capitalist expansion and the self-organising logic of the industrial working class. That class, slowly but surely realising its interests and its true position in capitalism, progressively organised itself — through the factories, the unions, the working-men's associations, political parties and so on. In other words, its self-organisation depended in large measure on those institutions and emerging traditions to which the free-floating lumpen proletariat, by definition, were not connected. The revolutionary struggle under 'definite conditions' of capitalism spawned the 'swamp flower' of the peasant lumpen proletariat and the urban 'scum of bourgeois society' (ibid.: 368, 383).

In Marx's account, then, a certain kind of social 'refuse' is a manufactured part of the process of capitalist transformation. Whatever the moral or ethical flaws of Marx's vitriolic attack on a class that included some of the most impoverished, excluded and socially disenfranchised populations of nineteenth century capitalism, he nonetheless posits a *mechanism by which such a category of social refuse is produced*. The lumpen proletariat are not 'matter out of place', excess, or concealed values — they are an active agent in the historical struggle to transform capitalism. However much he may have detested their actions and however much he disparaged their ways of life he was fully aware that they had a very particular historical role to play in Bonapartism and the stuttering emergence of French industrial capitalism. History repeats itself 'the first time as tragedy, the second as farce', Marx wrote, and the 'substitute' Bonaparte is swept to power by a 'substitute' army to rule over a state machine that is 'at once loathsome and ridiculous' (ibid.: 360, 388). Social refuse they may have been but the lumpen proletariat were no less historically significant for that and, what is more, they were generated as a *material force* in the ongoing class struggle.

When it comes to the production of *objective* as opposed to *human* 'refuse', however, the appealing logic of the mechanism breaks down and things become much more complicated. An important part of the reason for the added complication is that, except in relation to the lumpen proletariat, Marx makes little reference to refuse or waste, underscoring the moral thrust of his criticisms of that group. When he does use the term 'waste' he often qualifies it, as we shall see, with the rider 'so-called'. In fact, the production of waste under capitalism as opposed to the over-production of total output or the misapplication of capital, is not really seen as wasteful or, at least, Marx is much more ambivalent about its wasteful character.

Where social scientists have been able to derive a critique of the material waste of capitalism this has been based largely on Marx's scattered (and contradictory) comments on 'over-production'. Here, the mechanism that generates excess within the capitalist system is different to the mechanism that generates the social refuse of the lumpen proletariat. In general, Marx's comments have been taken to imply that capitalism produces too many commodities such as cars, 'phones, shoes — or books for that matter — and is, therefore, 'wasteful'. But whilst this is true in a limited sense, for Marx over-production meant much more than simply an overabundance of consumer goods: it meant an excess of the total capitalist system and all of its constituent parts. Discussing the crises that regularly afflict bourgeois society, Marx and Engels propose that:

> In these crises, there breaks out an epidemic that, in all earlier epochs, would have seemed an absurdity — the epidemic of over-production. Society suddenly finds itself put back into a state of momentary barbarism; it appears as if a famine, a universal war of devastation, had cut off the supply of every means of subsistence; industry and commerce seem to be destroyed; and why? Because there is too much civilisation, too much means of subsistence, too much industry, too much commerce. (Marx & Engels, 1981: 86)

It seems an extraordinary claim to make — that there is 'too much civilisation, too much means of subsistence' — since it appears to imply, at first sight, a world satiated with a copious bounty not only of life's necessities but also their civilised luxuries. It seems to portray a society hung-over from excessive self-indulgence, unable to gorge upon even the smallest extra morsel. This sense of consumerist decadence certainly circulates today and is a cornerstone of the 'throwaway society' thesis. But this is Marx and Engels writing in mid-nineteenth century England and, anyway, Marx later argued, in the *Grundrisse* and elsewhere, that consumption is itself productive both in the sense that production consumes raw materials and labour and in the sense that individual consumption is a necessary characteristic of capitalist production. So, whilst the major focus of Marx's observations on over-production are concerned with commodities as such, the critique is also levelled at the unplanned, uncoordinated and immoderate nature of capitalism as a whole — its political, social, cultural as well as economic dimensions. The excessive predisposition of capitalism derives both from its character as a revolutionary economic system and from the anarchic disorganisation of its production system 'which turns every progress into a social calamity' (Capital, I: 457–8). The bourgeois epoch, Marx and Engels assert in *The Communist Manifesto* (1981: 83), is distinguished by 'constant revolutionising of production, uninterrupted disturbance of all social conditions, everlasting uncertainty and agitation'. As a distinctively agitated historical epoch, capitalism is:

> a society that has conjured up such gigantic means of production and of exchange, [that it] is like the sorcerer, who is no longer able to control the powers of the nether world whom he has called up by his spells. (ibid.: 85–6).

Since the means of production are not under the direction of society as a whole there is no collective control over how much of what should be produced. Coupled with fierce competition between individual capitalists to maximise profit regular gluts of commodities are inevitable. 'For this reason', writes Marx (Capital III: 187), 'these commodities must be sold below their market value, and a portion of them may be altogether unsaleable' — a situation that exposes the 'squandered labour' that is applied in producing commodities 'in excess of the existing social needs'. Although the 'accumulation of commodities in great masses' in some instances might also be due to a 'stoppage of circulation' (Capital I: 532) or 'under-consumption' (see Sweezey, 1942, and below) it is clear that, as Ernest Mandel points out, crises of over-production are understood by Marx as one of the 'fundamental laws of motion' of capitalism (Mandel, 1983: 208).

The reason for floods of commodities in capitalist societies, for Marx, is not fundamentally because individual consumers have been duped into buying things they do not need. Indeed, we should remind ourselves that it was the experience of nineteenth century capitalism, rather than our postwar 'throwaway society', that was the basis for Marx's analysis of overproduction. The reason for the flood is that uncoordinated capitalists own the means of production and exploit labour for no other reason than to produce more capital or, as Marx puts it: 'Capital produces essentially capital, and does so only to the extent that it produces surplus value' (Capital, III: 880). Since it is in each capitalist's interest to produce things for profit rather than according to social need and since, in order to succeed in the face of competition from other capitalists, each is required to manufacture more and more goods at cheaper and cheaper prices then over-production is a constituent part of the productive process and not a reactive consequence of individual consumer choices. In this sense, if capitalism is wasteful it is so in its *misuse* of the industrial and social means at its disposal. Those industrial and social means are not necessarily waste-producing in themselves. Thus, the mechanism for the production of capitalist excess — in terms of commodities, means of subsistence, 'civilisation' — is different to the mechanism that produces the social refuse of the lumpen proletariat. Where the latter derived from the conditions of the class struggle and the social disintegration attendant on the transition from one mode of production to another, the former derives from the logic of capitalist accumulation itself. It is a consequence of the perverse way in which the means of production are applied not to the satisfaction of human needs but to the perpetual generation of more capital.

In this critique of misuse and misappropriation, some have been tempted to view Marx as a proto-ecologist whose recognition of society's relationship with nature can be used as the basis for a kind of socialist environmentalism. Again, scattered comments throughout Marx's work can be marshalled in support of the view. In fact, one can read in *Capital* a draft script of the 'sustainable development' principle propounded by the World Commission on Environment and Development (1987). Discussing surplus profit and ground rent, Marx writes:

> Even a whole society, a nation, or even all simultaneously existing societies taken together, are not the owners of the globe. They are only its possessors, its usufructuaries, and, like *boni patres familias*, they

must hand it down to succeeding generations in an improved condition. (Capital, III: 776).

Elsewhere (Capital, I: 474–5) Marx accuses 'capitalist agriculture ... not only of robbing the labourer, but of robbing the soil; all progress in increasing the fertility of the soil for a given time, is a progress towards ruining the lasting sources of that fertility.' Without denying or dismissing the red-green project as a whole it is also true that, in other places, Marx is rather less useful as a source of ecological inspiration. For example, in the same chapter where Marx expounds a proto-Brundtlandian vision of sustainable development, he takes caustic issue with the *Edinburgh Review* for its assertion that 'all England cannot be fed through the cultivation of Soho Square' (Capital III: 780–81). Nonsense! Cries Marx. The fundamental problem with this 'shallow conception' — which misunderstands the nature of soil as an instrument of production — is that it fails to take into account improvements in agricultural chemistry because the soil, 'if properly treated, improves all the time. The advantage of the soil, permitting successive investments of capital to bring gains without loss of previous investments, implies the possibility of differences in yield from these successive investments of capital' (ibid.: 790–91). Of course, Marx is not saying here that it is *really* possible to feed the whole of England from the soil of Soho Square. What he is saying is that scientific and technological advances can increase the productivity of the soil as a whole and, when rationally applied, can thereby enhance the yield on initial investments. The polemical attack on the *Edinburgh Review* reveals an underlying theme in Marx's ambiguous critique of capitalism. On the one hand, here in relation to agriculture and the soil and following the lead provided by the German chemist von Liebeg, Marx warns of capitalism's rapacious and unsustainable exploitation of natural resources (see Foster, 2000, for an extended discussion of Marx's use of von Liebeg). On the other hand, Marx nonetheless retained some faith in the science and technology that capitalism developed to improve the output of instruments of production (like the soil) and the efficiency of the production process as a whole. Thus Marx does not produce a critique of the scientific-technological society as such, only its perverted capitalistic organisation. This tension is the main reason why, when it comes to capitalism's objective waste products, Marx's analysis moves in yet another direction.

This new direction becomes visible in the first instance when comparing Marx's comments on machinery or commodities with his comments on wastes. Whilst the former are the subject of extensive and passionate reflection, the latter are dryly recounted as technical elements of the level of industrial efficiency. Where Marx's writing on machinofacture is filled with florid prose about the 'vampire-like', 'werewolf hunger' of capital that converts the worker into a 'crippled monstrosity' (Capital, I: 224, 252, 340), it also explores in great detail the constituents and operations of the machinery itself — the 'fly-wheels, shafting, toothed wheels, pullies, ropes, bands, pinions and gearing', and so on (Capital, I: 353). As well as having 'recourse to the mist-enveloped regions of the religious world' in order to explain how a table, as a commodity, 'stands on its head, and evolves out of its wooden brain grotesque ideas' about the 'magic and necromancy that surrounds ... commodities' (ibid.: 76, 77, 80–81), he also goes to inordinate lengths to describe and explain the complex relationships by which commodities acquire and release values (Capital, I: 43–144).

When it comes to waste, however, not only does the passionate prose disappear but so also does the intricate description of its physical and economic forms. In several short passages, Marx observes that material that is 'wasted' in the production process nonetheless enters into the value of a commodity and is an element of its exchange value. So, for example, in Capital I (198–9) he supposes that for every 115 lbs of cotton used in the manufacture of yarn 15 lbs are wasted. In this 'normal and inevitable circumstance' he continues:

> [Although] the 15 lbs of cotton never becomes a constituent element of the yarn ... its value is just as surely transferred to the value of the yarn, as is the value of the 100lbs that form the substance of the yarn ... The destruction of this cotton is therefore a necessary condition in the production of the yarn. (Capital I: 198)

However, this disappearance of a raw material from the final product is inevitable *only* when 'such refuse cannot be further employed as a means in the production of new and independent use values' as may be seen:

> ... in the large machine works at Manchester, where mountains of iron turnings are carted away to the foundry in the evening, in order the next morning to re-appear in the workshops as solid masses of iron. (ibid.: 199).

There are other scattered references and allusions to waste throughout Marx's writings, but the topic is only treated in any kind of detail in small sections in Capital III in the chapter on 'economy in the employment of constant capital' and, in particular, in the subsection on the 'utilisation of the excretions of production' (Capital III, 77–104; see also 108–110). This latter subsection opens by claiming that the capitalist mode of production 'extends the utilisation of the excretions of production and consumption' (ibid.: 101). The use of the neutral term 'excretion' is intended to signal both that the generation of 'so-called waste' (ibid.: 79) is inevitable and that it is a natural process of exchange of matter — initially in the human body but by extension in the productive system as a whole. In relation to the bodily excretions, Marx complains bitterly that in London 'they find no better use for the excretion of four and a half million human beings than to contaminate the Thames with it at heavy cost'. He makes the complaint because, with the application of the right technology, the 'excretions of consumption are of the greatest importance for agriculture' (ibid.: 101). Similarly, the term 'utilisation' also implies that dealing with the 'excretions' of production and consumption is a fundamentally technical issue. This same word was used by Simmonds (1876) in his technical treatise on 'waste products and undeveloped substances' and, later, by Koller (1902/1918) in his textbook on 'the rational utilization, recovery, and treatment of waste products of all kinds'. I include these examples only to situate Marx in a particular late-nineteenth century world-view that construed science and technology as unalloyed goods capable of resolving problems of industrial efficiency — if only their application were placed under rational control.

In this regard, it may be tempting to suggest that, for Marx, the capacity of science and technology to deliver rational responses to problems of inefficiency and/or waste is dependent on its socialistic organisation. However, Marx is keen to stress that scientific progress under capitalism is itself a 'general requirement' for the 're-employment of these excretions'. He proposes that 'so-called waste' is an important element of almost all branches of large-scale industry and its progressive 'reconversion ... into new elements of production' leads to a reduction in the costs of manufacture and 'increases *pro tanto* the rate of profit' (Capital III: 79, 80). Whilst Marx is keen to assert that capitalism is characterised by a 'great waste of the productive forces' (Capital II: 176), he nonetheless discovers that in many branches of industry the re-working and reconversion of used elements of production is simply a mundane reality of capitalist enterprise. Thus, he includes extracts from reports on the operation of the Great Western Railway whose 'wasteful' capitalist owners re-use wheels, axles and portions of engines in order to avoid purchasing new rolling stock in which case ' ... the old materials of coaches or engines are more or less worked up into other vehicles or engines, and *never totally disappear* from the road. The movable capital therefore may be considered to be in a state of continual reproduction [...] a constant state of rejuvenescence' (ibid.: 182-3. My emphasis). In consequence, Marx is forced to concede that:

> The capitalist's fanatical insistence on economy in means of production is therefore quite understandable. That nothing is lost or wasted and the means of production are consumed only in the manner required by production itself, depends partly on the skill and intelligence of the labourers and partly on the discipline enforced by the capitalist for their combined labour. (Capital III: 83)

He goes on immediately, and somewhat feebly, to suggest that the enforced discipline will 'become superfluous under a social system in which the labourers work for their own account'. But it is too late: he has already acknowledged that 'waste' is antithetical to capitalism and there is no reason to suppose that further capitalist development will witness any reversal of this inbuilt tendency. Anyway, the claim is not an isolated or contradictory musing that undermines Marx's real intent since it reaffirms what he had demonstrated in Capital I. Explaining why 'our friend [the capitalist] has a penal code of his own', Marx asserts that it is because:

> ... all wasteful consumption of raw material or instruments of labour is strictly forbidden, because what is so is so wasted, represents labour superfluously expended, labour that does not count in the product or enter into its value. (Capital I: 190–91)

To return to a theme first introduced in Chapter 3, Marx is particularly impressed by the great technological strides made by the chemical industry — the very emblem of Rachel Carson's critique of the callous character of modern environmental destruction. For Marx the chemical industry is 'the most striking example' of technological progress in waste utilisation. This industry, he opines, 'utilises not only its own waste, for which it finds new uses, but also that of many other industries.' Then, in what can only be described as wide-eyed wonder, he continues: 'For instance, it converts the formerly almost useless gas-tar [i.e., coal tar — see Chapter 3] into aniline, dyes, alizarin, and, more recently, even into drugs' (Capital III: 102). In case these observations are taken to imply that capitalist industry obsessively searches for means to reconvert its used raw materials whilst post-consumer discards pile high in the streets and dust heaps, it needs to be noted that Marx was also well aware of the extent of the late nineteenth-century recycling industries and saved particular opprobrium for the rag trade. Here, observing that the sorting of rags comprises 'one of the most dirty, and the worst paid kinds of labour, and one on which women and young girls are by preference employed' he carefully notes that this utilisation of the excretions of consumption is a truly international undertaking — i.e., a developed sector of the capitalist economy — that sees rags 'reconverted' into manure, bedflocks, shoddy and paper (Capital I: 436).

So, in relation to both the 'waste' of capitalist industry and the 'waste' produced by individual consumption Marx discovers that there is nothing intrinsically wasteful about capitalism in its use of raw materials, its repairs and reconversions or in the final consumption of the products of capitalist manufacture by consumers. What he finds, in fact, is an incredibly complex arrangement of practices and processes for initially preventing waste and then, where this is not possible, for managing, sorting, and exploiting it in order to put it to useful work. Where such 'excretions' are unused and left to despoil the environment (as in the example of the pollution of the Thames) this is an inefficiency that generates 'heavy costs' but one that merely awaits the right application of technology in order to service greater productivity.

What emerges from this exploration of Marx's examination of material waste is that, in generic terms, he is keen to castigate capitalism for its waste of the forces of production but, in specific terms, he is forced to a set of countervailing conclusions. The generic critique targets the gross inequality between those who own the means of production and those who do not. This division simultaneously robs the labouring classes of the fruits of their labours and 'wastes' those labours by applying them to the expansion of capital rather than the satisfaction of human needs. But the specific critique finds that, in relation to any given site of production, the expansion of capital results in conditions of efficiency and a reduction in waste either through inventions or intensified working practices or through the 'reconversion' of waste products facilitated by either scientific and technological advances or the consolidation of international waste recovery industries.

There are, then, three different theses on waste to be derived from Marx. The first is the antagonistic production of 'social refuse' as a consequence of the combined forces of the class struggle and social disintegration. The second is the anarchic 'over-production' of goods, 'civilisation', industry and commerce — in short the over-production of capitalism itself as a consequence of the 'perverse' application of capital to generate more capital rather than satisfying human needs. The third is the reappropriation or reconversion of materials into new use- and exchange-values in the means of production in a continuing spiral of technologically mediated productive efficiency. In this case, the production of social refuse is inevitable, the over-production of commodities is inescapable but, except in some special circumstances, the production of waste materials is not. It is paradoxical that, along with Engels, Marx observed and condemned the squalor and filth in which the proletariat was forced to subsist but could not explain the generation of the substance of that filth — in what it materially consisted or where it came from — as an inbuilt logic of capitalist production.

The conundrum of waste in Marx's statement of materialism encouraged later theorists to travel in rather different directions although they are united in shifting the theoretical focus from the process of production to the process of consumption. In fact, ingenious as each reworking of the conundrum is, none of them have provided a satisfactory theoretical response to the problem of waste in capitalist society. In considering the shift of focus I begin with a critical outline of Thorstein Veblen, move onto the ways that his work was incorporated into a more systematic Marxist framework by Paul Baran and Paul Sweezy before addressing recent work by Zygmunt Bauman.

## CONSPICUOUS WASTE

'When my students in the College at the University of Chicago read *The Theory of the Leisure Class*', wrote David Riesman in 1953:

they are anything but shocked at its unmasking of the lifestyles of the bourgeoisie; rather, they act as if they had always known that. Several years ago, they insisted with vocal unanimity that nobody bought a Cadillac for any reason save show [...]. So thoroughly are these students and others like them at some of our Universities indoctrinated with Veblenism that they cannot allow themselves much pleasure of variation in dress: the blue-jeans garb accompanies them not only to class but to their evening folk-dancing dates. (Riesman, 1960: 176)

This indoctrination into Veblenism, Riesman proposes, is not merely a characteristic of social science students at some prestigious American Universities. Veblen's language, ideas and 'moral grammar', to borrow Varul's (2006: 107) expression, have become deeply embedded in cultural constructions of the consumer society. The phrases 'conspicuous consumption' and 'invidious distinction', Riesman (1960: 171) suggested, were 'so current in our talk' even by 1953 that they, and the book from which they derived, had 'lost the power to clarify the contemporary scene'.

Veblen, influenced by Marx, is no less scathing than the latter in his criticism of the social degeneration and decay wrought by capitalism but the target of Veblen's, at times brutal, satire of its wastefulness is rather different. Where Marx had asserted an image of classes in historic struggle, of the crippling, 'vampire like' exploitation of collective labour, Veblen, in *The Theory of the Leisure Class* (1899/1961), visualised a world that had descended into magniloquent exhibitionism. According to Veblen, those historic, or less developed contemporaneous, societies 'where the population [...] is relatively homogeneous, stable, and immobile' demonstrate a natural law governed by human instinct, namely that 'all wastefulness is offensive to native taste' (ibid.: 131, 132). In contrast, in the perverted industrial society of the turn of the twentieth century, wastefulness has become the very infrastructure of the social and economic order. Whilst the book's title and undeniable focus centres on the growth of a parasitic class of unproductive emulators — the 'leisure class' — who seek nothing more than recognition of their 'pecuniary ability to afford a life of idleness', the general thesis — that 'waste' is the foundation of modern consumption — is applied to all classes and all situations. Thus, writes Veblen:

> Any consumer who might, Diogenes-like, insist on the elimination of all honorific or wasteful elements from his consumption, would be unable to supply his most trivial wants in the modern market. (ibid.: 117)

The reason for this sorry state of affairs is that the 'modern market' is saturated with the merchandise of misapplied industrial production — industrial production that has been turned (warped, even) to service and sustain the ostentatious display of the 'non-productive consumption of time (ibid.: 34). Such wasteful consumption does not amount to indolence — indeed, it takes concerted effort to fritter away a society's productive resources, a feat achieved by the leisure class partly through its 'characteristic occupations' of 'government, war, sports, and devout observances' (ibid.: 32). Veblen vacuums into his doleful attack on modern industrial society everything from clothing through holidays to architecture: all aspects of expenditure and consumption are lambasted for the wastefulness both of the forms they take and the motives behind those acts of expenditure and consumption. Chastising members of the upper classes who make charitable bequests for the provision of 'schools, libraries, hospitals and asylums for the infirm or unfortunate', Veblen concludes that even this practice adheres to the 'law of conspicuous waste' that drives the modern world. In these cases, the 'diversion of expenditure' from any useful purpose 'is not uncommon enough to cause surprise or even raise a smile' because:

> An appreciable share of the funds is spent in the construction of an edifice faced with some aesthetically objectionable but expensive stone, covered with grotesque and incongruous details, and designed, in its battlemented walls and turrets and its massive portals and strategic approaches, to suggest certain barbaric methods of warfare. The interior of the structure shows the same pervasive guidance of the canons of conspicuous waste and predatory exploit. The windows, for instance, to go no farther into detail, are placed with a view to impress their pecuniary excellence upon the chance beholder from outside, rather than with a view to effectiveness for their ostensible end in the convenience or comfort of the beneficiaries within. (ibid.: 258)

This passage, which I have quoted at length, is a prime example both of Veblen's method in *The Theory of the Leisure Class* and of the yardstick against which he measured the decay of the modern order. In terms of method, from cover to cover the book is an extended polemical diatribe against frippery and ostentation *in general*. There is no particular case anywhere in the text that is deeply analysed so that the variety and intricacy of the scrutinised practices can be evaluated by readers. Every case discussed simply epitomises the more general principle that conspicuous waste is the ordering rule of modern consumption and expenditure. The cases are all *types* — which is to say that whilst they may exist in reality there is no evidence that any of them individually actually conform to Veblen's general description. Reality does indeed contain clothing and holidays, manners and servants, 'dram-drinking, "treating", and smoking in public places' (ibid.: 67) as well turreted buildings and charity work. But Veblen does not delve into any of these instances empirically to demonstrate their inherent wastefulness or, equally appropriately in this particular text, immorality. Instead, they are fused together in a kind of pointilist portrait of a total culture: the whole is convincing, often amusing, always erudite but step closer to the canvas and the details become confusing, blurred and indistinct. In the case of the 'aesthetically objectionable' stone-faced building above it is pertinent to ask which building Veblen is discussing and by whose standards is it 'objectionable'? In similar vein, it is clear that he did not ask the 'beneficiaries within' whether they appreciated the windows or found them convenient or comfortable.

In relation to Veblen's yardstick it is also clear that the cultural decay and moral dissolution of modern industrial society could not be measured in its own terms. Instead, Veblen needed an external standard, an abstract commitment or tenet that could stipulate the contrast between society *as it was* and society *as it ought to be*. For example, in his condemnation of ostentatious architecture above, Veblen proposes that the windows in these objectionable buildings are placed so as to emphasise their 'pecuniary excellence' rather than their 'effectiveness'. So expenditure that is 'wasteful', in this instance, contradicts effective utility. From the point of view of economic theory, he acknowledges, 'the expenditure in question is no more and no less legitimate than any other expenditure'. It is not wasteful 'from the standpoint of the individual consumer who chooses it'. Rather:

> It is here called "waste" because this expenditure does not serve life or human well-being on the whole. (ibid.: 73)

'Wastefulness' and 'usefulness' are qualities 'seen from the point of view of the generically human' not from the point of view of the individually human (ibid.: 74). What is useful produces well-being, what is wasteful undermines it.

It is true, says Veblen, that all objects tend to be 'useful and wasteful both' but his focus on consumption, rather than production, is justified on the grounds that:

> ... in a general way, the element of waste tends to predominate in articles of consumption, while the contrary is true of articles designed for productive use. (ibid.: 75)

There is a very strong sense running throughout the book that luxury, idleness and display are the enemies of social progress, that such psycho-cultural qualities of the industrial order sap the collective will and hold back the potential of science, technology and industry to deliver ever-more useful and ever-more productive solutions to economic and social needs. Do away with the frippery, it suggests, and human life will prosper and grow — although what kind of prosperity and growth might ensue from the disposal of frippery, and whether anyone would want it, is not made clear. As Riesman wittily notes in this regard:

> If Veblen were around now, his friends would almost certainly, with the best will in the world, urge him to consult a psychoanalyst. (Riesman, 1960: 186. First published 1953)

Whether Veblen should be considered a candidate for therapy or not, it is certainly true that he put his finger on a central problem in Marxist theory. As I noted above, Marx had expended some energy on the nature of commodities and their fetishistic character but did not depict in any detail how the fetishism manifested itself socially. Veblen, on the other hand, seemed to provide an historically grounded account of how that fetishism became socially effective. The things that were products of human labour took on strange meanings and embodied statuses that were distinctly different from what the objects comprised materially. Their conspicuous consumption and conspicuous waste sent cultural signals about social status and worth, about class hierarchies and gender relations. The uncoupling of consumption from need and the perversion of production to support ostentation rather than well-being chimed well with Marx's original comments and indicate the 'soft materialism' that Veblen developed in his critique of Marxian economics (Veblen, 1990a; 1990b).

## SURPLUS CONSUMPTION

The importance of Veblen's contribution, however, should be understood not only in terms of the role of conspicuous waste in sending cultural signals about status and worth. For *The Theory of the Leisure Class*, and later writings, also called attention to another fundamental question in Marx's work: if societies are characterised by the 'epidemic of over-production', by 'too much civilisation, too much means of subsistence, too much industry, too much commerce' as Marx and Engels had claimed, then where was it all? Even a leisure class fanatically dedicated to conspicuous waste on a full-time basis could not dissipate the gigantic surplus generated by capitalist industry. Where was this excess and why had it not brought capitalism finally to its knees in a 'universal war of devastation'? Veblen did not provide a detailed answer to the conundrum but he pointed the way towards an intriguing set of arguments and analyses that were taken up most influentially by Paul Sweezy (see Sweezy, 1962; 1981) and Paul Baran (see Baran & Sweezy, 1970). The answer to this Veblenian conundrum, according to Baran and Sweezy, is that capitalism 'wastefully' — even 'ostentatiously' — uses up the surplus in order to stave off collapse. The waste of capitalism, in true Veblenian spirit, is visible not in what it *excretes* but in what it *expends*.

Like Veblen, Sweezy followed Marx in arguing that modern industry generates an enormous surplus that is neither consumed efficiently nor put to productive use and, furthermore, that the surplus disproportionately accrues to the bourgeois class. However, where Veblen had attributed the discrepancy between production and use to the emulative culture of 'invidious comparison' — in which self-respect, esteem and personal worth are socially ranked in terms of accumulated property — Sweezy argued that the discrepancy is a structural condition of the workings of capitalism. The argument was first put forward systematically in 1942 in *The Theory of Capitalist Development* (see Sweezy, 1962). In this groundbreaking work, Sweezy supplemented Marx's comments on 'over-production' with a theory of 'underconsumption' (1962: 162–89). The core of the thesis is that the 'competitive capitalism' analysed by Marx has given way to 'monopoly capitalism' the fundamental contradiction of which is a tendency 'to expand the capacity to produce consumption goods more rapidly than the demand for consumption goods' (ibid.: 180, 189. See also Sweezy, 1981: 39). The contradiction arises because the purpose of capitalism is the perpetual expansion of capital — for this, according to Marx, is 'the motive and purpose of production; that production is only production for *capital*' and not for the '*society* of producers' (Capital III: 250. Emphasis in original). In consequence, production is expanded 'without any reference to the consumption which alone can give it meaning' (Sweezy, 1962: 175). As a corollary to the general expansion of production regardless of need, capitalism also actively restricts the consumption power of labour to a 'variable minimum' — through depressed wages, primarily, but also by the 'greed for an expansion of capital and a production of surplus value on an enlarged scale' (Capital III: 244). The effect of the contradiction is an economic system overburdened with a surplus of capital — a burden that renders the economy liable to prolonged stagnation unless some means can be found to transform the surplus into profitable use or, at least, enable it to support the continuation of capitalism.

Thus, stagnation, according to Sweezy, is 'the norm towards which capitalist production is always tending' but the tendency is offset by a range of 'counteracting forces' (Sweezy, 1962: 218) that both stimulate demand and provide a range of uses for the surplus. These forces include new industries and population growth but most importantly they consist in 'wasteful', non-productive expenditures, including an expanded 'machinery of selling and distribution' which 'softens the contradictions':

> ... not by making it possible for capitalism to harness the expanding productive forces, but rather by diverting their use into socially unnecessary and hence wasteful channels. (Sweezy, 1962: 286)

Clarifying and explaining this proposition is a crucial but relatively small part of *The Theory of Capitalist Development* — which deals also with Marx's method, capitalist crises, the state, imperialism and fascism in order to ground the 'case of capitalism' in 'a careful study of the state, monopoly, and world economy' (ibid.: 236).

In *Monopoly Capital* (Baran & Sweezy, 1970) the question of wastefulness takes on a much more central role. The book's focus remains true to Sweezy's original work — the description and explanation of a specific phase of capitalism characterised by monopoly. However, much more attention is devoted to an account of why the surplus of capitalism is generated and how it is absorbed in order to counteract the threat of stagnation. In typically straightforward style Baran and Sweezy describe the 'topsy-turvy, and fetishistic' (ibid.: 326) appearance of monopoly capitalism from the individual's point of view in the following terms:

> The self-contradictory character of monopoly capitalism — its chronic inability to absorb as much surplus as it is capable of producing — impresses itself on the ordinary citizen in a characteristic way. To him, the economic problem appears to be the opposite of what the textbooks say it is: not how best to utilize scarce resources but how to dispose of the products of super-abundant resources. (ibid.: 114).

Surrounded by goods and services of every imaginable description, the dilemma facing the individual citizen is not the fact that there is 'too little' but its precise opposite, that there is 'too much'. 'This condition of affairs', Baran & Sweezy continue:

> … is peculiar to monopoly capitalism. The very notion of "too much" would have been inconceivable to all precapitalist forms of society; and even in the competitive stage of capitalism, it described a temporary derangement, not a normal condition. (ibid.)

In order to explain how 'too much' becomes the normal state of affairs in conditions of monopoly, Baran and Sweezy devote one chapter to the characteristics of 'the giant corporation' and one to 'the tendency of surplus to rise'. In the first case, citing Veblen's (1904: 24) comments on the 'strategic control of the conjunctures of business', they argue that modern monopolistic corporations are rational calculators that, far from competing in a free market, are geared towards manipulating and controlling markets in an 'institutionalization of the capitalist function' (Baran & Sweezy, 1970: 55). So, whilst 'the way the system works is still the unintended outcome of the self-regarding actions of the numerous units that compose it' (ibid.: 63), nonetheless, the competitive game has subtly altered. The key task under monopoly capitalism is not to grow by driving other capitalists out of business through increased efficiency of production and cheaper prices. Instead, the task is 'the creation and expansion of markets' (ibid.: 115): the intensification and deeper penetration of existing markets and the opening up of previously non-market situations to capitalist exchange.

This characteristic of giant corporations feeds directly into the second quality of monopoly capitalism. Such corporations do not compete with each other in a finite market but in one that, theoretically at least, is infinitely expandable — existing consumers may be persuaded to purchase more or different commodities or new consumers can be added by either selling things that were nominally 'free' (such as water or public services) or by selling existing commodities in new regions or countries. These logics of expansion under monopoly conditions mean that the growth of one industry or business does not have to take place at the expense of another: monopoly capitalism is not a 'closed' system that is able to distribute only a fixed quantity of goods or realise a fixed quantity of profit. On the contrary, the ever-increasing capacity to produce goods coupled with the theoretical facility to expand markets indefinitely means that the total amount of goods and services — and consequently the total 'surplus' of capitalism — grows ever greater.

Baran and Sweezy suggest that, in order to prevent the surplus from resulting in economic stagnation it must be utilized or absorbed. 'In general', they write:

> ... surplus can be absorbed in the following ways: (1) it can be consumed, (2) it can be invested, (3) it can be wasted' (ibid.: 87).

Whilst it is certainly the case that capitalists' consumption has grown in absolute terms, they suggest, it has declined 'as a proportion of surplus': in other words, capitalists' consumption cannot keep pace with the overall rate of growth of that surplus. Nor, similarly, can investment keep pace. For, every investment in new technologies in the production process or in the expansion of markets either reduces the costs of production or stimulates demand for what capitalists produce: in both cases the investment simply adds to the problem of increased surplus — either in the form of goods and services themselves or, more importantly, in the form of investment-seeking income. Consequently, the single most important conduit for absorbing the ever-growing surplus of the capitalist economy is to expend it in non-productive or wasteful ways. Baran and Sweezy provide many examples of such expenditures including, in an updating of Veblen's complaint against ornate architecture, the construction of:

> ... grandiose headquarters buildings, providing [ ... ] functionaries with offices which grow plusher by the year, transporting them in fleets of jet planes and Cadillacs, granting them unlimited expense accounts, and so on and so on. (ibid.: 56).

But these practices are mere triflings when compared with the real wastes of the capitalist system. However much they show off the 'pecuniary excellence' of the corporation and its members, no amount of 'grandiose' building work and attendant luxuries could absorb the accumulated (and ever accumulating) surplus. Instead, this surplus must be absorbed in non-productive activities of the capitalist system itself. Baran and Sweezy place most of their emphasis on expenditures in the sales effort and in military expenditures. In the first case, they propose that Veblen's analysis of the role of 'salesmanship' in conspicuous waste is '100% on target' when applied to post-war America in the sense that the huge order of difference between what it costs to produce an object and the price for which it sells is chiefly a consequence of 'the production of saleable appearances' rather than any intrinsic utility in the object itself (ibid.: 136). Whilst Veblen concerned himself primarily with the tendency of consumers to be influenced by 'the finish and workmanship of the goods [rather] than by any marks of substantial serviceability' (Veblen, 1961: 118), Baran and Sweezy examined the sales effort as a whole — including, as listed in the appendix by Joseph D. Phillips, 'advertising, market research, expense account entertaining, the maintenance of excessive numbers of sales outlets, and the salaries and bonuses of salesmen' as well as 'public relations, lobbying, the rental and maintenance of showy office buildings, and business litigation' (Baran & Sweezy, 1970: 365). When a consumer buys a product or service in monopoly capitalism, most of the price paid is absorbed by this institutional, social and political framework, i.e., by its 'non-productive', 'wasteful' packaging, and only a fraction represents the 'value' of the product or service itself.

In relation to militarism they argued that, in the American case, huge increases in expenditure were driven partly by the desire to contain the threat of Soviet socialism and partly by the drive to expand and consolidate an (American led) empire of 'free enterprise'. But even if specific historical factors are absent, they implied, military spending provides jobs, incomes and technological investment that is capable of absorbing a significant portion of the surplus. It is 'wasteful' in the sense that it contributes nothing useful to the social system as a whole — a proposition that, on its own, indicates Baran and Sweezy's heavy intellectual debt to Veblen. Whereas, in the United States at least, 'the means already exist for overcoming poverty, for supplying everyone with the necessities and conveniences of life' the bare facts of life for millions are poverty, ill health, ghettoisation, lack of education and criminalisation. It is possible to achieve 'the utmost perfection in the manufacture of weapons of mass destruction' but, in the context of American social reality, such perfection 'does not make their production rational' (ibid.: 330, 349). It merely betrays the irrationality of a system that wastes the vast resources at its disposal rather than apply them judiciously to social improvement.

## SURPLUS EXCLUSION

Where Veblen was concerned with the ostentatious waste of goods and time and Baran and Sweezy with the non-productive expenditure of resources as a means to prop up capitalism, Zygmunt Bauman, in his book *Wasted Lives*, proposed that '[separation] and destruction of waste was [...] the trade secret of modern creation' (Bauman, 2004: 21. Emphasis omitted) and that the 'destination of waste is the waste-yard or the rubbish heap' (ibid.: 12). Whilst this particular book is ostensibly about a superfluous population of 'migrants, refugees and other outcasts' — the 'downtrodden or the underdog' as he put it in the interview with Richard Kilminster and Ian Varcoe (see Bauman, 1992: 206) — it is clear that the analysis is meant to apply also to material objects because waste 'is the dark, shameful secret of all production' (Bauman, 2004: 27). In this definition, 'material objects, whether human or inhuman' amount to the 'superfluous, unnecessary, unneeded and unwanted' which 'tends to be piled up indiscriminately on the same refuse tip' (ibid.: 22, 40, 78) — a passage undoubtedly indebted to Marx's description of the lumpen proletariat as a 'whole indefinite, disintegrated mass, thrown hither and thither'.

The specific origin of this approach to waste is to be found in Bauman's intellectual shift from a concern with a 'postmodern' social order characterised by indeterminacy, ambivalence, 'inconclusiveness, motility and rootlessness' (Bauman, 1992: 192, 203) to a concern with a 'liquid modern' social order characterised by fluidity, disengagement and interchangeability (Bauman, 2000: 6, 11, 13. See also Bauman, 2004: 117, 123). What drives the analytical shift is Bauman's increasing focus on consumerism and its pervasive impact on all social relations and personal ambitions. Already, in *Life in Fragments* (1996), Bauman had argued that where 'modern' society engaged citizens as producers, 'postmodern' society engaged them as consumers. This distinction became increasingly relevant to Bauman's project so that by 1998 he abandoned the modern/postmodern dichotomy altogether, arguing instead, that:

> In its present late-modern, second-modern or post-modern stage, society engages its members — again *primarily* — in their capacity as consumers. (Bauman, 1998: 24)

Here, the 'late', 'second' or 'post' quality of society is no longer of any relevance and any label is as good as any other. Instead, Bauman draws the distinction between 'then and now' in terms of the (old) emphasis on producerism and the (new) emphasis on consumerism: consumerism becomes the defining and substantial characteristic of the contemporary world and all relationships, experiences and phenomena are explained in its terms.

Although these intellectual developments seem a world apart from Veblen or Baran and Sweezy — indeed, Veblen is rarely invoked and Sweezy is never referred to — Bauman nonetheless remains partial heir to both traditions. In relation to Veblen, Bauman follows the underlying thrust of *The Theory of the Leisure Class* exactly, arguing that 'a society of consumers is one of universal comparison — and the sky is the only limit'. 'The main concern is therefore', he continues, 'that of *adequacy* — [...] of having the ability to rise to the new opportunity as it comes, [...] to "get in" more than before' (Bauman, 2000: 76, 77). Thus, personal worth, self-esteem, social standing are all, as Veblen had argued, rooted in acquisition, the display of ability ('prowess') and conspicuous consumption. In relation to Baran and Sweezy, he readily acknowledges that 'the production of consumers itself devours an intolerably large fraction of the total costs of production — a fraction which the competition tends to enlarge further, rather than cut down' (ibid.: 75). In this case, 'consumerism' reaches way beyond individual experiences, choices, behaviours or relationships and is a structural component of socio-economic activity on a grand scale. To describe this kind of structural impact as an instance of 'the petrification of the cultural products of cultural activity' (Bauman, 1992: 210), as Bauman defines 'structure', would be stretching the concept of 'petrification' beyond breaking point. Rather, it is precisely the interweaving of structural and cultural analysis that marks Bauman, like Veblen before him, as a 'soft materialist' in the sense that he eschews all historical determinism yet retains an emphasis on the particularity of historically rooted conditions of action.

For Bauman, 'to consume' objects does not mean simply 'wearing them, playing with them and otherwise causing them to satisfy one's needs and desires':

> To consume also means to destroy. In the course of consumption, the consumed things cease to exist, literally or spiritually. Either they are "used up" physically to the point of complete annihilation [...] or they are stripped of their allure [...] and so become unfit for consumption. (Bauman, 1998: 23)

Elsewhere he proposes that consumerism:

> ... is not about *accumulating* goods (who gathers goods must put up as well with heavy suitcases and cluttered houses), but about *using* them and *disposing* of them after use to make room for other goods and their uses. (Bauman, 2003: 49. Emphasis in original)

Of course, as we have seen in Chapter 5, this sentiment is very far from the reality of consumption and disposal behaviour — cluttered houses, for example, are very common indeed and discarding things is a complex series of activities that are not necessarily or simply about making room for more goods. But Bauman has little — if any — interest in the empirical reality of waste objects and what people (or organisations) do with them. Rather, his interest is in the 'waste' that is 'liquid modern culture' which:

> ... no longer feels like a culture of learning and accumulation like the cultures recorded in the historians' and ethnographers' reports. It looks

instead like a *culture of disengagement, discontinuity and forgetting'* (Bauman, 2004: 117. Emphasis in original)

So, whilst the subtitle of Bauman's (2004) book is 'modernity and its outcasts', the real target of its analysis is not the wasted lives of the 'superfluous populations', nor the wasted objects of rampant consumerism but the wasted lives of ordinary citizens whose embracing of the new 'Big Brother' ideology of exclusion is rooted in the paucity of their culture and the detachment of their politics. In this lament for a lost world of engagement in which 'our ancestors fought back against the awesome powers of Big Brother', (ibid.: 132--3) Bauman seeks a material symbol that encompasses the decay of modern political culture. The 'huge volumes of waste' (Bauman, 2003: 123) spawned by the contemporary 'addiction' to consumption (Bauman, 2000: 74–6) are the physical and human remnants of a society built on discarding and excluding the flawed, the incomplete and the redundant by-products of consumerism (Bauman, 2004: 12–14).

If, for Veblen and for Baran and Sweezy, the waste of capitalism consists in what it expends, for Bauman this waste consists in what it ejects and excludes. But it is not the material objects themselves — 'whether human or inhuman' — that are the real waste of a consumption-addicted capitalism. The real waste lies in the *process* of ejection. Like Douglas, Bauman construes this process as a by-product of creating order — like a factory that 'turns out waste alongside its intended product' (Bauman, 2003: 128). But, unlike Douglas the by-product is not an outcome of the differentiating activity of the mind. Instead, it is a social process (see Bauman, 2004: 22, 30–31): the (im)morality of ejection is a social fact of consumer capitalism. In this regard, where Marx had vilified the 'refuse of all classes' Bauman offers society's outcasts sympathy and pity — the 'surplus population', the 'immigrants', the 'flotsam and jetsam of the planetary tides of human waste' (ibid.: 57) — are casualties of modernization, globalization and consumerism. They serve no purpose in historic class struggles, and their 'ever rising quantities' have 'no useful function' (ibid.: 69, 77) other than to clean up behind callous consumers or play the role of scapegoat for society's tensions and anxieties. Rather than absorbing the waste of capitalism, they stand as visible reminders of just what a waste contemporary capitalism is.

Characteristically more subtle and more poignant, Bauman's argument is, at base, a restatement of the 'throwaway society' thesis: 'waste' exposes the moral void at the heart of consumer culture. For Bauman, 'wasting' is not fundamentally a sociological process — except in the Durkheimian sense that all social facts are really moral facts — and it is not differently organised and co-ordinated through varying contexts, conditions and relationships. Nor is it a socially orchestrated process of production that generates this or that waste in different material forms in different times and places. Instead, waste is the inevitable by-product of a consumerist logic that consigns all imperfections, defects and flaws to the same (late/second/post-modern) refuse tip of exclusion. Where Veblen had sought to unpick the minutiae of displays of ostentation and the cultural contamination these symbolised, and Baran and Sweezy the wasteful expenditure of capitalist surplus as a means of propping up a stagnating economy, Bauman invokes the 'wasteful' material and human consequences of mass addiction to the logic of consumerism. For Bauman, then, the waste of modern society is an emblem of moral decay: a dematerialisation — even destruction — of social and political engagement in a world in thrall to the baubles and trinkets, the shiny, gleaming but hollow promise of consumer freedom.

# Conclusion
## Rubbish Society!

Where there's muck there's brass (Old Yorkshire aphorism)

In April and May of 2002, *The Guardian* (UK) newspaper carried a series of articles by Emma Brockes on waste. They touched on issues of consumption, waste disposal and management, and included the views of the waste industry, refuse collectors and Green activists. I put down the last of this series of articles (*The Guardian G2* Section, Wednesday, 22/05/2002) expecting the following day's letters page to be filled with comment, rebuttal, fascination and outrage. What I had forgotten was that every time a major newspaper publishes an analysis of waste disposal and recycling it is inevitably ignored, in the major British Dailies, at least: an almost total wall of silence has surrounded every example since the mid-1990s. More people are willing to tell tales about their personal infidelities, pathologies and diseases than are willing to contribute to a debate about waste. Newspapers have become virtual confession media in which a national outpouring of sinful and reprehensible behaviour has become an expected part of the daily literary diet. Yet, it is a rarity indeed for waste to occupy even one hundredth of the column inches devoted to personal aberration. Perhaps it is a sign of our times that people are in the shadow of a greater awe and in the abyss of a greater guilt about waste than they are about their sexual, psychological and biological malfunctions.

An important reason for this lies in just how closed and narrow is the public debate about waste. Whilst a century of psychoanalysis, personal liberations and medical advances have opened the confessional floodgates of personal angst, the utter absence of any sophisticated public reflection on the nature, causes and consequences of wasting has resulted in only two possible positions. One abandons the question of rubbish to the tiny expert and technical echelons of scientific and scholarly institutions. The other abandons it, as a societal-wide moral failure, to the Green movements in order that they may induce in government, economy and society a new and ecologically sound way of doing business as usual. In both cases, the complexity of waste and the many different roles it plays in industry and in social life are ignored. Waste is treated, in these abandonings, as the end of value and worth.

Yet, we should remind ourselves that 'where there's muck there's brass' and add to this aphorism that where there's brass there's muck. For brass and muck, or wealth and waste, are not two contradictory substances, two different 'things' that oppose each other in eternal social and economic struggle. They are two dimensions of the same thing: two proportions of value and utility that inhere in the material objects of the world, in the industrial production and collective consumption of those objects. The wastes of production and consumption have played crucial roles in social and economic change, they have been, and are, objects of personal, industrial and political significance. They are not things that can be got rid of by the invention of new technologies because they are central players in the development of technology. They cannot be tidied away by more and more bureaucratic rules and regulations because those rules and regulations express vested interests in the exploitation and continued social circulation of wastes. Certainly, waste products of many descriptions are personally injurious, environmentally degrading and socially menacing. But the 'wastes' themselves are no more injurious, degrading or menacing than many of the objects of desire whose 'by-products' they ostensibly are. To get hung up about a contemporary 'crisis' of post-consumption waste, rather than the injurious, degrading and so often fatal means by which consumer objects are produced in the first place is to put a relatively small cart before a very large horse.

This idea — that contemporary society faces a 'waste crisis' — is deeply embedded in popular consciousness and a central element in much policy and scholarly rhetoric. It is an idea that has to forget history in order gain any purchase on the contemporary scene. But paying attention to historical stories about waste suggests that the relationship between waste and society has always been critical (see Chapter 1). It has been critical in terms of the invasion of filth and detritus into every nook and cranny of urban life, its accumulation in streets, waterways, houses, 'in alleys, at the foot of milestones, in cabs'. Its festering, stinking, disease-carrying and health-harming qualities have persisted alongside urban populations for centuries and so normalised has it been in certain times and places that some of its constituents passed (and continue to pass) virtually unnoticed. Waste's apparently excessive presence, its over-abundance, has stimulated many and diverse schemes for its exploitation — from profit-turning sewerage projects through double payment for its removal and management to shady deals and political manipulations to build airports, parks and boulevards. There is nothing specifically modern about the problem of waste and, indeed, many modern developments — including waste recovery and conversion processes, clean and safe sewerage systems, and regulated waste management organisations — might be viewed with a sense of relief when even recent experiences with waste are held up to scrutiny. Furthermore, the idea that consumerism is the harbinger of a waste crisis rooted in a callous disinterest in the value of materials and objects misconstrues the benefits that consumerism brought to some of the most disadvantaged members of the industrial world. Whilst some have argued that consumerism has been accompanied by a changed relationship between people and the material objects that passed through their lives, it is most definitely true that it was accompanied by enormous gains in health, education, leisure and social rights at the same time that the urban environment became more hygienic and, at least in terms of effluents and debris, spectacularly more congenial. The four historical stories that I outlined in Chapter 1 lend weight to the idea that waste has always been, and remains, a critically important dimension of, especially urban, social experience. What has happened to waste historically reveals something basic about the social and political changes that have characterised the emergence of modern, industrial, consumer society. The emergence of this social order was dependent on the changing nature of both its understanding of and its means of dealing with the wastes that were being produced. In Chapters 2 and 3, I outlined some of the aesthetic (Chapter 2) and industrial (Chapter 3) characteristics of waste in the modern social world.

I made stories of waste the central theme of Chapter 2 because to imagine waste in any systematic sense is to imagine the world in which it is produced. It is to invoke a moral and sociological assessment of personal worth, social organisation and societal development — it invariably involves a judgment about the 'health' or otherwise of society at large. The four stories outlined in this chapter represent significant transition points in the emergence of contemporary understandings of waste. They are all fictions, of one kind or another, but I suggest that they capture the spirit of how wider social understandings of waste have altered from the late nineteenth century to the present day. I am not arguing that each story has successively displaced its predecessor so that there is nothing left of Dickens's dust-filled vision or Eliot's loss of value in the contemporary world. Rather, like the wastes that are recounted within the stories, each is an accretion upon or accumulation of imaginary contents, consequences and relationships of or with waste. However, I would also propose that each vision exhibits, in part, the dominant images in which waste has been portrayed historically during the emergence of modern industrial society. They reflect something of the real experience of waste at particular times and in particular places.

Dickens's sketch of the moral worth buried within the 'accumulated scum of humanity' connects to sets of relationships that Victorians had with waste. When street scavengers and gatherers, as we saw in Chapter 3, hourly and daily picked the streets and accumulated dust heaps for objects of value, they demonstrated systematically and irrefutably that the dust of the cities contained all manner of useful and valuable things. When eight and a half acres of accumulated debris could be sold to 'rebuild Moscow' here was clear evidence that even the last, seemingly desperate dregs and leftovers of urban life retained some measure of worth. As with the dust piles, so with the lowliest inhabitants of London's social hierarchy — here too, for Dickens, is value in abundance. It is not the low or high status of the individual that determines their moral worth, any more than it is the dusty or discarded status of materials that determines their usefulness. Rather, moral worth is either built into the individual or it is not and social standing cannot and does not alter that fundamental fact. Dickens's use of London's dust and filth to narrate a story about usefulness and value makes sense precisely because Victorian London lived intimately, side-by-side with that filth. The distance between respectability and disrepute was as thin as the 'stickey' polish that clung to the Veneerings and even in this case to venture beyond the protective walls of the respectable household was immediately to enter the grime and murkiness of the metropolis.

By the time that Eliot published *The Waste Land* the social fabric recounted by Dickens had been torn apart. Many of the worst slums that had characterised London in Dickens's time had been torn down. Motorised transport had reduced the enormous volumes of equine waste that slimed the highways of central London. With the exception of the continued threat of the 'London particular' — the choking smog that regularly settled over the city — the urban environment had been transformed immensely. Sewerage systems had been laid, municipal waste operations were systematically removing rubbish from doorsteps, the street scavengers were mostly out of business as new, chemically synthesised materials replaced the economic function the former had provided. The essential dustiness of life that had underpinned Dickens's tale of redemption and demise was far less visible in Eliot's urban experience. So, for Eliot, 'dust' or waste — the debris and detritus of life — was not a source of moral worth, a foundation of life, a value in itself. Instead, Eliot sees waste as absence, as the loss of sets of values that held together an old order, even as an emptiness or deficiency of value that can be refilled or revitalised only through concerted and personally difficult decisions and action. The waste in *The Waste Land* invokes a challenge to post-war Europe and references a wider sense of economic and social deficiency in the aftermath of the Great War that is also captured by Talbot's (1919) and Kershaw's (1928) complaints about the loss of value that waste represents and the efficiency and dynamism that would ensue from reversing this loss in a new industrial order.

The dissonant, uncertain, valueless terrain of *The Waste Land* is overturned in Philip K. Dick's dystopian vision of the consequences of industrial excess. Here, in the kipple and the dust that slowly but inexorably covers the earth and infects its inhabitants is not a Dickensian redemption or an Eliotian ambiguity. Instead, there is only the certainty of destruction and disintegration. The industrial system that floods the world with technological marvels also rains deadly dust on its inhabitants — it is responsible both for the invention of new life forms and the obliteration of existing life forms: the creative destruction of modern technology has devastated the natural world and poses an immanent threat to all life on planet earth. Waste is a lethal consequence of technological progress and the rapacious consumption of and callous disregard for nature's bounty. Where Dickens had presented London's dust as an element of life itself and Eliot had presented waste as the absence of value, Dick (and Harrison and Brunner) grasps waste as the excessive menace of pollution. It consists in the 'slop and swill' that Dorothy Sayers had lambasted but inflected by Rachel Carson's vision of a dying environment choking on the ever-increasing toxicity of society's detritus.

The very title of Don DeLillo's monument to the twentieth century — *Underworld* — reveals the different imagination of waste that the book invokes: underneath the world of appearances is a shadow world of values and objects. Whilst these values and objects are rarely observed or scrutinised they are, nonetheless, the 'flesh and breath' of a people's history. What connects the past to the present in everyday culture is not the artistry, poetry or literature of greatness: it is the scraps, the 'patches and adumbrations' of mundane life. It is these scraps and patches that connect each person to 'what they did before you'. The scraps might comprise pocket litter, an old, stained baseball, a Styrofoam cup or any object that, on the surface, appears useless. The value of these junk items subsists in the fact that they are the material residues of ordinary life. Whilst their meanings may be hidden or obscured by the journeys they have taken from initial use to final disposal, they remain filled with cultural significance. This significance promotes a reverential relationship to the discarded objects of desire that fill the landfills and caverns where America's quotidian culture is interred. It persuades the character Nick Shay to handle his garbage 'esoterically' — like 'preparing a Pharaoh for his death and burial' — and obsessively to sort and separate the valuable from the valueless. Just as there can be no certainty that any object is an authentic piece of history so there can be no certainty that any object has lost all its authenticity and value. The waste of the modern world is represented here not as the certainty of destruction and disintegration but as the shadow existence of everyday life.

These four narratives are not the strange imaginings of socially disconnected isolates. They draw on features of the social contexts of their production in order to tell stories about the state of the world and its personal and social meanings. Dickens's story expresses not only an injunction to consider moral worth in its own terms, it also delves deeply into the dustiness of Victorian London and recounts vibrant relationships between society, its wealth and its wastes. Those wastes, as Chapter 3 explained, were crucial sources of technological and industrial development and, for many of the poorest members of the population, a source of income and usable resources. Large numbers of the poor lived on, from and with the dust of Victorian England and scavenged the streets and dust heaps for materials that could be returned to industrial production. Many Victorian industries depended absolutely on this socially organised practice — the paper industry and the tanning industry being particular cases in point. But this does not mean that mid-Victorian England was less 'wasteful' than what followed it. It means that this era was characterised by one way of organising the social circulation and transformation of wastes and what followed it was characterised by a different method of organising that circulation and transformation. For, by the time that Dickens's novel was published, the reliance on armies of independent scavengers was already giving way to the synthesis of new products from dangerous and injurious industrial wastes or the discovery of new uses for what had, for long, been considered useless. Medicines and dyes from coal tar; automotive transport from petroleum spirit; air travel from 'waste' hydrogen; moisturisers, lubricants and, eventually, explosives from glycerin: all of these technological wonders persuaded some that industrial and domestic refuse might become the foundation for economic and social progress in the aftermath of the Great War. The economic value of these rubbish resources implied that the careless disposal of fats, rags, cinders, paper, shells, glass and all of the other 'wastes' from industry and households represented a tremendous loss of national resources. If only these wastes could be collected and exploited in a systematic, rational way, economic stagnation could be avoided and technological progress assured. But the confidence in modern industry's ability to transform industrial and domestic wastes into ever-increasing quantities of useful goods was short lived. This loss of confidence was not, initially, because of a perceived failure of industry to deliver on its recycling potential. From the 1930s to the 1960s the value and scale of industrial and agricultural recycling operations continued to grow. The loss of confidence was initially rooted in a moral complaint about where society was headed: the 'gluttony' and greed, the selfishness and social disconnection that characterised economic growth; the destruction of moral values attendant on the 'artificial stimulation' of consumption that was Keynesian economics. Rather than a loss of resources and economic values the 'trash and waste' of the burgeoning consumer society consisted in its excesses, its over-production and over-consumption of needless goods. By the 1960s, the critique of greed, gluttony, selfishness, and excess was joined by a sense of menace: the excess of waste became a threat to planetary life partly through the gluttony of consumerism but more importantly through the toxicity of industrial production itself. Unregulated releases of industrial effluents, illegal dumping of noxious contaminants, the increasing toxicity of consumer products themselves — the evidence on the environmental impacts of a chemical culture mounted quickly. Thus, two sets of ideas were merged into the now familiar 'crisis of waste' outlook: consumerism breeds gluttony, gluttony breeds profligacy, profligacy breeds waste, waste poisons the planet, therefore consumerism is the cause of the crisis of waste in both its excessive and toxic guises.

Notwithstanding that rapacious exploitation of natural resources and the — regulated and unregulated — deposition of toxins is responsible for an environmental catastrophe on a global scale, the 'consumerism equals waste crisis' proposition should still be subjected to scrutiny and not merely taken as an article of faith. It is not easy to investigate the validity of the proposition empirically because the relevant data are thin. However, what data are available suggest that consumerism and profligacy are not as strongly associated as has been assumed. When the disposal practices of modern households are compared with those of our parents and grand-parents it appears that today's consumers do not in fact wantonly waste a great deal more than our forebears. When these disposal practices are set in their proper social and industrial contexts, and when changing waste management methods are taken into account, today's consumers are not the comparatively callous wastrels they have been made out to be. Looking at the numbers (Chapter 4) — that is, the quantities of materials discarded — over time, the methods of counting these quantities and the means by which the quantities entered various disposal routes indicates that our non-consumerist grandparents were as likely to 'waste' valuable resources as we are today. Whether rags, paper, wood, cinders, food, glass or metals the disposal rates for these items from the beginning to the end of the twentieth century did not grow as significantly as is implied in the claim that con-sumerism is responsible for a waste crisis. Moreover, when contemporary relationships with various wastes are investigated (Chapter 5) it transpires that 'callous disposal' does not accurately depict the richness and intimacy of people's relationships with wastes of many different kinds. In fact, alleg-edly profligate consumers go to extraordinary lengths to revalue, restore or pass on carefully all manner of 'excess' items. As in Dickens's London, con-temporary consumers live *with* the wastes that pass through their lives and apply energy and effort to uncover or discover any values they might have. The energy is applied not only to large and obviously useful objects — fur-niture, white goods, clothes, electrical items — but also to the 'junk' that accumulates as life progresses — the old books and video tapes, the plastic bottles, the paper, and so on. These things, as Don DeLillo so poignantly portrayed, comprise the 'flesh and breath' of people's histories: they are meaningful, 'spiritual' objects of desire that invoke memories and signal personal events and relationships. So far from being wantonly profligate, people invest the material 'shadow' of their lives with value and virtue and seek useful and meaningful sites where it can continue to serve needs and desires. It is not ordinary people who divest these materials of meaning and significance. Rather, it is the political and commercial institutions charged with waste management. Here, no sense of the intrinsic value of waste is to be found — the only value that counts is waste's commodity value. Instead of attaching life's junk to familial and communal contexts of experience, the commercial exploitation of waste *detaches* it from these human milieus and inserts it into impersonal channels of profitable enterprise. It is engaged not in the socialisation of waste but in its commodification.

In sociology, the bewildering variety of meanings, relationships and values in which waste is embroiled has represented a major theoretical dilemma — one so problematic that few have attempted to tackle it. Where sociologists have attempted to theorise waste two different directions have been pursued. Some have depended on a transposition of Mary Douglas's anthropological study of dirt to the modern scene. Here, the focus has been on classification, categorisation, naming — on the mental constructs by which waste is symbolically ordered and represented. As Chapter 6 explained, however, the transposition of Douglas's thesis to modern waste is fraught with difficulties dealing with which demands that the original thesis is supplemented with an array of additional propositions, hypotheses and arguments. Thus, whilst waste, following Douglas's understanding of dirt, is a construed as a cognitive matter it is also the sticky reminder of mortality, the consequence of a clash of worldviews, the 'abjectivity' of modern excess, the 'bourgeois habitus' of excretory manners, or the 'haunting shadow' of modern reason. These additions to Douglas's original thesis are necessary because there is no theoretical connection between the cosmological universe of the 'primitive' cultures to which the thesis applied and the endless cultural variability of modern society. The random hotch-potch of 'different fields of symbolic action' that makes up the cognitive landscape of modernity means that the latter's total culture cannot be grasped through its pollution and cleanliness rituals. This is precisely why Douglas did not include any consideration of dirt and pollution in her account of modern consumption. What Douglas's followers demonstrate most clearly is that her portrayal of the cultural variability of modern society applies to its sociological theories as well as its everyday symbols. In some modern places waste symbolises abjectivity or excess, in others a sticky indication of mortality, in others again a habitus or a haunting shadow. These are not incorrect or somehow deficient representations. On the contrary, they each signal the divergence of the symbolic fields in which waste attains meaning and significance in modernity and provides an affirmation of Douglas's original claim that the divergence engenders disjointed, rather than unified, cognitive constructions. Modern idealism is as endlessly variable as the cultural contexts in which its claims are made meaningful.

The second direction that has been pursued in the attempt to develop a theory of waste has been to connect waste to the social and economic relations of capitalism. Beginning with the work of Karl Marx this materialist analysis has also produced a disjointed collection of concepts and constructs. Marx himself did not develop a systematic theory of capitalist waste and, as I showed in Chapter 7, three different theses on waste can be derived from his writings. These are the social production of a class of human 'refuse', the overproduction of capital, and the 'reconversion' of the 'excretions of production'. In each case the underlying process that generates these 'wastes' is different. The lumpen proletariat emerge as a consequence of social disintegration and the logic of class struggle; the over-production of capital arises from the anarchic organisation of industry and the disconnection of production from social need; the excretions of production (and consumption) represent either resources for manufacture or inefficiencies that await the application of new technological solutions. The heirs to this materialism have tended to take the process of capitalist production for granted and focus attention on wasteful consumption. Veblen's theory of conspicuous waste castigates the perversion of industrial production to satisfy 'non-productive consumption'. Whilst his (1899) book focused on the norms and practices of a 'leisure class', it is clear that the thesis applies to consumption in general: 'invidious comparison' has infected the whole of society with the consequence that social standing and personal worth are measured by the ostentatious display of waste. But capitalist society produces so much surplus that such individual consumption could never account for it all. Instead, according to Baran and Sweezy, the gigantic surplus is 'wasted' by reconverting it into non-productive expenditures — in the sales effort, in the military, and in government bureaucracy. For Veblen and for Baran and Sweezy, the 'waste' of capitalism is measurable by what it non-productively expends — either in a culture of invidious comparison or in a concerted effort to prop up an economy constantly under the threat of prolonged stagnation. For Bauman, on the other hand, the waste of capitalism consists not in what it expends but in what it ejects and excludes. In an updating of Packard's 'throwaway society' thesis he argues that the modern 'addiction' to consumption has engendered a 'culture of disengagement' in which any imperfection, incompletion or redundancy is consigned to the human or material scrap heap.

In both the idealist and materialist constructions waste always stands for something other than itself: the abjection of technological culture or the shadow of Western reason, the emulative practice or the structural absorption of non-productive expenditure. Waste, here, has no dimensions of its own, no characteristics that mark it as this or that kind of thing or relationship, no contexts through which its variety and abundance is visible. In short, it has no existence in and of itself. To speak of waste is too often to decontextualise the processes that sustain different kinds of wastes in different kinds of relationships. The consequence of the decontextualisation is an image of waste as something that can be disappeared if only the right technology, bureaucratic rule or moral standpoint were adopted — if only we could be like our parents and grandparents, if only we were not addicted to the logic of consumerism, if only industry were organised socialistically, if only government would encourage us to 'do all the obvious things' — then we could make the nasty waste disappear! What is rarely suggested, and even more rarely openly debated, is that 'waste' will *never* go away. No technical, bureaucratic or moral fix is available to cure the wastage of society because waste is not the excess, remainder, or surplus of what modern societies produce and consume. We need to construe waste as *what* societies produce and consume or, at least, to grasp that the production and consumption of waste is as important, as central to social life as the production and consumption of anything else in modern society. Producing, managing, storing, routing, organising, sorting, mining, recovering, reprocessing and trading rubbish is an integral and expanding element of modern economies. Only when this fact is acknowledged will it be possible openly and honestly to conduct a rational debate about how waste can be socially valued in ways that determine that good things, rather than bad things, happen to it.

Contemporary society organises its wastes in different ways to those of its immediate and not so immediate predecessors, but it is wrong to suggest that today's citizens are more callous and disdainful of the consequences of their wasting activity. Throughout the history of industrial society there have been vested interests in the production, circulation and consumption of waste substances of very many kinds — whether in the dust heaps of Dickens's London, the synthesis of industrial by-products into valuable resources or the conversion of scrap plastics, metals, glass and agricultural debris into useable goods and services. In today's world there remain vested interests in the production, circulation and consumption of waste substances: industries and bureaucracies thrive on this production, circulation and consumption. The peculiar, historically unique character of modern society's wastefulness cannot be changed without simultaneously refashioning those industries and bureaucracies. The target of attack cannot be the throwaway mentality of ordinary citizens. To propose that unproblematic moral lessons from the past can be applied in the present — that earlier phases of modern history were characterised by relations of 'stewardship' and 'guardianship' of material goods and resources in contrast to our own repugnant profligacy — is a truly bizarre misconstruction of the historical record. It is also a somewhat blinkered approach to the significance of waste in contemporary social, economic and political life.

In developing a sociology of waste, I have concentrated on the variety of stories, experiences, practices and processes that entangle waste in many different kinds of relationships and imbue it with many shades and forms of value. In part, my aim has been to challenge the idea that waste can be understood only in terms of the excesses of a 'throwaway society' and partly to expose its deep and meaningful roots in social life and in industrial development. Waste is truly a paradox of modern society. It simultaneously expresses value and non-value, repugnance and desire. It motivates the search for usefulness and stimulates national and international political and economic alliances and organisations, valuation schemes and trading arrangements. It is everywhere: in the home, the street, the factory, the office, the soil, the seas and the atmosphere. It is produced and reproduced, managed and routed, valued, devalued and revalued in countless shapes and sizes. To waste is to engage in a complex social process characterised by diverse social meanings and social practices, orchestrated through multiple networks and institutions, revealing desire, spirituality and beauty as well as profits, resources and commodities. To rubbish society, then, is to install this fundamental quality of our connection to the wastes we produce and consume as a central and necessary dimension of social organisation.

In this respect it is true that I live in a throwaway society, but so too did my parents, and their parents, and their parents before them, and so on, all the way back to Adam and Eve — who must have discarded the apple core carelessly since the Bible makes no mention of fruit juice, citrus oil or pectin recovery operations. I dread to think what Edwin Chadwick would have done with a few thousand gallons of the toxic by-products of the contemporary chemical industries, and the vision of my Tudor ancestors managing several tonnes of nuclear waste is too nightmarish to contemplate. All societies, not just the modern 'consumer' version, are 'throwaway societies.' The issue is not whether contemporary society throws things away *in contrast* to a past which stewarded objects and reused and recovered resources. The issue is whether the throwing away can be organized better and made to serve purposes that are at least as beneficial as they are harmful. There is no way of responding to this question without understanding the contribution that throwing things away has made in the past, and continues to make in the present, to social, economic and industrial development.

Waste is not the 'dark, shameful secret of all production', as Bauman claims (see Chapter 7). How can there be anything 'dark' or 'shameful' about the inevitable generation of debris and detritus? Waste can only be grasped as a reprehensible material form if it is construed as the accidental or callous by-product of something else. But, as I have been at pains to show throughout this book, not only is waste ultimately unavoidable — a *normal* constituent of social life — it is, simultaneously, the spur and means to incredible technological, economic and social transformation. Individually, it may be that we are what we eat but collectively it is more appropriate to aver that we are what we excrete. When we realise how *absolutely central* to life is the process of wasting then, and only then, might we be able to do something rational and collectively desirable with the intrinsic richness, variety and abundance of modern waste and value it for what it is. Waste is useful and always has been. It is time to get a proper intellectual and political grip on the rubbish reality that drives social change.

# Notes

## INTRODUCTION

1. Eurostat Statistics in Focus, Environment and energy, no. 7/99: 'Hazardous waste in the European Union' (1999).

## CHAPTER 1

1. http://www.bedoyere.freeserve.co.uk/FUMIFUGIUM.HTM. Retrieved August 2003
2. See http://www.museumoflondon.org.uk: 'Urban Grime Exhibition'
3. Parliamentary Sessional Papers, 1865, viii (171): iii. London: HMSO
4. See Inglis, 2001: 269, 279, *et passim*. For a discussion of the rise of American indoor plumbing in the nineteenth century, see Ogle, 1996.
5. http://www.ci.nyc.ny.us/html/dcp/html/fkl/ada/competition/2_0.html. Retrieved August 2003.

## CHAPTER 2

1. Unattributed page numbers in this section refer to Dickens (1997).
2. Unattributed page numbers in this section refer to Eliot (1963).
3. Unattributed page numbers in this section refer to Dick (1999).
4. Unattributed page numbers in this section refer to DeLillo (1998).

## CHAPTER 3

1. Examples of research on hazardous waste and pollution since the 1960s include the Agricultural Research Council (1967), Clayton and Chilver (1973), McCormick (1985), Franklin, Hawke & Lowe (1995).
2. See *USA Today* 'Space junk traffic jams could clog Earth's paths' (17/05/2002). See also http://www.csmonitor.com/durable/1999/06/28/fp2s2-csm.shtml. (Retrieved 18/08/2003).

## CHAPTER 4

1. Interestingly, this figure is almost exactly the same as that provided by Wylie for the year 1954–55 in his treatise on the agricultural and commercial value of town wastes where Wylie finds himself unknowingly in striking agreement with Talbot in proposing that each person produced 1.68 lbs of refuse daily (Wylie, 1955: 84, 200–1).

# Bibliography

Adburgham, A. (1989). *Shops and Shopping, 1800–1914: Where, and in what manner the well-dressed Englishwoman bought her clothes*, London: Barrie & Jenkins. Second Edition. First published 1964.

Agnew, J-C. (1983). 'The consuming vision of Henry James' in R. W. Fox & T.J. Jackson Lears (eds) *The culture of consumption: critical essays in American history, 1880–1980*, NY: Pantheon Books, p.69.

Agricultural Research Council (1967). *The effects of air pollution on plants and soil*, London: Agricultural Research Council.

Alexander, J.H. (1993). *In defense of garbage*, Westport, CT: Praeger.

Appadurai, A. (1986). 'Commodities and the Politics of Value', in A. Appadurai, ed, *The social life of things: commodities in cultural perspective*, Cambridge, Cambridge University Press.

Atlas, M. (2002). 'Few and Far Between? An environmental equity analysis of the geographic distribution of hazardous waste generation,' *Social Science Quarterly* 83 (1): 365–78

Baran, P.A. & Sweezy, P.M. (1970). *Monopoly capital: an essay on the American economic and social order*, Harmondsworth: Penguin. First published 1966.

Bataille, G. (1991.) *The accursed share: an essay on general economy. Volume I: Consumption*, New York: Zone Books.

Bauman, Z. (1992). *Intimations of postmodernity*, London: Routledge.

—— (1996). *Life in fragments*, Cambridge: Polity.

—— (1998). *Work, consumerism & the new poor*, Buckingham: Open University Press.

—— (2000). *Liquid modernity*, Cambridge: Polity.

—— (2003). *Liquid love: on the frailty of human bonds*, Cambridge: Polity.

—— (2004). *Wasted lives: modernity and its outcasts*, Cambridge: Polity.

Beck, U. (1992). *Risk society: towards a new modernity*, London: Sage.

Benjamin, W. (1973). *Illuminations*, London: Fontana. First published 1955.

Berman, M. (1983). *All that is solid melts into air: the experience of modernity*, London: Verso.

Blackmur, R.P (1991). 'T.S. Eliot' in Cuddy, L.A. & Hirsch, D. H. (eds) (1991) *Critical essays on T.S. Eliot's the waste land*. Boston, MA: G. K. Hall & Co., 73–82. (First published 1928).

Booth, W. (1890). *In darkest England, and the way out*, London: International Headquarters of the Salvation Army.

Brindle, D. (1998). 'Council in waste product insult to dead censured', *The Guardian*, 7th August 1998.

Brunner, J. (1968). *Stand on Zanzibar*, New York: Doubleday.

Carson, R. (1994). *Silent Spring*, New York: Houghton Mifflin Co. With an introduction by Al Gore. First published 1962.

Clapp, J. (2001). *Toxic exports: the transfer of hazardous wastes from rich to poor countries*, Ithaca, NY: Cornell University Press.

Clayton, K. M & Chilver, R.C. (eds) (1973). *Pollution abatement*, New York: McGraw Hill.

Colten, C.E. & Skinner, P.N. (1996). *The Road to Love Canal: managing industrial waste before EPA*, Austin: University of Texas Press.

Cooper. T. (2005). 'Slower consumption: reflections on product lifespan and the throwaway society', *Journal of Industrial Ecology 9* (1-2): 51–67.

Corbin, A. (1986). *The foul and the fragrant: odor and the French social imagination*, Leamington Spa: Berg Publishers. Trans Marian L. Kochan, Roy Porter and Christopher Prendergast. First published 1982, Aubier Montaigne.

Cuddy, L.A. & Hirsch, D. H. (eds) (1991). *Criticalesssays on T.S. Eliot's the waste land*, Boston, MA: G. K. Hall & Co.

Dant, T. (1999). *Material culture in the social world: values, activities, lifestyles*, Buckingham: Open University Press.

———— (2005). *Materiality and society*, Buckingham: Open University Press.

DeLillo, D. (1985). *White noise*, New York: Viking.

———— (1998). *Underworld*, London: Picador.

Department for Environment, Food and Rural Affairs (2003). 'Waste statistics 2003' http://www.defra.gov.uk/environment/statistics/wastats/ (Retrieved February 2004).

———— (2005). 'Municipal Waste Management Statistics 2003/04', http://www.defra.gov.uk/news/2005/050308b.htm (Retrieved July 2005).

Department of Environment (1971). *Refuse disposal: report of a working party on refuse disposal*, (Chaired by J. Sumner) London: HMSO.

Dick, P.K. (1999). *Do androids dream of electric sheep?* London: Millenium Books. Gollancz S.F. Masterworks Series. First published 1968.

Dickens, C. (1997). *Our mutual friend* London: Penguin. Edited with an introduction and notes by Adrian Poole. (First published 1865).

Douglas, M. (1978). *Natural symbols*, Harmondsworth: Penguin. First published 1970.

———— (2002). *Purity and danger: an analysis of the concepts of pollution and taboo*, London: Routledge. First published 1966.

Douglas, M. & Isherwood, B. (1979). *The world of goods: towards and anthology of consumption*, London: Allen Lane.

Durning, A.T. (1997). *How much is enough?: the consumer society and the future of the earth*, Worldwatch Environmental Alert Series. New York: W. W. Norton and Co.

Engels, F. (1974). *The condition of the working class in England. From personal observation and authentic sources*, St. Alban's, Herts: Panther. With an Introduction by Eric Hobsbawm. Fist published 1845.

Eliot T.S. (1922). *The waste land* in T.S. Eliot (1963) *Collected Poems 1909–1962*, London: Faber and Faber.

Ferrell, J. (2006). *Empire of scrounge: Inside the urban underground of dumpster diving, trash picking and street scavenging*, New York: New York University Press.

Flintoff, F. & Millard, R. (1969). *Public cleansing: refuse storage, collection, and disposal; street cleansing*, London: McLaren & Sons.

Foster, J.B. (2000). *Marx's ecology*, New York: Monthly Review Press.

Franklin, D., Hawke, N. & Lowe, M. (1995). *Pollution in the U.K*, London: Sweet & Maxwell.

Gabor, D. & Colombo, U. (With A. King & R. Galli). (1978). *Beyond the age of waste: a report to the Club of Rome*, Oxford: Pergamon Press.

Gandy, M. (1993). *Recycling and waste: an exploration of contemporary environmental policy*, Aldershot: Avebury.

—— (1994). *Recycling and the politics of urban waste*, London: Earthscan.

Girling, R. (2005). *Rubbish! Dirt on our hands and crisis ahead*, London: Transworld Publishers.

Gregson, N. & Crewe, L. (2003). *Second hand cultures*, Oxford: Berg.

Gregson, N., Metcalfe, A. & Crewe, L. (2006). 'Identity, mobility and the throwaway society' http://www.sheffield.ac.uk/content/1/c6/04/72/08/Identity%2 0Mobility%20and%20the%20Throwaway%20Society.pdf (Retrieved October 2006).

Haley, B. (1978). *The healthy body and Victorian culture*, Cambridge, MA: Harvard University Press.

Hansen, K. Tranberg. (2000). *Salaula: the world of second hand clothing and Zambia*, Chicago: University of Chicago Press.

Harrison, H. (1986). *Make Room! Make Room!* Harmondsworth: Penguin. First published in 1966 by Doubleday, New York.

Harrison, R. M (1996). *Pollution: causes, effects and control*, London: Royal Society of Chemistry, 3rd edition.

Hertwich, E.G. (2003). 'Editorial: Consumption and industrial ecology', *Journal of Industrial Ecology* 9 (1–2): 1–6.

Hetherington, K. (2004). 'Secondhandedness: consumption, disposal and absent presence', *Environment & Planning D: Society & Space*, 22: 157–73.

Hicks, J. & Allen, G. (1999). *A century of change: trends in UK statistics since 1900*, House of Commons Research Paper 99/111, London: House of Commons.

Hills, R.L. (1988). *Papermaking in Britain, 1488–1988: A short history*, London: The Athlone Press.

Hunter, D. (1957). *Papermaking: the history and technique of an ancient craft*, London: The Cresset Press

Inglis, D. (2001). *A sociological history of excretory experience: Defacatory manners and toiletry technologies*, Mellen Studies in Sociology, volume 30. Lewiston, NY: The Edward Mellen Press.

Jones, A. (1967). *War on waste*, London: Conservative Political Centre. CPC number 369.

Kershaw, J.B.C. (1928). *The recovery and use of industrial and other wastes*, London: Ernest Benn, Ltd.

Koller, T. (1918). *The utilization of waste products: A treatise on the rational utilization, recovery, and treatment of waste products of all kinds*, London: Scott, Greenwood & Son. 3rd edition, translated from the 2nd revised German edition. First published (in English) 1902.

Kyd, T. (1996). *The Spanish tragedy*, New York: St. Martin's Press. First published 1592.

Lash, S. and Urry, J. (1987). *The end of organised capitalism*, Cambridge: Polity.

Leadbeater, C. (2000). *Living on thin air: the new economy*, Harmondsworth: Penguin.

Lipsett, C.H. (1963). *Industrial wastes and salvage: Conservation and utilization*, New York: The Atlas Publishing Co., Inc. 2nd edition. First published 1951.

Luckin, B. (2000). 'Pollution in the city' in M. Daunton (ed) *The Cambridge history of Britain, volume III: 1840–1950*, Cambridge: University Press.

Lynch, M.J., Stretesky, P. & McGurrin, D. (2001). 'Toxic crimes and environmental justice,' in G. Potter (ed) *Controversies in white collar crime*, Cincinatti, OH: Anderson

Mandel, E. (1983). 'Economics' in D. McLellan (ed) *Marx: the first 100 years*, London: Fontana, pp. 189–238.

Marx, K. *Capital: a critique of political economy*, London: Lawrence & Wishart.

—— (1977). Volume I: *The process of production of capital*. Translated by Samuel Moore & Edward Aveling. Edited by Friedrich Engels. First published 1867.

—— (1974). Volume II: *The process of capitalist circulation*. Edited by Friedrich Engels. First published 1885.

—— (1977). Volume III: *The process of capitalist production as a whole*. Edited by Friedrich Engels. First published 1894.

Marx, K. & Engels, F. (1976). *Basic writings on politics and philosophy*, London: Fontana. Edited by Lewis S. Feuer. First published 1959.

—— (1981). *The communist manifesto*. Introduction by A.J.P Taylor. Translated by Samuel Moore. Harmondsworth: Penguin. First published 1848.

Mayer, J.T. (1991). 'The Waste Land: Eliot's Play of Voices', in Cuddy, L.A. & Hirsch, D. H. (eds) *Critical essays on T.S. Eliot's the waste land*, Boston, MA: G. K. Hall & Co., 265–78.

Mayhew, H. (1981). *The Morning Chronicle survey of labour and the poor: the metropolitan districts. volume 2*, Horsham: Caliban Books. First published 1849–50.

—— (n.d.). *Mayhew's London: being selections from 'London labour and the London poor' by Henry Mayhew*, London: Spring Books. [Attr. W. Kimber, 1951. First published 1851]

McCormick, J. (1985). *Acid earth: the global threat of acid pollution*, London: International Institute for Environment & Development.

McLaughlin, T. (1971). *Coprophilia: or, a peck of dirt*, London: Cassell & Co.

Melosi, M.V. (1983). *Garbage in the cities: refuse, reform and the environment, 1880–1980*, College Station: Texas A&M University Press.

Miller, B. (2000). *Fat of the land: garbage of New York, the last two hundred years*, New York: Four Walls Eight Windows.

Mims, C. (1998). *When we die: the science, culture and rituals of death*, New York: St Martin's Press

Mitchell, R.J. & Leys, M.D.R. (1964). *A history of London life*, Harmondsworth: Penguin. First published 1958.

More, C. (1997). *The Industrial Age: economy and society in Britain, 1750–1995*, Harlow, Essex: Addison Wesley Logman. Second edition. First published 1989.

Moyers, B. with The Center for Investigative Reporting (1991). *Global dumping ground: the international traffic in toxic waste*, Cambridge: The Lutterworth Press.

Mumford, L. (1934). *Technics and civilization*, New York: Harcourt & Brace.

Murphy, R.E. (1991). 'Considering Phlebas: The poetry of *The Waste Land*' in Cuddy, L.A. & Hirsch, D. H. (eds) *Critical essays on T.S. Eliot's the waste land*, pp.248–56. Boston, MA: G. K. Hall & Co.

Murray, R. (1999). *Creating wealth from waste*, London: Demos.

O'Brien, M. (1999a). 'Rubbish Power: Towards a Aociology of the Rubbish Society', in J. Hearn & S. Roseneill (eds) *Consuming cultures: power and resistance*, Basingtoke: MacMillan, 262–77.

—— (1999b). 'Rubbish Values: Reflections on the Political Economy of Waste', *Science as Culture* 8 (3): 269–95.

Ogle, M. (1996). *All the modern conveniences: American household plumbing, 1840–1890*, Baltimore: Johns Hopkins University Press.

Orwell, G. (1989). *Coming up for air*, Harmondsworth: Penguin. First published 1939.

Packard, V. (1957). *The hidden persuaders*, New York: McKay.

—— (1967). *The waste makers*, Harmondsworth: Penguin. First published 1960.

Palmer, J. (1988). *War on waste*, London: Dryad Press, Ltd.

Pearce, F. & Tombs, S. (1998). *Toxic capitalism*, Aldershot: Ashgate.

Pinkney, T. (1988). 'The Aristocracy in *The Waste Land*' in L. Cookson & B. Loughrey (eds) *Critical essays on the waste land. T.S. Eliot*, Harlow: Longman.

Poole, A. (1997). 'Introduction' in Charles Dickens, *Our mutual friend*, London: Penguin, pp. ix–xxiv.

Rathje, W. & Murphy, C. (1992). *Rubbish! The archaeology of garbage*, New York: Harper Collins.

Riesman, D. (1960). *Thorstein Veblen: a critical introduction*, New York: Charles Scribner's Sons. First published 1953.

Riis, J. (1890). *How the other half lives*, New York: Charles Scribner's Sons.

Roach, M. (2003). *Stiff: the curious lives of human cadavers*, London: Penguin

Robbins, R. (1999). *Global problems and the culture of capitalism*, London: Allyn & Bacon.

Roszak, T. (1972). *Where the wasteland ends: politics and transcendence in post industrial society*, New York: Doubleday.

Salusbury, G.T. (1948). *Street life in mediaeval England*, Oxford: Pen-in-Hand Publishing Co. Second Edition. First published 1939.

Sayers, D. (1948). *Creed or Chaos? And other essays in popular theology*, London: The Religious Book Club.

Scanlan, J. (2005). *On garbage*, London: Reaktion Books.

Schlosser, E. (2000). *Fast food nation: What the all-American meal is doing to the world*, London: Penguin.

Schoon, N. (1996). 'Significant shorts,' *The Independent*, 15th July p.2.

Sehgal, H.S. & Sehgal, G.K. (2002). 'Aquacultural and socio-economic aspects of processing carps into some value-added products' *Bioscience Technology*, 82: 291–3.

Simmonds, P.L. (1876). *Waste products and undeveloped substances: a synopsis of progress made in their utilisation during the last quarter of a century at home and abroad*, London: Hardwicke & Bogue.

Skitt, J. (1972). *Disposal of refuse and other waste*, London: Charles Knight & Co.

Smith, G. Jr. (1991). 'Memory and Desire: *The Waste Land*' in Cuddy, L.A. & Hirsch, D. H. (eds) *Critical essays on T.S. Eliot's the waste land*, Boston, MA: G. K. Hall & Co. 122–39. (First published 1956).

Soper, G.A. (1909). *Modern methods of street cleaning*, London: Archibald Constable & Co. Ltd.

Spears Brooker, J. & Bentley, J. (1991). 'The defeat of symbolism in "Death by Water"' in Cuddy, L.A. & Hirsch, D. H. (eds) *Critical essays on T.S. Eliot's the waste land*, Boston, MA: G. K. Hall & Co., 239–47. (First published 1989).

Spooner, H.J. (1918). *Wealth from waste: elimination of waste, a world problem*, London: George Routledge & Sons, Ltd.

Standage, T. (1999). *The Victorian internet: the remarkable story of the telegraph and the nineteenth century's online pioneers*, London: Weidenfeld and Nicolson.

Stearns, P.N. (2002). *Consumerism in world history: the global transformation of desire*, New York: Routledge

Strasser, S. (1982). *Never done: A history of American housework*, New York: Pantheon Books.

——— (1989). *Satisfaction guaranteed: the making of the American mass market*, Washington, DC: Smithsonian Institute Press.

Strasser, S. (1999). *Waste and want: a social history of trash*, New York: Henry Holt & Co.

Stretesky, P. & Hogan, M. (1998). 'Environmental justice: An analysis of super-fund sites in Florida,' *Social Problems* 45: 267–87.

Sweezy, P.M. (1962). *The theory of capitalist development: principles of Marxian political economy*, London: Dennis Dobson Ltd. First published 1942.

Sweezy, P.M. (1981). *Four lectures on Marxism*, New York: Monthly Review Press.

Talbot, F. (1919). *Millions from waste*, London: T. Fisher Unwin, Ltd.

Tammamagi, H. (1999). *The waste crisis: landfills, incinerators, and the search for a sustainable future*, Oxford: University Press.

Teynac, F., Nolot, P. & Vivien, J-D. (1981). *Wallpaper: a history*, London: Thames & Hudson. Trans from the French by C. Lloyd Morgan

Thompson, M. (1979). *Rubbish theory: the creation and destruction of value*, Oxford: Oxford University Press.

United Kingdom Environment Agency, 'Managing Waste' (http://www.environment-agency.gov.uk/subjects/waste. Retrieved June 2003).

Van der Ryn, S. (1978). *The toilet papers: recycling waste and conserving water*, Sausalito, CA: Ecological Design Press.

van Loon, J. (2002). *Risk and technological culture: towards a sociology of virulence*, London: Routledge.

Varul, M.Z. (2006). 'Waste, Industry & Romantic Leisure: Veblen's theory of recognition', *European Journal of Social Theory*, 9 (1): 103–117

Veblen, T.B. (1904). *The theory of business enterprise*, New York: Scribner's.

Veblen, T.B. (1961). *The theory of the leisure class: an economic study of institutions*, New York: Random House (The Modern Library Edition). Foreword by Stuart Chase. First published 1899.

Veblen, T.B. (1990a). 'The Socialist Economics of Karl Marx and His Followers. 1. The Theories of Karl Marx', *The Quarterly Journal of Economics* 20. Reprinted in Thorstein Veblen, *The Place of Science in Modern Civilization and Other Essays*. Introduction by Warren Samuels. London: Transaction Publishers, pp. 409–430. First published 1906.

Veblen, T.B. (1990b). 'The Socialist Economics of Karl Marx and His Followers. 2. The Later Marxism', *The Quarterly Journal of Economics* 21. Reprinted in Thorstein Veblen, *The Place of Science in Modern Civilization and Other Essays*. Introduction by Warren Samuels. London: Transaction Publishers, pp. 431–456. First published 1907.

Wohl, A.S. (1983). *Endangered lives: public health in Victorian Britain*, London: J.M. Dent & Son.

Womack, J.P. & Jones, D.T. (1996). *Lean thinking: banish waste and create wealth in your corporation*, NY: Simon & Schuster.

Woodward, D.H. (1991). 'The Hidden years of *The Waste Land* manuscript' in Cuddy, L.A. & Hirsch, D. H. (eds) *Critical Essays on T.S. Eliot's The Waste Land*, pp.60–5. Boston, MA: G. K. Hall & Co. (First published 1989).

Wright, A. (1984). *The literature of crisis, 1910–22: Howards End, Heartbreak House, Women in Love and The Waste Land*, London: MacMillan.

Wright, L. (1960). *Clean and decent: the fascinating history of the bathroom and the Water Closet*, London: Routledge & Kegan Paul.

Wylie, J.C. (1955). *Fertility from town wastes*, London: Faber & Faber.

Wylie, J.C. (1959). *The wastes of civilization*, London: Faber & Faber

Young, J.E. (1991). *Discarding the throwaway society*, Washington, DC: Worldwatch Institute. (Worldwatch Paper 101).

# Index

Adburgham, A. 29
Agnew, J-C. 28
Agricultural Research Council. 181
Airship 66–67
Alexander, J.H. 87
Alkali Act 22
Appadurai, A. 120–121
Archaeology xi, 6, 12
Atlas, M. 88

Baran, P.A. (see Sweezey)
Bataille, G. 47
Bauman, Z. 9, 164–168, 177, 179
Beck, U. 3
Benjamin, W. 145
Berman, M. 43
Blackmur, R.P. 46
Body tissues 78–79
Booth, W. 31
Bricolage 31
Brindle, D. 78
Brunner, J. 35, 51
Bubonic plague 13, 14, 16, 17
Bunters 60

Capitalism (see chapter 6); economy of
        waste in 154–155
Carson, R. 48, 50–51, 75, 125
Chadwick, Edwin 17–18, 22, 179
Clapp, J. 75
Clayton, K. M & Chilver, R.C. 181
Coal ash 15, 95–96, 97, 100–102
Coal tar (gas tar) 67–68, 155
Colten, C.E. & Skinner, P.N. 75
Commodification 8, 119–124 175
Consumerism 6, 28–33, 84, 88, 98,
        107, 108, 111, 119, 131–133,
        156–160, 165–167, 171
Cooper. T. 111

Corbin, A. 17
Corpses 37–38, 77–78
Crisis of waste 12, 83–84, 88, 91–93,
        99, 170, 175
Crossing sweepers 18

Dant, T. 110
Defecation 17, 139–140 (see sewers &
        sewerage)
DeLillo, D. 7, 36, 52–56, 118, 174, 175
Department for Environment, Food
        and Rural Affairs 89–91, 92, 94
Department of Environment 95,
        98–99, 104
Dick, P.K. 1, 7, 48–52, 172–173
Dickens, C. 7, 36, 37–43, 44, 47,
        51, 54–55, 56, 64, 125, 128,
        171–172
Dirt 9, 25, 26; as cognitive construct
        126, 128; as indication of
        mortality 134, 136; as risk 139
        (see chapter 6)
Douglas, M. xii, 4, 9, 125–133, 134,
        135–136, 137, 138–139, 140,
        141, 142, 143, 145, 167, 176
Durning, A.T. 111, 115–116
Dust 7, 37–43, 48, 50–51, as
        foundation of life 42, 47–48,
        171–172
Dust collectors 20–21, 26, 40
Dustbin 89, 90

Eliot T.S. 7, 36, 44–48, 51, 172
Engels, F. 18–19, 24 (see also Marx)
Erythropoietin 78–79
Excretions of production 153–155, 177

Ferrell, J. 8, 108–112, 113
Filthy streets 18, 24–25

Fleet River 13
Flintoff, F. & Millard, R. 94, 95,
    101–103, 104
Fly tipping 67, 93, 104
Forces of production (waste of) 151,
    156
Foster, J.B. 152
Franklin, D., Hawke, N. & Lowe, M.
    181

Gabor, D. 28, 84
Gandy, M. 12, 185–186
Garbage 'laws of' xii; metaphysics
    142; as shadow 7, 52–56, 82,
    141–142, 173, 175, 176
Girling, R. 86–87
Gluttony 70–72, 174
Glycerin 68–70, 174
Goodwill Industries 31
Great War 23, 45, 46, 47, 99
Gregson, N. 8, 112–115, 116
Gunpowder 68–69

Haley, B. 19
Hansen, K. Tranberg 112
Harrison, H. 51–52
Harrison, R. M.
Hertwich, E.G.
Hetherington, K. 137
Hicks, J. & Allen, G. 95
Hills, R.L. 59, 60
Horne, R.H. 42
Horses 25, 104
Hunter, D. 59
Hygiene (*see* public health)

Incineration 121–123
Industrial revolution 64–70
Inglis, D. 11, 126, 133, 139–141
Internal combustion engine 65–66

Jones, A. 74, 76
Junk 115–119; 'Law of' 117

Kershaw, J.B.C. 32, 69, 73
Kipple 2, 48–49, 51
Koller, T. 1, 154
Kyd, T. 46
Landfill 30, 54, 121
Leadbeater, C. 78
Leisure class 157–158
Lipsett, C.H. 72–73
Luckin, B. 22, 23

Lumpen proletariat 147–149, 164–168,
    176
Lynch, M.J. 87–88

Mandel, E. 151
Marx, K. xii, 9, 70, 146–156, 157,
    160, 161, 167, 176–177
Mayer, J.T. 44, 46
Mayhew, H. 18, 19, 20–21, 24, 60,
    62–63
McCormick, J. 181
McLaughlin, T. 11, 12, 13, 14, 42,
    126, 133, 134–136
Mediaeval era 12
Melosi, M.V. xi, 11, 24–25
Miller, B. 11, 21, 26–27, 68
Mims, C. 78
Mitchell, R.J. & Leys, M.D.R. 14
Modernism 45–46, 47–48
More, C. 29
Moyers, B. 75
Mumford, L. 70
Murphy, R.E. 44, 45–46
Murray, R. 76, 84, 86, 89–91, 93,
    103–104

Night soil 23, 40–41
Non-productive (wasteful)
    consumption 157, 159, 160, 163

O'Brien, M. xii, 115–124
Odour 13, 15, 17, 19
Ogle, M. 181
Organic wastes 79–81
Orwell, G. 107, 125
Overproduction 29, 149–151, 160,
    162, 176–177

Packard, V. 28, 71–72, 74, 84, 88, 111
Palmer, J. 76
Paper 58–61, 63, 73, 155
Paraffin 64–5
Pearce, F. & Tombs, S. 88
Perfume (*see* odour)
Petroleum spirit 64–66, 174
Pinkney, T. 45
Politics of waste 23–28, 86–87
Pollution 26, 127–128, 129 174 (*see*
    waste); as aesthetics 137
Poole, A. 37, 39
Population 91–92, 94–95, 99
Pound, Ezra 44
Primitive culture 126, 129–130

Public health 11, 17–18
Public Health Acts 22, 23
Pure 61–64

Rag and Bone Collectors 2, 64
Rags 58–60, 61, 63, 73, 155, 174
Rakers 13
Rathje, W. & Murphy, C. xi, 6, 75,
    83, 117
Recycling 8, 69, 89–90, 92, 94,
    100–101, 109–111 (*see also*
    waste recovery)
Riesman, D. 156–157, 159–160
Riis, J. 24
Roach, M. 78
Robbins, R. 29
Roszak, T. 75

Salusbury, G.T. 16
Salvation Army 31
Sayers, D. 71–72, 84, 111
Scanlan, J. 126, 133, 141–143, 147
Scavengers 7, 18, 37–38, 59–64,
    108–109, 173
Schlosser, E. 79
Scientific revolution 61–64
Scrounge economy 108–112
Second hand consumption 112–114;
    and household disposal
    practices 114–115
Sehgal, H.S. & Sehgal, G.K. 81
Sewers & Sewerage 20, 21, 22–23, 26,
    141, 153–154
Simmonds, P.L. 32, 61, 64, 67, 154
Skitt, J. 94, 95, 101–103, 104
Smith, G. Jr. 46
Smoke pollution 14, 15, 23
Soper, G.A. 32, 81, 99
Space programme 77
Spears Brooker, J. & Bentley, J. 46
Spooner, H.J. 33, 68, 73, 100
Standage, T. 60
Stearns, P.N. 29
Strasser, S. 11, 15, 30–31, 133
Street cleansing 18, 25
Stretesky, P. 88
Sustainable development 151–152
Sweezy, P.M. 9, 151, 160–164,
    165–166, 167, 177

Talbot, F. 57, 65, 67, 68, 69, 70, 73,
    94, 96
Tammamagi, H. 12, 84, 85, 86, 87–88

Teynac, F., Nolot, P. & Vivien, J-D. 60
Thames River 13, 37, 154
Thompson, M. xi, 109, 126, 133,
    136–138
Throwaway society xii, 6, 28, 71, 84,
    103, 105, 107, 114, 124, 150,
    167–168
Tudor era 14
Typhoid 17, 19

Underconsumption (*see*
    overproduction)

Van der Ryn, S. 80
van Loon, J. 126, 133, 138–139
Varul, M.Z. 157
Veblen, T.B. 9, 111, 156–160, 162,
    163, 164, 165, 167, 177

Waste: collection systems 32;
    consumption 4, 10; garden
    104; household 8, 30–31, 175
    (*see* chapter 4); household
    incineration 32, 70, 87,
    100–102; litter 92, 99; matter
    out of place 9; miscellaneous
    103–104; municipal (*see* chapter
    4); packaging 86; producer
    waste 33; production 4, 10;
    recovery 32, 72–73; sanitary 86;
    separation of 22, 23; statistics
    (*see* chapter 4); values of 21,
    69–70, 136–138 (*see* chapter
    5); vegetable 94, 96–100,
    102–103; war on 3, 73–74; and
    capitalism 9 (*see* chapter 7); as
    ejection 167; as excretion 179;
    as loss of value 7, 44–48, 172;
    as pollution 26, 50–52, 74–76,
    172–173; as social criticism (*see*
    chapter 2); as social sensibility
    36; as symbol of social
    degeneration 86–87; as what
    societies produce 177–178.
White, Alfred 26–27
Wohl, A.S. 11, 18, 19, 22
Womack, J.P. & Jones, D.T. 76
Woodward, D.H. 44, 46
Wright, A. 44, 46
Wright, L. 11, 13
Wylie, J.C. 11, 15, 69, 97, 100–101

Young, J.E. 28, 111